CHEMICAL INDUSTRY
with special reference to the U.K.
General Editors: J. DAVIDSON PRATT AND T. F. WEST

Heavy Organic Chemicals

A

Heavy Organic Chemicals

BY

A. J. GAIT

PERGAMON PRESS

OXFORD · LONDON · EDINBURGH · NEW YORK
TORONTO · SYDNEY · PARIS · BRAUNSCHWEIG

PERGAMON PRESS LTD.,
Headington Hill Hall, Oxford
4 & 5 Fitzroy Square, London W.1

PERGAMON PRESS (SCOTLAND) LTD.,
2 & 3 Teviot Place, Edinburgh 1

PERGAMON PRESS INC.,
44–01 21st Street, Long Island City, New York 11101

PERGAMON OF CANADA, LTD.,
6 Adelaide Street East, Toronto, Ontario

PERGAMON PRESS (AUST.) PTY. LTD.,
20–22 Margaret Street, Sydney, New South Wales

PERGAMON PRESS S.A.R.L.,
24 rue des Écoles, Paris 5e

VIEWEG & SOHN GmbH
Burgplatz 1, Braunschweig

Printed in Great Britain by Page Bros. (Norwich) Ltd.

Contents

Editors' Preface

WE were asked by Sir Robert Robinson, O.M., P.P.R.S., to organize the preparation of a series of monographs as teaching manuals for senior students on the chemical industry, having special reference to the United Kingdom, to be published by Pergamon Press as part of the Commonwealth and International Library of Science, Technology and Engineering, of which Sir Robert is a Chairman of the Honorary Editorial Advisory Board. Apart from the proviso that they were not intended to be reference books or dictionaries, the authors were free to develop their subject in the manner which appeared to them to be most appropriate.

The first problem was to define the chemical industry. Any manufacture in which a chemical change takes place in the material treated might well be classed as "chemical". This definition was obviously too broad as it would include, for example, the production of coal gas and the extraction of metals from their ores; these are not generally regarded as part of the chemical industry. We have used a more restricted but still a very wide definition, following broadly the example set in the special report (now out of print), prepared in 1949 by the Association of British Chemical Manufacturers at the request of the Board of Trade. Within this scope, there will be included monographs on subjects such as coal carbonization products, heavy chemicals, dyestuffs, agricultural chemicals, fine chemicals, medicinal products, explosives, surface active agents, paints and pigments, plastics and man-made fibres.

A list of monographs now available and under preparation is appended.

We wish to acknowledge our indebtedness to Sir Robert Robinson for his wise guidance and to express our sincere appreciation of the encouragement and help which we have received from so many individuals and organizations in the industry, particularly The Association of British Chemical Manufacturers.

The lino-cut used for the covers of this series of monographs was designed and cut by Miss N. J. Somerville West, to whom our thanks are due.

J. DAVIDSON PRATT $\Big\}$ *Editors*
T. F. WEST

Author's Foreword

THIS book is one of a series on the chemical industry which is, itself, rather a conglomeration of industries than a single industry. It is, moreover, about a part of the industry which is growing rapidly and, at the same time, undergoing great technological changes. From the constantly moving picture the author has tried to describe a "still" for the period about October 1965, together with a description of the developments which led up to the situation at this time and some estimates of the future course of events.

Information on which the book is based has been drawn from many sources; mainly it is based on the author's accumulated experience of some thirty years in the organic chemical industry supplemented by regular reading of scientific publications and technical journals. The author has also received much help from friends and colleagues in the industry and especially from the Directors of Shell Chemical Co., whose approval and encouragement made the work possible, from Mr. E. G. Hancock and many other colleagues in Shell who filled the gaps in the author's knowledge, from Mr. W. A. Dickie and Dr. W. Tyerman of British Celanese Ltd. who helped with information on the early history and current operations of their company and from Mr. H. Bradley and his colleagues at Price's (Bromborough) Ltd. who greatly enlarged the author's meagre knowledge of oleo-chemicals. To all of these people the author expresses his grateful thanks for their help and interest.

Introduction

ORGANIC chemistry is a vast and complex subject and it is estimated that, up to the present time, well over one million organic compounds have been prepared and characterized. Many of these are no more than the by-products of research projects designed to elucidate fundamental principles, reaction mechanisms, structure of complex compounds and so on; they are, and are likely to remain, laboratory curiosities. Of this vast number of compounds some 15,000 are listed by H.M. Customs and Excise as being of commercial importance, indicating that there has been some international trade in them which may only have amounted to a few pounds or even a few ounces. Many of these, and others not listed, will have been evaluated in research laboratories for therapeutic activity, insecticidal or herbicidal properties or growth-regulating power and rejected for various reasons. In such a list how is one to differentiate between heavy organic chemicals and others which, although produced in substantial quantities, will fall to be dealt with in one of the other volumes in this series?

There is no clear-cut answer to this question; selection will depend on the type of chemical, how it is made and the use to which it is put. In general, it can be said that a heavy organic chemical is one which is produced in quantities of at least hundreds of tons per annum; more usually, annual production will be measured in thousands or even in tens of thousands of tons. Some compounds produced on a relatively small scale will, however, be described, either because they are by-products from a large manufacturing complex or because they are closely related to an important product. On the other hand, some chemicals produced in large tonnage from traditional sources, or for traditional uses, such as coal tar chemicals or dyestuffs intermediates, have been omitted because they will be described in other volumes of the series. In some cases the older methods for production of these compounds have been supplemented or superseded by new processes based on different raw materials; these newer processes will be described in the present volume.

The cut-off point at the other end of the manufacturing chain is much clearer. The work has been confined to descriptions of the production of commercially pure chemicals to the point where they enter into other manufactures. Thus the production of poly-merizable monomers and of detergent raw materials is described but not the production of plastics, artificial fibres or detergents.

Although this book is specifically about the British heavy organic chemicals industry it has been necessary, in order to present a balanced treatment of the subject, to give some des-cription of developments abroad, both in the U.S.A. and in Europe. The establishment of a manufacture in one place rather than another, or the choice of one process in preference to another, usually depends on a combination of factors—geographi-cal, technical, legal, etc.—which change with time so that the distribution of industry does not remain constant.

The chemical industry in the U.K. is notable for the lack of reliable published statistics about it, especially when compared with similar industry in the U.S.A. Wherever possible, figures have been quoted for plant capacities and production and sales tonnages; these are based partly on factual information from published and private sources and partly on estimates derived from indirect evidence. They are believed to be reasonably reli-able, but obviously their accuracy cannot be guaranteed.

In deciding on the layout of the book the author had to choose between classifying chemicals according to their structure, as is done in the standard textbooks of organic chemistry, or according to the primary raw material or process used in their manufacture. Since, in industry, chemical manufactures tend to be grouped together according to raw material availability or manufacturing process, the second method has been adopted. In those cases where several commercial routes to a given end product are in use, the author has made his own assessment of the one likely to become dominant in selecting the chapter in which to deal with it; this assessment may well prove to have been wrong.

The general treatment of the subject is orientated strongly towards the technical and economic factors which have led to the establishment of certain processes and to the type, size and location of plant used. Enough chemical formulae and equations have been given for the reactions involved to be understood, but for a detailed study of the chemical, physical and mathematical problems involved, the student must refer to the many textbooks and other publications available; a reading list is given at the end of each chapter as a guide for further study.

Mixed systems of measurement are in common use in industry and no effort has been made to achieve an academic uniformity of units and nomenclature. Tonnages are in long tons of 2240 lb, gallons are Imperial gallons, temperatures °C and, for the rest, the standard English foot/pound/second system has been used except where stated to the contrary. For chemicals the common name in use in the industry has been used where one exists and, in most cases, the formula given will make the meaning clear. Where doubt could arise, particularly with the more complex compounds, the International Union of Pure and Applied Chemistry (I.U.P.A.C.) rules for nomenclature, as interpreted in in the Chemical Society *Handbook for Authors*, have been adopted.

Similarly, the names of many companies and products have become so well known in the industry that names are commonly shortened or even initials are used. It is, for instance, fairly common knowledge that I.C.I. stands for Imperial Chemical Industries Limited, but others may not be so widely known. Since it would be unduly cumbersome to quote the name in full on every occasion it has been written in full the first time it is mentioned and the shortened form is used thereafter. A list of abbreviations is given at the end of this introductory section.

Finally it must be said that the heavy organic chemical industry is now so large and complex that a complete description of its products and processes would require several volumes. Moreover,

B

the industry is growing and changing so rapidly that any book on it is out of date by the time it is published; regular study of the current technical journals is the only way of keeping abreast of new developments.

It is hoped that the present volume will provide a good starting point for students and newcomers to industry and, at the same time, give a satisfactory overall picture of an important branch of chemical industry for workers in other fields.

READING LIST

General Information

1. *The Petroleum Chemicals Industry*, by R. F. Goldstein. E. & F. N. Spon, London, 1958.
2. *The Petroleum Chemicals Industry*, by H. M. Stanley. The Royal Institute of Chemistry Lecture Series, 1963, No. 4.
3. *Chemicals from Petroleum*, by A. Lawrence Waddams. John Murray, London, 1962.

Process Information

1. *Industrial Chemicals*, by W. L. Faith, Donald B. Keyes and Ronald L. Clark. John Wiley, New York, 1957.
2. *Organic Chemical Processes*, by Marshall Sittig. The Noyes Press, New York, 1962.
3. Kirk Othmer, *Encyclopaedia of Chemical Technology*, 2nd edition. Interscience Publishers, a Division of John Wiley, New York, and London.

ABBREVIATIONS

B/B	butane/butene.
ft^3	cubic foot or cubic feet.
F.B.P.	final boiling point.
I.B.P.	initial boiling point.
IMS	industrial methylated spirit.
I.S.O.	International Standards Organization.
I.U.P.A.C.	International Union of Pure and Applied Chemistry.
K.I.D.	Key Industries Duty.

LPG	liquefied petroleum gas.
MEK	methyl ethyl ketone.
PTFE	polytetrafluoroethylene.
psig	pounds per square inch gauge.
PVC	polyvinyl chloride.
SBR	styrene/butadiene rubber.
t/a	tons per annum.
U.K.	The United Kingdom of Great Britain and Northern Ireland.
U.S.A.	the United States of America.

COMPANY NAMES

The relationship between companies in the chemical industry is confusing. There have been many mergers in recent years, some American companies have bought shares in, or taken over, British concerns and much reorganization and rearrangement is still going on. Students to whom this information is important should consult the current edition of *Who Owns Whom*, published by O. W. Roskill & Co. Reports Ltd., 14 Great College Street, London, S.W. 1. Brief information on most of the companies mentioned in the book is given below.

Albright and Wilson	A very old established company which has diversified recently and taken over a number of other chemical companies, the most important of which are: A. Boake Roberts & Co. Ltd., W. J. Bush & Co. Ltd., Marchon Products Ltd. and Stafford Allen & Sons Ltd. Midland Silicones Ltd. also is a subsidiary.
Alchemy Ltd.	A subsidiary company of Burts & Harvey Ltd. which is, in turn, a subsidiary of Burt, Boulton & Haywood Ltd.
American Cyanamid	The American Cyanamid Co., with subsidiaries all over the world, the British

	company being Cyanamid of Great Britain Ltd.
B.A.S.F.	Badische Anilin und Sodafabrik of Ludwigshaven am Rhein, one of the constituent groups of the pre-1945 I. G. Farbenindustrie combine in Germany.
B.H.C.	British Hydrocarbon Chemicals Ltd., joint company owned 50/50 by D.C.L. and B.P., making chemicals from petroleum.
B.O.C.	The British Oxygen Co. Ltd. and its subsidiaries.
B.P.	The British Petroleum Co. Ltd.
Courtaulds	Courtaulds Ltd., a large group of companies with many subsidiaries in the textile, chemical, paint and plastics industries. British Celanese Ltd. is one of its subsidiaries.
D.C.L.	The Distillers Company Ltd., a group of companies originally engaged in the production of Scotch whisky but now greatly diversified into the manufacture of industrial alcohol, foods, chemicals and plastics.
Degussa	The Deutsche Gold und Silber-Scheideanstalt.
Esso	The Esso Petroleum Co. Ltd., the British subsidiary of the Standard Oil Co. of New Jersey.
Hoechst Farbwerke Hoechst	A group of companies operating at Hoechst, near Frankfurt am Main. At one time part of the I.G. Farbenindustrie combine.
H.I.A.G.	Holzverkohlungs Industrie Aktiengesellschaft. A German company originally interested in wood distillation.
I.C.I.	Imperial Chemical Industries Ltd., the

largest chemical company in Europe. It has many associated and subsidiary companies and engages in a wide range of chemical manufacturing activities.

Laporte

Laporte Industries Ltd., a group of companies which has taken over a number of smaller chemical manufacturers recently, including Howards of Ilford Ltd. of Ilford and Peter Spence & Sons Ltd. of Widnes.

Monsanto

The Monsanto Chemical Co. of the U.S.A., and its British subsidiary, Monsanto Chemicals Ltd.

Pfizer

Charles Pfizer & Co. Inc. of the U.S.A., and its British subsidiary, Pfizer Ltd.

duPont

E. I. duPont de Nemours & Co. of Wilmington, Delaware, the world's largest chemical company. Its British subsidiary is duPont Co. (United Kingdom) Ltd.

Shell

A word used loosely to refer to any member of the Royal Dutch Shell group of companies. The British company for chemicals is Shell Chemicals U.K. Ltd.

Union Carbide

The Union Carbide Corporation of the U.S.A., and its British subsidiary, Union Carbide Ltd.

CHAPTER 1

Historical Introduction

MAN has, perforce, always been interested in natural animal and vegetable materials since he depends on them for his life and well-being; it is in man's efforts to change these materials to meet his growing needs that the roots of the organic chemical industry can be seen to lie. Details of man's first attempts to bring about chemical changes are lost in the mists of antiquity, but it can be inferred with reasonable certainty that they will have been confined to such simple operations as boiling or calcining and, later perhaps, treatment with other materials readily available such as wood ashes or natural earth. It is certain that two processes which have survived to the present day have been known from very early times. These are the fermentation of sugars to produce alcohol—first for potable purposes and later for a host of other uses—and the destructive distillation of wood for production of charcoal in the first instance and later for the recovery of wood tar and other distillation products.

The identity of the human benefactor who first discovered the fermentation process will never be known, but it is fairly certain that, as soon as man had pots in which sugary materials could be left standing, some primitive housewife who could not be bothered to do the washing up will have created the right conditions for the discovery. After this it would only be a matter of time before the changes taking place were noticed, the beneficent effects of imbibing the resultant liquid brought to light and the foundations of one of our most ancient industries firmly laid. After this the discovery of the concentrating effects of distillation may have had to wait for many centuries; it is certain that the process was known to the ancient Greeks, but it is thought that reasonably pure alcohol did not become available until the twelfth century A.D. As the discoverer of fermentation is unknown so, likewise, is the identity of the less beneficent individual who first thought of putting a tax on the products of the industry; this must have happened quite early in the existence of organized societies and the fermentation industries have been a fruitful source of revenue to various rulers and governments ever since. In spite of its long history as a beverage, alcohol did not begin to assume importance as a chemical until the time of the Industrial Revolution in the late eighteenth and early nineteenth centuries. The art of fermentation was given a great boost by the work of Louis Pasteur (1822–95) who showed that the reactions were brought about by the action of microscopic living organisms. Improvements in distillation methods kept pace with improvements in knowledge of the fermentation process and culminated, in 1830, in the introduction of the still designed by Coffey which remained virtually unchanged as a standard piece of equipment in distilleries until well into the twentieth century. In the early nineteenth century pure alcohol was still very expensive due to the high excise duties levied on it. It was quickly realized that this high cost was not only retarding the growth of the industrial alcohol industry, but was also hindering the development of other industries which needed alcohol as a raw material or solvent. In 1855 the Board of Customs and Excise made an order sanctioning the sale of duty-free alcohol for industrial purposes, provided it was first mixed with a small proportion of wood naphtha (methanol) and other materials to make it unpalatable as a potable spirit, and so methylated spirit was born; most other European countries enacted similar legislation at about the same time. This provision has since been broadened and extended by various legal enactments and by regulations issued by H.M. Customs and Excise so that, today, duty-free alcohol can be made available, subject to the appropriate physical controls, in a sufficient state of purity for any chemical process carried out on a substantial scale.

The origins of the wood distillation process, like those of fermentation, are lost in prehistory, but the early Iron Age smelters are known to have used large quantities of charcoal in their operations. Wood tar, also, has been used for caulking the seams of boats and for similar purposes from very early times. Wood distillation has never attained the same importance as an industrial process as fermentation, probably because the yield of chemicals is relatively small, and because developing technology permitted the same products to be made by other means from different raw materials as the demand for them increased.

Already in 1709 Abraham Derby (1677–1717) had substituted coal for wood in iron smelting and in 1796 it is recorded that von Reden in Germany used coke in a blast furnace for the production of iron. However, during the late eighteenth and early nineteenth centuries, the pyroligneous acid from wood distillation was the only source of methanol and was a convenient source of acetic acid and, by calcination of calcium acetate, of acetone. It is interesting to note that in Germany, where the alcohol duties were not as high as in Britain, acetic acid was made by the oxidation of alcohol in the late eighteenth century; this was clearly the most practicable method by which the growing demands for acetic acid could be met, but it appears to have been some time after the introduction of duty free methylated spirit before the process became widely adopted. Although charcoal has been entirely replaced by other forms of carbon for most applications, certain specialized uses for it remain and wood distillation is still carried out on a small scale in Britain today.

It has been shown above how the fermentation industry changed through the period of the Industrial Revolution, roughly from 1750 to 1850. During this period the whole chemical industry, organic and inorganic, experienced a similar growth and development—in fact without it the Industrial Revolution would have been greatly slowed down. In the 1780's Berthollet investigated the nature of oils and fats and Scheele showed that glycerol is a by-product of the saponification reaction.

Shortly afterwards the classic work of Chevreul (1786–1889)

demonstrated the nature of the raw materials and the reactions used in soap making. During this period also the process of coal carbonization developed rapidly, the emphasis being more and more on the chemical products rather than the coke; for example, the Earl of Dundonald was granted a patent in 1781 for the production of a substitute for wood tar by the destructive distillation of coal. The by-product gas had already been the subject of investigations since the time of van Helmont in the late sixteenth century and its adaptation for industrial and domestic use by Murdock and by Winsor and Clegg led to greatly increased production of coal tar. Elucidation of the composition of coal tar by such workers as Kekule, Runge and, especially, Hofmann facilitated the development of the dyestuffs industry which was complementary to the enormous growth of the textile industry in the nineteenth century. It is to the pressure put on these early processes by the immense industrial growth of the first half of the twentieth century that the modern heavy organic chemical industry owes its development.

These great developments in technology were only made possible by parallel developments in knowledge. The early chemists believed that organic compounds differed from inorganic in containing some mystic life force derived from their origin in living matter and, even though Berzelius showed in 1814 that organic compounds obeyed the same laws of multiple proportions in their molecular composition as inorganic, he held that they could only be made by living organisms. This belief began to be more and more assailed by chemists until, in 1828, Frederick Wohler produced an undeniably organic compound—urea—from an undeniably inorganic compound—ammonium cyanate. Even then the belief persisted and was finally dispelled in 1862 when Berhelot showed that carbon and hydrogen will react in the electric arc to produce acetylene.

The simple unsaturated hydrocarbons had been discovered quite early—ethylene by Deiman in 1795 and acetylene by Edmund Davy in 1836. Their reactivity made them of great interest to the early chemists and the study of their reactions played a large part in developing an understanding of organic compounds. After 1855 ethylene could be easily and cheaply made from methylated spirit and, after calcium carbide, which had been discovered by Wohler in 1862, became commercially available when Willson established its manufacture in the electric furnace in 1892, acetylene too could be made cheaply on a large scale. Thus, by the end of the nineteenth century, commercial manufacture of two of the most important raw materials of the modern heavy organic chemicals industry was already established.

The nineteenth century was a period of exploitation of natural products; resources in many parts of the world were mobilized to provide for the ever-growing needs of industry in Europe and North America, and the chemical industry grew to provide the means of processing and transforming these materials into finished products. So far, the age of substitution had not arrived and wood, coal, wool and cotton were staple raw materials for many processes. Rubber also became important during this period although it was not until the East Indian plantations, established in the 1870's, began to come into full production about 1895 that the industry could rely on a firmly based supply of raw material. However, this coincided well with the establishment of the motor car industry which is, today, the largest user of rubber and absorbs some 50% of total world production.

Mention of the motor car industry brings us to the exploitation of petroleum and to the development of the great oil industry which has done so much to supply the energy and transport needs of the twentieth century and which has, almost as an afterthought, provided the basic raw materials needed for the growth of the organic chemicals industry.

The existence of petroleum has been known from very early times, but the industry is generally considered to have begun with the completion of Drake's well in Pennsylvania in 1859. As with other naturally occurring materials, the establishment of supplies was only the first stage; finding out how best to use the material is a continuing process and, even today, more than 100 years after the completion of Drake's well, there is still much that is not known about this astonishing material. For an account of the early searches for oil in many parts of the world, the establishment of refining methods and the gradual extension of knowledge on the composition of various crude oils the student is referred to the many excellent books on the subject, of which a selection is given in the reading list at the end of this chapter.

It was quickly found that, in spite of the varied composition of different crude oils, fitting the pattern of products which could be produced to the pattern of demand for them in the market was an ever-present and ever-changing problem. It is to the oil industry's efforts to solve this problem by changing the unwanted oil fractions into useful products that we owe great advances in chemical and engineering technology, especially in the handling and treatment of hydrocarbon gases and liquids in vast quantities, which have found applications in other industries, and especially in the chemical industry.

At first the major demand was for kerosine for lighting and the light petrol fractions were a waste product which was regarded as dangerous and difficult to dispose of. The motor car, which may be said to have been established with the construction of usable vehicles by Daimler and Benz in 1885, was at first seen as providing a God given outlet for the unwanted petrol. The internal combustion engine developed, however, and became more demanding in the quality of its fuel and, by the second decade of the twentieth century, the demands for motor fuel were already creating problems in product pattern for the oil refining industry. These problems were intensified by increasing demands for fuel for aircraft and, to-day, the major part of the industry's technical effort is directed to satisfying the vast but fastidious appetites of these two consumers.

Changes in product pattern from crude oil are usually brought about by breaking down, or "cracking", the long chain hydrocarbons in the high boiling fractions into shorter chain hydrocarbons of lower boiling point and many ingenious methods of carrying out this process have been devised. The importance of these developments from the chemical industry point of view was that, in addition to the desired low boiling petrol fractions, substantial yields of by-product gases were obtained which, unlike natural gas, contained significant proportions of the lower olefins ethylene, propylene and the isomeric butylenes.

It has already been noted that the reactions of these gases had been extensively studied by chemists and it was quickly realized that these by-product streams offered a raw material from which commercially important chemicals might be made on a large scale. Further, the oil refining industry had started by borrowing the techniques and equipment of the chemical industry and had developed them for continuous operation on a vast scale. Construction of the necessary plant, therefore, presented no insurmountable difficulty and the first plant for the production of isopropyl alcohol from a propylene rich refinery gas stream was built by the Standard Oil Co. at Bayway, New Jersey in 1920. Other plants and products soon followed, encouraged by the ready availability of refinery gases and the increasing cost of the traditional raw materials so that, by the outbreak of the Second World War in 1939, the U.S.A. had a large and well-established organic chemical industry based on petroleum and natural gas, which was of vital importance to the Allies during the struggle.

In Great Britain development proceeded along different lines. As a great maritime and colonial power in the late nineteenth and early twentieth centuries, Britain had access to all the natural raw materials of the world and had established vast interests overseas. At home, she had emerged from the Industrial Revolution with great industries based on these raw materials, but with coal as her main indigenous natural resource. Her organic chemical industry consisted chiefly of the manufacture of dyestuffs from the by-products of coal carbonization and of a few simple aliphatic chemicals from the products of fermentation and wood distillation; even in this limited field the initiative was lost to Germany, which had become a great centre of organic chemical research and of industry. Thus, the outbreak of war in 1914 found Great Britain with a small, rather inefficient, organic chemical industry, quite unable to meet the additional demands of the war and not well suited for rapid expansion. The most immediate shortage was of acetone, essential for the manufacture of cordite, which had been mainly imported from Germany. The existing method of manufacture was cumbersome and expensive but, fortunately, in 1912 Dr. Chaim Weizmann had discovered that certain strains of bacteria—the Clostridia—could convert sugars and starches into alcohols, ketones and acids and that one strain—*Clostridium acetobutylicum*—produced mainly acetone and butanol. This process had been set up on a commercial scale by Messrs. Strange and Graham in 1913/14 and clearly offered the best prospects for rapid expansion. It attracted the attention of Mr. Lloyd George, at that time responsible for expanding the production of military supplies, who is reported to have waved a test tube of acetone during a speech in the House of Commons —surely one of the earliest instances of a governmental interest in science. Although a plant was built at the Royal Naval cordite factory at Holton Heath, the greater availability of raw materials in North America, as in the 1939 war, made it advantageous to carry out the process there and plants were built in Canada and, later, in the U.S.A. at Terre Haute, Indiana. The latter plant was erected by the U.S. Government and, when it was offered for sale at the end of the war, a company named Commercial Solvents Corporation was formed to buy and operate it.

Another pioneering effort at this time was the establishment by H. A. Dreyfus in 1916 of the British Cellulose and Chemical Co., later to become British Celanese, at Spondon, near Derby. This company produced cellulose acetate lacquers for doping the fabric used for covering the aircraft of that day. The acetate had the advantage of being less inflammable than the nitrocellulose used up to that time; it is for its work in the development and manufacture of cellulose acetate fabrics and plastics that the company has continued to be best known up to the present day. In order to supply the acetic anhydride required for cellulose acetate manufacture, the company built a plant for production of calcium carbide and it was, in fact, the availability of coal for power production and of coke and lime as raw materials for the carbide which caused the company to choose the Spondon site. The processes by which the acetylene was converted to acetic anhydride will be referred to later; their use by this company at such an early date represents a considerable achievement. Indeed this company has never been a major factor in the marketing of chemicals but the development work which it has carried out in its efforts to manufacture its own requirements of organic chemicals has undoubtedly stimulated the British chemical industry as a whole.

After 1918, as the country began to recover from the war, the great upsurge of industrial activity engendered by it spilled over into civil life as manufacturers tried to develop peacetime applications for plant and products designed to meet war needs. It was found, of course, that other countries had similar problems and British industry, struggling to adapt itself to peacetime conditions, became subjected to severe competition from imports, especially from Germany and the U.S.A. Britain had, up to this time, been essentially a free trade country, but the memory of the shortages of vital materials in the early stages of the war now persuaded the Government to introduce protective legislation, and the Safeguarding of Industries Act, 1921, imposed a $33\frac{1}{3}\%$ *ad valorem* duty—the Key Industries Duty or K.I.D.—on many industrial products including most organic chemicals. This was followed in 1928 by the Import Duties Act which imposed a 10% *ad valorem* duty on virtually all imports, including most chemicals not already covered by K.I.D., except foodstuffs and basic raw materials not indigenous to Britain. The Act imposing K.I.D. also included provisions for dealing with appeals against the inclusion or exclusion of particular materials in the schedules of products subject to the duty. There were also arrangements for temporary exemption from the duty where a material was not made in the U.K. or where home production was inadequate Applications and appeals under this procedure have been a feature of the chemical business for nearly forty years. One of the first was the plea by the British Cellulose and Chemical Co.

in December 1921 that calcium carbide had been improperly excluded from the list of organic chemicals covered by the Act, and one of the last that by I.C.I. and others, just before the Act was repealed in 1958, that polyethylene had been similarly treated. In both cases it was decided that the materials were not organic chemicals as defined by the Act. Although much of the earlier legislation dealing with import duties was consolidated in the new Import Duties Act in 1958, this did not alter the incidence of duties at that time, but provided a somewhat different and more uniform procedure for dealing with changes in, and exemption from, duty.

Behind the protective tariffs industry began to develop; American production line methods were introduced into the motor car industry and the growing output of cars and lorries made demands on other industries, especially for steel sheet, rubber and paint. Nitro-cellulose lacquers became the standard finish for vehicles and these, in turn, needed ketone and ester solvents unknown to the conventional paint industry. It was found that these new finishes tended to be brittle, but could be made more flexible by having "plasticizers" incorporated in them and so another important branch of the organic chemical industry became established.

Companies with "know how" in the aliphatic chemical field were quick to take advantage of this growing market and the names of A. Boake Roberts & Co. and Howards of Ilford appear often in the advertisements for lacquer solvents of that period. The Distillers Co. Ltd. erected a factory at King's Lynn for the production of n-butanol and acetone by the Weizmann fermentation process; this plant was unfortunately wrecked by an explosion and fire almost before it had attained full output. Instead of rebuilding it, the company pursued its efforts to gain a share of the solvents market by the formation, jointly with the German H.I.A.G. company, of a new company, British Industrial Solvents Ltd. A factory was built near Hull in 1929 for the production of acetone, acetic acid and n-butanol, using ethanol drawn from the adjacent D.C.L. owned Hull Distillery Co. and processes and "know how" provided by its German parent. After the war the German interest was bought by D.C.L. and this site has now developed into a major centre for heavy organic chemical production.

The Weizmann fermentation process was again established in the U.K. by the Commercial Solvents Corporation (Great Britain) Ltd., a subsidiary of the U.S. company which had pioneered the civil development of the process in the U.S.A. after the first war. A plant was built in 1935 on a site at Bromborough on the Mersey estuary to run on molasses as raw material; it continued in production through the war years and into the 1950's. After the war the plant was bought by the D.C.L. and was eventually closed down because it could not compete with the newer processes based on petroleum.

Another important event of the inter-war years was the formation in 1926 of I.C.I. by the merger of a number of companies prominent in the manufacture of heavy inorganic chemicals, explosives and dyestuffs. This great company has expanded its interests into many fields not covered by the original mergers and has played a dominant part in the British chemical industry for the past forty years; its activities will be referred to again and again in the ensuing chapters of this book.

So far the U.K. organic chemical industry had followed a more or less predictable pattern of development based on coal and natural raw materials and the stage would seem to have been set for the change to petroleum feedstocks in the same way as in the U.S.A. The change was, however, delayed by more than twenty years by what appeared, at the time, to be a relatively unimportant piece of legislation. This was the imposition in the Finance Act of 1928 of a Customs Duty of 4*d*. per gallon on light hydrocarbon oils (then called the Petrol Tax). The duty was designed, in the first instance, to provide protection for the Scottish shale oil industry and the benzole industry against competition from imported petrol. Once the machinery for collecting the tax had been established, however, successive chancellors found it such a convenient and, with the growth of motor car usage, expanding source of revenue that the tax has been increased over the years until it reached its present level of 3s. 3d. per gallon. The protective effect was maintained by fixing a differential between the Excise Duty on indigenously produced oils and the Customs Duty on imported oils. This differential was finally removed at the end of 1964 in order to comply with the provisions of the convention setting up the European Free Trade Association, thus dealing the final death blow to the Scottish shale oil industry and exerting a profound effect on the economics of benzole recovery from coal carbonization.

The provisions of the legislation imposing light hydrocarbon oil duty made the use of these oils, or of gases produced from them, for chemical synthesis prohibitively expensive and had a profound effect on the development of their use as solvents. They also had the effect of creating two kinds of oil, indigenous oil and imported oil, which had to be stored and accounted for separately for Customs and Excise purposes while being held in bond. This created formidable difficulties in plants and storage installations where both kinds of oil were processed and still further hindered development of chemical uses for hydrocarbons. On the outbreak of war in 1939, as in the First World War, the relatively retarded state of development of the U.K. organic chemical industry compared with that of the U.S.A., coupled with the greater availability of raw materials there, caused the major expansion of organic chemical production required by the war to take place in North America. It is worthy of note, however, that a start was made on the use of petroleum as a chemical raw material when British Celanese built a plant at Spondon in 1942 to crack gas oil, which boiled above the range set for light hydrocarbon oils and so was not subject to the duty, for production of ethylene and propylene and their conversion into solvents and chemical intermediates. A little earlier Shell too had completed at Stanlow, Cheshire, a project which had been started before the war for the production of secondary alkyl sulphate detergents from olefins derived from the cracking of paraffin wax, which was also free from the light oil duty.

Towards the end of the war the Government had again learned the lesson that a well-developed and efficient chemical industry is essential for national security, and in 1944 a committee was set up under the chairmanship of Sir John Ayre to examine the effect of the hydrocarbon oil duties on the British chemical industry. As the result of the recommendations of this committee legislation was introduced in the Finance Acts of 1945 and 1946 which cleared the way for the use of light hydrocarbon oils in chemical synthesis without payment of duty. This marked the beginning of the phenomenal expansion of the production of heavy organic chemicals, shown graphically in Fig. 1, which has

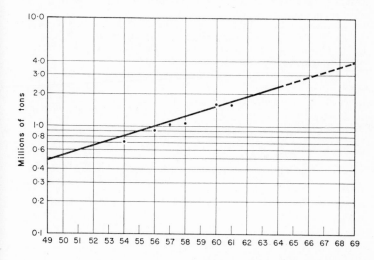

Fig. 1 U.K. Production of Heavy Organic Chemicals 1949-1964 with projection to 1969.

taken place since the last war and which will be the main theme of this book.

This expansion has been facilitated by a greater readiness on the part of government to introduce amending legislation where this can be shown to be in the interests of expansion. Science has become politically fashionable and it now remains to be seen

whether the industry will be as greatly embarrassed in the future
by too much interest from government as it has been in the past
by too little.

READING LIST

Industrial History

1. *Short History of Technology*, by T. K. Derry and T. I. Williams. Clarendon
   Press, Oxford, 1960.
2. *A Short History of the Art of Distillation*, by R. J. Forbes. E. J. Brill, Leiden, 1948.

History and Technology of Petroleum

1. *Studies in Early Petroleum History*, by R. J. Forbes. E. J. Brill, Leiden, 1958.
2. *More Studies in Early Petroleum History* 1860–1880, by R. J. Forbes. E. J. Brill,
   Leiden, 1959.
3. *The Science of Petroleum*, Edited by A. E. Dunstan, A. W. Nash, B. T. Brooks
   and H. Tizard. Oxford University Press, 1938. Revisions 1950–3.
4. *The Chemistry of Petroleum Derivatives*, by Carleton Ellis. The Chemical
   Catalog Co., 1934.

Chemicals from Petroleum

1. The Petroleum Chemicals Industry in the United Kingdom, by H. P.
   Hodge. The Institute of Petroleum Review 1962, Vol. 16, pp. 114–21.

CHAPTER 2

Primary Transformations and Separations

CHEMICAL synthesis, by definition, consists of the building up of more complex molecules from simpler ones and usually starts from relatively pure elements or compounds. Natural raw materials, on the other hand, are usually complex mixtures of chemical entities and some initial step of physical separation or chemical transformation is necessary to produce from them the relatively simple compounds which are the starting points for organic chemical synthesis proper. On account of the many common features of these operations, and of the diversity and multiplicity of their products, it is convenient to bring the descriptions of them together into one chapter and to treat them as unit operations which produce the bricks on which further building operations depend.

1. WOOD DISTILLATION

This ancient process is still carried out in this country on a modest scale although the simple earth-covered wood stacks of the early charcoal burners have been replaced, first by portable externally heated retorts, then by fixed kilns operating batchwise and, finally, by continuously operating wood distillation plants. All four methods of operation may still be found but direct charcoal burning and portable kilns account for only a very small proportion of the total output. It was only at the fixed retort stage that recovery of the volatile products of the distillation became practicable and maximum recovery of these products is important in the economics of the modern plants. One of the most modern plants is operated by Shirley Aldred and Co. Ltd. at Worksop, Notts. The feed to this plant consists of branches, misshapen trunks, plantation thinnings, etc., of such woods as beech, birch, oak, ash, sycamore and chestnut. The wood is cut into lengths of about 1 ft and pre-dried to about 15% water content before being fed to the retort. This is a vertical cylinder some 55 ft high and 6 ft in diameter heated internally by non-condensable gas from the process. Charcoal is removed intermittently from the bottom of the retort and is stabilized by being held in a controlled stream of air for 24 hr before being graded and packed for sale.

The volatile products pass out of the top of the retort and are recovered in condensers and scrubbers while the non-condensable gases pass on and are used as fuel. The condensate, after separation from tar, is known as pyroligneous acid and is first split by distillation into two fractions—crude wood spirit and stripped acid. The crude wood spirit is further distilled to produce three crude solvents:

1. Boiling up to 60°C and containing methyl acetate, acetone and some methanol.
2. Boiling from 60°–65°C and consisting mainly of methanol with some acetone.
3. Boiling from 65°–90°C—a crude denaturing spirit containing allyl alcohol.

The dilute stripped acid is separated from tar and concentrated to produce a formic acid fraction, a pure 99–100% acetic acid fraction and a fraction containing higher acids. Charcoal production in this country approaches 10,000 t/a and represents only about one-third of total requirements.

2. FERMENTATION

The production of aliphatic chemicals such as ethanol, acetone and n–butanol by the microbiological fermentation of carbohydrates was, for many years, the most economic commercia method of manufacturing these compounds. Increase in cost of the carbohydrate raw materials, however, has made the processes uneconomic in comparison with processes based on petroleum and they have declined in importance. Production of acetone and n–butanol by this method ceased in the U.K. some years ago and the output of ethanol from fermentation has declined sharply since 1950. The Distillers Co. has one distillery working at Hull at a level far below its potential capacity and another small distillery in Liverpool is believed to be still operating; apart from these all industrial ethanol is petroleum based.

Microbiological processes are still used for the production of some pharmaceuticals and fine chemicals and the versatility of micro-organisms, combined with the accuracy with which they can pick out the right raw material from a complex mixture, has de to a substantial amount of research into the possibility of producing suitable cultures for specific syntheses difficult to achieve by direct chemical means. The production of the simpler aliphatics by this process may also become economic again and a brief description of the two fermentation processes most widely used in the recent past is given below.

The basic steps in all industrial fermentations are similar. First a pure culture of the desired organism is prepared by careful selection of a strain known to have high activity for the reaction concerned. This culture is then increased by growing it on a suitable nutrient medium until sufficient material is available for inoculation of the bulk fermenters; the greatest care is necessary at this stage in order to keep the culture pure and free from foreign organisms. The bulk fermentable solution, or "wort", is prepared simultaneously and sterilized. After inoculation the fermentation is allowed to proceed at a controlled temperature, selected according to the organism being used, until no further end product is being made. The product is then separated from the spent solution, or "wash", by conventional means such as distillation, solvent extraction or crystallization.

The best known fermentation process is the production of

ethanol by fermentation of sugars with yeast. The yeasts are unicellular organisms lying between the animal and vegetable kingdoms; there are many species and, for the production of ethanol, a species known as *Saccharomyces cerevisiae* is preferred since it has been found by experience to give the highest conversion of sugar to alcohol. The cells of this species are almost spherical and about 10 μ in diameter; the pure culture is started by picking out, under a microscope, a single perfect cell from a laboratory culture, known to be of high fermenting power, and transferring it on a platinum wire to a test tube of sterile nutrient solution containing sugar and small quantities of other growth substances such as phosphates and nitrates. The culture is then incubated at 30°C for some hours while the cells multiply by division. This culture is then used to inoculate a larger quantity of nutrient and the procedure repeated; in this way the culture is carried through a number of stages, increasing in volume at each stage, until some thousands of gallons of culture are obtained over a period of up to a week. The piping and vessels of the pure culture plant, usually referred to as the seed yeast plant, are of copper tinned on the inside.

The bulk fermentation is carried out in large mild steel vessels of up to 100,000 gal capacity, equipped with coils for heating and cooling, and with means for blowing in air to agitate the contents. The raw material most commonly used is molasses— the syrupy material remaining after the recovery of sucrose from sugar cane or sugar beet. The raw molasses, containing about 55% of sugars, calculated as invert sugar, is first diluted with water to reduce the sugar content to about 32%, the pH is adjusted to about 4·5 by addition of sulphuric acid, and the solution is then sterilized by heating to 77°C. This operation could perhaps better be described as pasteurization since the temperature is not high enough for complete sterilization. Cold water is then added to reduce the invert sugar content of the wort to about 12·5% and the temperature is adjusted to 35·5°C. Air agitation is now started and the ready prepared pure culture added. A distillery will normally have a number of fermenters in operation simultaneously and the number and size will determine both the amount of pure culture to be prepared for each series of fermentations and the total output of which the plant is capable. As fermentation proceeds the temperature will rise and cooling become necessary to hold the temperature as near constant as possible and definitely below 38°C; also, with the increasing rate of conversion of sugar to alcohol, the evolution of carbon dioxide, which is a by-product of the reaction, will provide sufficient agitation for the solution and air agitation may be stopped. Fermentation may last for up to 72 hr before all the available sugar has been converted and the "wash", as the fermented solution is called, is then sent forward to the distillation plant for recovery of the ethanol and small quantities of other alcohols. It will be seen that fermentation is essentially a batch process and the normal method of working is to prepare a batch of pure culture for a fixed number of fermenters. When the fermenters are under way, the pure culture plant can proceed with the preparation of the next batch of pure culture, against the time when the fermentation cycle has been completed and the fermenters are again ready for inoculation.

The wash, containing 5·5–6·0% by weight of ethanol, is fed to a preliminary distillation column where the ethanol and by-products are distilled over as a 50–60% aqueous solution and the spent wash runs to waste from the bottom of the column. A stream from a tray near the bottom is run through a phase separator to recover any higher alcohols which have not distilled over. The crude alcohol from the wash column is next fed to an aldehyde column which removes volatile low boiling products, and then to the rectifying column. The overhead distillate from the rectifying column still contains traces of aldehyde and is returned to the aldehyde column; the pure rectified spirit, containing 95·5% ethanol, is taken off as vapour a short distance from the top of the column, condensed, cooled and run to storage. As described for the wash column, the higher boiling alcohols, or "fusel oil" are recovered from a tray near the bottom of the column. Because of the high rate of excise duty (about £25 per

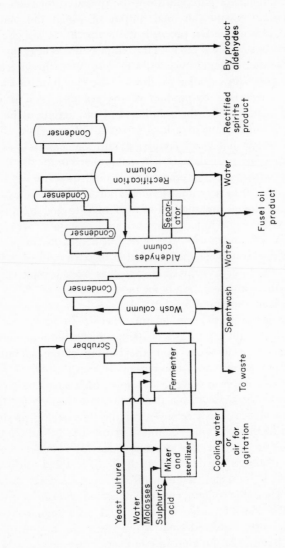

Fig. 2 Production of Ethanol from Molasses by Fermentation.

gallon) on pure ethanol, the whole process is carried out under strict Customs and Excise supervision and the finished spirit is stored in bonded warehouses until it is denatured according to an approved formula and released from Excise control. One pound of 100% ethanol is produced from 2·353 lb of invert sugar; the by-products amount to approximately 5 gal of fusel oil and 6000 lb of carbon dioxide per 1000 gal of rectified spirit. A diagrammatic flow sheet of the process is shown in Fig. 2.

In the Weizmann fermentation for production of acetone and n–butanol, the organism used is a bacterium, *Clostridium aceto-butylicum*, for which the culture conditions are slightly different from those for yeast. Molasses is commonly used as the raw material and the gas evolved during the fermentation is a mixture of carbon dioxide and hydrogen; a little ethanol is also produced and the general procedure is very similar to that for the ethanol process.

When starchy raw materials are used for either of the above described fermentations, the ground material is first cooked with steam under pressure to about 120°C to solubilize the starch grains. Water and malt are then added, and the solution is allowed to stand while the starches are converted to sugars by enzyme action. More water is then added to adjust the sugar concentration and the wort fermented in the usual way.

3. HYDROLYSIS

Hydrolysis, or the splitting of molecules by the action of water, is a widely used chemical process; when applied to natural raw materials, it is usually the esters of carboxylic acids which have to be hydrolysed according to the reactions:

$$RCOOR' + H_2O \longrightarrow RCOOH + R'OH$$

The reaction may be catalysed by acids or alkalis; if sufficient alkali is used to form the alkali salt of the acid as it is released, the process is usually referred to as saponification, since this is the basic reaction when soap is produced by the action of alkalis on natural fats or oils.

The natural fats and oils consist mainly of glyceryl esters of long-chain fatty acids which, on hydrolysis, give glycerol and free acid:

$$
\begin{array}{l}
CH_2OOCR_1 \\
| \\
CHOOCR_2 \; + \; 3H_2O \; \longrightarrow \; CHOH \\
| \\
CH_2OOCR_3
\end{array}
\qquad
\begin{array}{l}
CH_2OH \\
| \\
CHOH \\
| \\
CH_2OH
\end{array}
$$
$$+ \; R_1COOH + R_2COOH + R_3COOH$$

In addition to their use in soap making the fatty acids are becoming important as heavy organic chemicals and, with the corresponding fatty alcohols, are often called oleochemicals. Some of these natural products have already been replaced by synthetic acids and alcohols derived from petroleum and this is likely to be a growing trend in the future. The products are described more fully in Chapter 8.

Many variants of the basic hydrolysis process have been devised in the soap industry for the splitting of natural fats but, when fatty acids for industrial use are required, splitting with water is the usual method. There are three common variants of this process—the Twitchell process, the autoclave process and the continuous splitting process.

In the Twitchell process the fat is simply boiled with water to which 0·5–3% of Twitchell reagent has been added. The Twitchell reagent is an acyl benzene sulphonic acid made by reacting a fatty acid, such as oleic acid, with benzene and sulphuric acid.

$$C_{17}H_{33}COOH + C_6H_6 + H_2SO_4 \longrightarrow$$
$$C_{17}H_{33}COC_6H_4SO_3H + 2H_2O$$

Boiling is carried out in a wooden vat and lasts from 24–48 hr.

The process has the advantage of being simple and requiring only small capital investment but it yields acids of inferior colour and is not now widely used.

The second, and still the most widely used process, consists simply in heating the fat with water in an autoclave to about 220°C until hydrolysis is complete.

The third, and the newest, method is continuous splitting with hot water at a temperature of 250–260°C and pressure of 700 psig in a vertical column about 75 ft high. Fat enters at the bottom and water at the top, the top and bottom sections of the column acting as heat exchangers in which feeds are heated and products cooled while the middle section is the actual splitting zone. The entering fat rises as droplets through the descending dilute glycerol (sweet water) to the water/fat interface; it then rises as a continuous phase and is further hydrolysed by descending water droplets. Live steam distributors are provided near the interface to heat the materials to reaction temperature and at the top of the column to heat the water for splitting. Sweet water is withdrawn continuously from the bottom of the column and the fatty acid product passes out at the top.

For some fatty acids, such as those from castor oil, low temperature splitting with caustic soda is still employed to avoid intra-esterification. The acid is recovered from its sodium salt by treatment with mineral acid.

Whatever the splitting process the subsequent operations are similar: the sweet water is concentrated for the production of pure glycerol and the fatty acids undergo a variety of after treatments according to the use for which they are required (see Chapter 8).

4. TREATMENT OF NATURAL GAS

Only relatively small quantities of natural gas are found in Britain but bulk importation of it in liquid form is now well established, although it is still rather expensive when compared with the liquid feed stocks currently available. It is to be expected that, as experience is gained in transporting and handling the material in liquid form, the imported gas will become cheaper and, in addition, there is a possibility that the preliminary discoveries of gas which have been made in the prospecting now going on under the bed of the North Sea may result in the proving of a major natural gas field. Natural gas must, therefore, be regarded as a potential raw material which may become available at prices comparable with those ruling in other producing areas in Europe such as the Po valley, the Lacq area of France and the most recently discovered gas fields in Holland.

Natural gas consists chiefly of methane but the other gaseous paraffins from ethane to butane may be present in varying proportions and these may add appreciably to its value as a chemical feedstock. In addition, most natural gases are contaminated with variable amounts of nitrogen; other diluents may also be present such as hydrogen sulphide and the oxides of carbon. Exceptionally, other gases may be present and certain American natural gas fields yield gases containing up to 5% of helium. Analyses of typical natural gases from different parts of the world are given in Table 1 below.

The analysis of the gas from the Slochteren field is particularly interesting since it may be anticipated that any gas fields discovered under the North Sea might be extensions of this field and yield gas of similar composition.

TABLE 1. Composition of typical Natural Gas Samples.

	Slochteren Holland	Lacq France	Po Valley Italy	Hasi R'mel Sahara	Oklahoma U.S.A.	McKamie U.S.A.
CH_4	81·9	69·3	95·9	83·5	83·9	68·3
C_2H_6	2·7	3·1	1·4	7·0	9·7	7·2
C_3H_8	0·4	1·1	0·4	2·0	3·9	3·3
C_4's	0·1	0·6	0·2	0·8	2·5	2·7
C_5's+	0·1	0·7	0·1	0·4		
H_2S	—	15·2	—	—	—	6·8
CO_2	0·8	9·6	0·2	0·2	—	—
N_2	14·0	0·4	1·8	6·1	—	11·1

Natural gas needs little preliminary treatment other than desulphurization when sulphur compounds are present; in some cases, as at Lacq, recovery of elemental sulphur may be an important part of the operation. Removal of the other contaminants and separation of the individual hydrocarbons may be necessary for some purposes, and this is especially the case when the gas contains significant quantities of ethane and propane which are particularly valuable as feedstocks for olefin production. Removal of hydrogen sulphide and carbon dioxide is accomplished by methods similar to those described for synthesis gas on page 49; separation of individual hydrocarbons is by low temperature distillation as described for the production of ethylene on page 37.

5. TREATMENT OF CRUDE OIL

Crude oil is frequently found together with natural gas and, when this occurs, the crude is first "stabilized" by the separation of both free and dissolved gas. The separated natural gas is treated as described in the preceding section. This operation is usually carried out in the production area and, when this is far removed from industrial markets, as much gas as possible is left dissolved in the crude oil and recovered by preliminary treatment in the refinery. After removal of dissolved gas the crude is subjected to a primary distillation.

Distillation is a fundamental process in the separation of chemical compounds and it will be referred to again and again in the following chapters; it has been assumed that the reader is familiar with the principles of distillation processes which have been described in much published work.

The process is carried out on a vast scale in the petroleum industry and present day knowledge of the chemical engineering principles applied to the design and construction of large-scale distillation plants owes much to the development work carried out by oil refiners, especially in the U.S.A. It is by the fractional distillation of crude oil, followed in some cases by further processing, that the most important feedstocks for the manufacture of organic chemicals are prepared. Some knowledge of the basic oil refining processes is essential to an understanding of the later chapters of this book.

A complete crude oil may be imagined as consisting of a full range of hydrocarbons from the simplest, methane, to the most complex known in Nature which may contain up to 125 carbon atoms; in practice crude oils contain only a small part of the range of possible hydrocarbons and vary considerably in composition, especially in the proportions of light and heavy hydrocarbons present. Paraffinic hydrocarbons predominate but aromatics and naphthenes may also be present and some crude oils are rich in these cyclic compounds; olefinic hydrocarbons do not occur. Much work has been done on the chemical composition of crude oils but it is only comparatively recently that, with the aid of mass spectrometry and chromatography, positive identification of some of the more complex hydrocarbons present has been possible. Separation of individual hydrocarbons in a pure state is, however, still impracticable except for the simple compounds where the possibilities of isomerism are limited or, in a few cases, where advantage may be taken of specific physical or chemical properties of some of the more complex compounds to effect a separation. For the oil refining industry, however, such separations are rarely necessary and splitting the crude oil into fractions of varying distillation range and specific gravity by fractional distillation is all that is required as a first step in refining; this process will also provide the naphtha fraction now largely used as a feedstock for chemical operations. A much simplified diagram showing the flow through a modern distilling unit and the approximate temperatures in the columns when distilling a typical Middle East crude oil are given in Fig. 3.

The stabilized crude feed is first pumped through a bank of tubes contained in a furnace, where about 40% of it is vaporized, and the mixture of liquid and vapour is injected into the first column of the distillation train. This column separates the residue, or "reduced crude", from the bottom, a heavy gas oil from a tray about half way up and the distillate passes on to the next column.

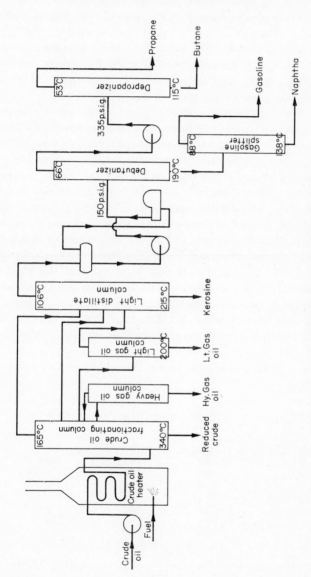

FIG. 3 Flow Diagram of a Modern Crude Oil Distiller.

C

The separation then continues in stages as shown; there are, of course, many heat exchangers in the system for heating or cooling the various streams so that maximum use is made of the heat, put in at high temperature in the primary evaporation, as the column operating temperatures fall when the lighter fractions are being separated. The approximate yields and distillation ranges of the products are given in Table 2.

The reduced crude may be further submitted to vacuum distillation for recovery of lubricating oil fractions, waxy distillates and, ultimately, bitumen or petroleum coke: residues from Middle East crudes are not generally preferred for this purpose but are blended off for use as fuel oil. The kerosine and gas oil fractions are partly used for domestic fuel and lighting purposes and as tractor, diesel and aviation turbine fuels but they, together with the naphtha, are important feedstocks for further processing and conversion to high octane gasoline, for conversion to olefins for chemical manufacture and for the production of gas by the nationalized gas industry. It will be noted that the yield of gasoline in the initial distillation of the crude was quite small, with a final boiling point of about 100°C, whereas commercial gasoline should have an end point of 205°C. It is only by blending the straight run gasoline with the products from secondary conversion

TABLE 2. YIELD OF PRODUCTS FROM A TYPICAL MIDDLE EAST CRUDE
OIL %/WT.

Product	Yield %/wt.	Sp. gr. 15°/4°C	Boiling range °C
Reduced crude	51·3	0·977	350
Heavy gas oil	8·8	0·876	300–350
Light gas oil	8·8	0·843	250–300
Kerosine	12·9	0·799	160–250
Naphtha	7·7	0·751	100–160
Gasoline	7·7	0·685	Up to 100
Butane	1·8	—	Gas
Propane	0·8	—	Gas
Crude feed		0·856	

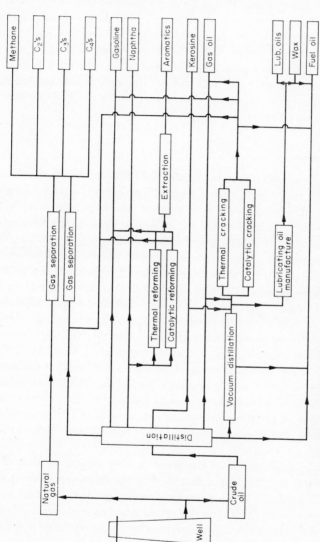

Fig. 4 Diagrammatic Scheme for Conversion of Crude Oils to Finished Products.

processes that the modern high octane gasolines are produced in the necessary quantity and quality. Figure 4 shows schematically how the secondary conversion processes fit into the overall pattern of refining processes and two of them, reforming and extraction, are described below. The cracking process is also of major importance to refiners but, because of its importance to the chemical industry also, it is treated separately in the next section of this chapter. Secondary processes are well described in modern books on oil refining.

Reforming

Reforming is a process in which light hydrocarbon fractions are heated to a temperature which is high enough to cause partial molecular breakdown, at a pressure which is high enough to encourage recombination and rearrangement of the molecular fragments; the process may be carried out with, or without, the aid of catalysts. The reformed distillate will be somewhat more volatile than the feedstock and will have a higher octane number. Straight thermal reformers usually work at temperatures up to 540°C and pressures up to 1,000 psi, whereas catalytic reforming may be carried out at pressures of 200–700, psi. and somewhat lower temperatures and hydrogen is mixed with the feed to minimize deposition of carbon on the catalyst. Catalysts are of two kinds—molybdenum or chromium oxide based or platinum based; in both cases the support is usually alumina but sometimes silica/alumina mixtures are used. Increase in temperature and decrease in pressure improve the octane number of the produced gasoline but increase the yield of the lighter hydrocarbon gases.

The arrangement of the plant is very similar to that of a naphtha cracking plant described in the following section; the whole process is really a cracking process carried out under mild conditions. The chief basis for octane number improvement is the formation of aromatic hydrocarbons by such processes as dehydrogenation and ring closure of n-paraffins:

$$n \; C_7H_{16} \longrightarrow \text{(benzene with } CH_3) + 4 H_2$$

and by dehydrogenation of naphthenes:

$$\longrightarrow \text{(benzene with } CH_3) + 3 H_2$$

Any olefins formed are quickly rehydrogenated by the hydrogen present and the gasoline produced, especially by catalytic reforming, is practically free from olefins. For modern high octane gasolines catalytic reforming is essential, and when the process is carried out in such a way as to give a very high conversion to aromatics, pure hydrocarbons may be separated from the resulting reformate for use by the chemical industry.

In the U.K., with one exception, all the catalytic reformers are operated by oil companies which supply aromatic hydrocarbons for the chemical industry. The exception is I.C.I. which has built its own reformer at Wilton, Yorks., to supplement the aromatics recovered from the liquid fractions produced by its naphtha cracking plants.

Extraction

Extraction processes consist of washing petroleum fractions with a selective solvent which dissolves specific hydrocarbon types and forms a two phase system with the insoluble portion which may be readily separated. The valuable portion may be in the solvent (the extract) or in the residue (the raffinate); frequently both fractions are upgraded in value. The process is widely used for the de-asphalting and dewaxing of lubricating oil fractions but, for the chemical industry, it is the recovery of aromatics which is of interest.

The first of these processes to achieve commercial importance was the Edeleanu process, invented in 1907, which used liquid sulphur dioxide as a solvent; it was a standard refinery process for many years but has now been largely replaced, first by the Udex process, which employs di-ethylene glycol as the selective solvent and is still probably the most widely used, and then by the recently invented Shell process which uses sulpholane (thiophan 1·1 dioxide) as its selective solvent. The arrangement of the process is simple; the solvent is allowed to flow down a specially packed tower where it contacts a rising stream of feed. The raffinate, free from aromatics passes out at the top of the tower and an aromatics rich solvent stream is withdrawn from the base; this is freed from aromatics by heating and returned to the process.

The extract will contain most of the aromatics and olefins from the original feed; its composition will clearly depend on the nature of the feed used. Platinum based reforming (Platforming) of light feedstocks can give high conversions to the lower aromatics, benzene, toluene and the xylenes and virtually no production of olefins. By tailoring the feed to the correct distillation range, the production of specific aromatic hydrocarbons may be favoured and this is frequently done when pure aromatics for chemical purposes are to be the main product of the process. The gasoline fraction from the high severity cracking of naphtha also contains substantial proportions of the lower aromatics which may be recovered by extraction and subsequently separated and purified.

As in the case of catalytic reformers, extraction plants in the U.K. are all owned and operated by oil companies with the exception of one owned by I.C.I. at Wilton which treats the gasolines from its own reformer and from its high severity naphtha crackers.

Finally, mention must be made here of urea dewaxing in which waxy distillates are treated. The urea forms a crystalline addition compound with straight chain waxes, which may be filtered off and decomposed to recover the urea for recycle and give a wax consisting mainly of straight chain paraffins. Although not yet operated in the U.K. the process is used by Shell in Holland to provide special wax feedstocks for the manufacture of detergent raw materials, which is carried out in this country (see page 182).

The series of operations described gives the refiner considerable flexibility in adapting his product pattern to market demand. In such a complex system, however, it is inevitable that some products will appear in surplus, and it is among these surpluses that the chemical and gas making industries must look for their feedstocks if they are to get them reasonably cheaply. In the U.K., at present, it is the naphtha fractions which are in surplus, and it is on this feedstock that the current operations and planned expansion of the heavy organic chemical industry and, to some extent, of the nationalized gas industry are based.

6. CRACKING

It has already been mentioned on page 6 that the process of cracking, or pyrolytic decomposition, was developed by the oil refining industry to break down the higher hydrocarbons into simpler ones and so improve the yield of petrol from a given crude oil, and that it was the presence of olefins in the by-product gases from these operations that led, in the first place, to the manufacture of chemicals from petroleum on a large scale. The demand for olefins for the production of chemicals, especially for ethylene, soon outstripped the availability from oil refinery by-product sources and, since the end of the last war, the tendency, even in the U.S.A., has been for olefins for chemical manufacture to be produced by cracking operations specially designed to maximize the yield of the desired gases.

All hydrocarbons become unstable if heated to a sufficiently high temperature, the degree of instability at a given temperature depending on the chain length and structure. The two chief decomposition reactions which occur in cracking are dehydrogenation and chain rupture of paraffins according to the general equations:..

$$C_nH_{2n+2} \longrightarrow C_nH_{2n} + H_2$$
$$C_{m+n}H_{2(m+n)+2} \longrightarrow C_mH_{2m} + C_nH_{2n+2}$$

Because the smaller hydrocarbon molecules are more stable, methane, and to a lesser extent, ethane, frequently appear as the paraffinic products of chain rupture, thus producing as large an olefin as possible from the molecule undergoing cleavage.

When, as is usually the case, a mixture of hydrocarbons is cracked, both of these reactions proceed simultaneously; the product mix is further complicated by additional reactions such as dehydrogenation of naphthenes, de-alkylation of aromatics, formation and recombination of free radicals and by the rehydrogenation, further decomposition and condensation reactions of olefins already formed.

TABLE 3. YIELD OF PRODUCTS FROM CRACKING PARAFFINIC NAPHTHAS

	Straight run light naphtha				Straight run heavy naphtha			
Boiling range:								
I.B.P.	26 °C				102 °C			
F.B.P.	102 °C				221 °C			
Sp. gr.	0·700				0·780			
Coil outlet Temperature	740 °C		765 °C		727 °C		763 °C	
Steam moles/ mole feed	3·05		7·50		3·50		8·20	
	Wt. %	Mol. %	Wt. %	Mol. %	Wt. %	Mol. %	Wt. %	Mol. %
H_2		11·2		14·6		10·5		15·5
CH_4		31·4		29·5		28·3		28·7
C_2H_2	}	25·2		0·6		0·1		0·6
C_2H_4				32·4		26·7		32·4
C_2H_6		8·5		5·7		9·1		3·4
C_3H_6		14·3		10·5		15·1		11·7
C_3H_8		1·2		0·7		1·1		0·4
C_4H_6		2·5		2·5		2·4		3·2
C_4H_8		5·5		4·3		5·8		3·9
C_4H_{10}		0·2		0·2		0·3		0·2
C_4 and lighter	70·3		73·8		57·5		59·0	
Distillate to 190 °C	24·1		17·8		35·2		30·5	
Fuel oil	5·6		8·4		7·3		10·5	
Ethylene on feed	17·7		23·9		15·4		19·1	

For production of the lower olefins the best feedstock is the corresponding paraffin since only a simple dehydrogenation is required and high yields and conversions are possible. In the U.S.A., therefore, natural and refinery gases are the preferred feedstocks. In the U.K., however, for reasons already described, naphtha is the chief raw material for chemical production. Naphtha is a somewhat indeterminate petroleum fraction boiling roughly within the range 40°–180°C and containing mainly paraffinic hydrocarbons from C_5 to about C_{12}. Cracking such a feedstock gives a broad spectrum of products which varies with the boiling range of the feed and the cracking conditions used. Table 3 is based on results published by Schutt and Zdonik in 1956[†] and shows typical yields.

The figures in Table 3 show clearly the higher yields of the valuable unsaturated gases obtainable from the lower boiling feedstock; they also demonstrate well the substantial effect on the yield of ethylene of a comparatively modest increase in cracking temperature at the expense of a very large increase in steam injection with the feed.

A typical cracking operation is shown diagrammatically in Fig. 5.

The feedstock is first vaporized and preheated by heat interchange with a hot process stream and then enters the convection section of the cracking coil, which is situated in the upper part of the furnace and is heated by the hot gases from combustion of the furnace fuel. At a convenient point in this section the steam is added to lower the partial pressure of the hydrocarbon vapour and to minimize coke deposition in the cracking coil; the steam/feed ratio may be as high as 1:1 by weight. From the convection section the steam/hydrocarbon mixture passes down into the radiant section in the lower part of the furnace where the coil is exposed to direct radiation from the burner flame and the hot brickwork of the furnace walls and roof. The layout of the cracking tube and furnace is designed to

† *Oil and Gas Journal*, 13 Feb. 1956, pp. 98–103.

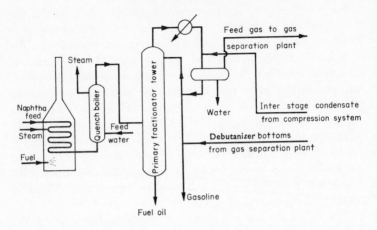

Fig. 5 Flow Diagram of a Modern Naphtha Cracker.

obtain a very high rate of heat input in the radiant section in order to raise the feed to its maximum temperature and to supply the heat required for the endothermic cracking reactions as quickly as possible. Once this objective has been achieved, the gases must be cooled, or quenched, rapidly in order to prevent further decomposition of the olefins already formed. The gases leaving the coil may be at a temperature of 800°C, or even higher when maximum ethylene yield is required, and they pass immediately to the quench exchangers where they are cooled rapidly to about 400°C by water which is converted to high pressure steam. This steam is used to drive a compressor in the gas separation section of the plant and is then discharged at a suitable pressure for injection as dilution steam in the convection section of the cracking coil. Any excess steam may be used for other process purposes. The hot flue gases leaving the convection section of the furnace are cooled by being passed through steam superheaters and boiler feed water preheaters before going to the stack.

The cracking process described above may be divided into three important and distinct stages:

1. Diluting the feed with steam and bringing it to a temperature of 560–600°C where cracking begins.
2. Cracking to the desired composition by rapid addition of heat.
3. Quenching rapidly to a temperature of about 400°C.

The major chemical engineering contractors, mostly with U.S. affiliations, who specialize in construction of cracking plants, have devoted much study to the design of furnaces to achieve these ends and each has his own "know how" on the subject. A version of the process, due to the M. W. Kellogg Co., supplies the heat required for cracking by mixing the feed, already heated to cracking temperature of about 600°C, with steam superheated to about 900°C. By this means high yields of ethylene can be obtained with minimum coke deposition and the process has been used successfully for many years by I.C.I. at Wilton. The most modern designs, however, favour the conventional methods of heating and achieve their results by concentrating on rapid heating to much higher cracking temperatures than would have been thought possible a few years ago, followed by rapid quenching. The new I.C.I. plant at Wilton is of this type.

The hot gases leaving the quench exchangers are further cooled in the primary fractionator tower where the heavy fuel oil fraction is separated from the bottom, a gasoline fraction is taken off near the top and the gas stream, consisting mainly of C_4 and lighter hydrocarbons, passes overhead to the gas separation section. Separation of pure hydrocarbons from this gas stream is a technically complex but theoretically simple operation. Two broad approaches to the problem are possible; the C_4 hydrocarbons may be removed first followed by C_3 removal, then C_2 as a composite stream which is subsequently split into ethylene and ethane in a separate column. When this method is adopted, it is common for the C_4's to be removed by selective oil absorption and for the remaining separations to be carried out by low temperature distillation. Many plants in the U.S.A. are still operating successfully by this method but, in the newest plants, it is usual to refrigerate the whole of the C_4 and lighter gases and to remove fractions in ascending order of molecular weight starting with a methane/hydrogen stream. The method of operation is shown schematically in Fig. 6.

The gas from the top of the primary fractionator is compressed in four stages to about 500 psig with cooling and removal of condensate between each stage. The gases must also be scrubbed with dilute caustic soda solution to remove traces of hydrogen sulphide and carbon dioxide and this may be done before compression or between the third and fourth stages. The inter-stage condensates are allowed to flash into the inlet to the preceding stage, that from the first stage being returned to the primary fractionator after separation of any condensed water. The final compressed gas stream is now free of unwanted impurities and has had most of its water and hydrocarbons above C_4 already removed. The water content is now reduced to a few parts per million in driers packed with activated alumina or molecular sieves. Generally there are three driers in series, interconnected so that any one may be first in sequence:

ABC or BCA or CAB.

As it becomes saturated, the first drier in the series is taken out of circuit and regenerated by having warm methane/hydrogen mixture from the top of the demethanizer column blown through it. The regenerated drier is then put back into circuit last in the series.

After drying, the gas is cooled by refrigeration until everything, except the hydrogen, part of the methane and a little ethylene, is liquefied and this gas/liquid mixture is fed in the demethanizer column in which a methane/hydrogen stream, still containing a little ethylene, is taken off the top and the remaining hydrocarbons are removed as liquid from the bottom. A refrigerated condenser maintained at a temperature of $-90°C$ to $-100°C$ supplies reflux to the column; the efficiency of ethylene recovery is very largely determined by the temperature and pressure conditions at this point. Some further cooling, which improves

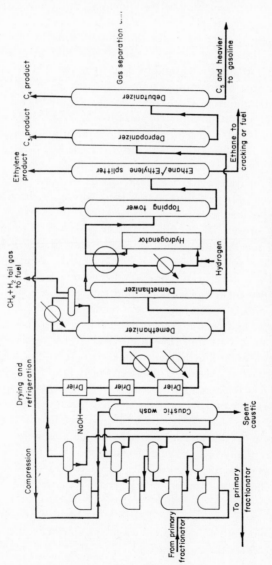

FIG. 6 Separation of Cracker Gas Stream into its components.

ethylene recovery, is sometimes obtained by passing the gas from the top of the demethanizer through an expansion turbine before it passes out of the plant.

From the demethanizer the liquid is fed into the de-ethanizer where a mixture of ethylene and ethane are removed as gas from the top and the C_3 and heavier hydrocarbons go on to the depropanizer where propylene/propane are taken off and then to the debutanizer which removes the C_4 hydrocarbons and leaves the column bottoms, consisting of C_5 and C_6 hydrocarbons, which are blended with the gasoline from the primary fractionator. The C_2 stream from the de-ethanizer is heated by exchange with suitable process streams, mixed with a little hydrogen which must be separately prepared, and passed over a hydrogenation catalyst, usually palladium on an inert base, to hydrogenate the acetylene which is always produced to a small extent in the cracking process. If the final ethylene produced is to meet the required specification, which is usually a maximum of 10 parts of acetylene per million, the acetylene content of the C_2 stream at this point must be substantially below this level. The hydrogenated stream is again cooled and subjected to a preliminary topping distillation to remove any remaining methane, together with excess hydrogen and inert gases. The gas mixture taken off is small in volume and rich in ethylene and is returned to the suction side of the fourth stage of the main cracker gas compressor. The purified C_2 stream is then separated into ethylene as top product and ethane as bottoms on the ethane/ethylene splitter.

In the above description reference has been made to refrigeration and to heat exchange with process streams without giving any details of the arrangements by which this is carried out. There are many such arrangements possible and the one chosen will depend on the composition of the cracked gas concerned, the specification of the finished products required and, to some extent, the whim of the individual designer. The general principles are as follows: the cracked gas is at its highest pressure after compression and refrigeration while the lowest temperature is required where the methane/hydrogen tail gas is separated from the more valuable constituents at the top of the demethanizer. As the gas stream passes through the series of columns, its pressure will fall and its temperature rise. The ethane/ethylene splitter can be regarded as a small subsidiary circuit to the main stream.

Each column requires heating for its reboiler and cooling for its condenser and these may be provided by exchange with process streams at the appropriate temperature or by heat or cold from external sources. The object is clearly to balance the heat flows within the plant so that the minimum heat or cold is required from outside. For refrigeration, liquid ethylene and propylene are employed and temperatures are controlled by controlling the pressures at which they evaporate. Propylene compressed to 130 psig may be liquefied by condensation with water at 15°C and, by evaporation at controlled pressures, will provide temperatures down to −40°C when the pressure will be down almost to atmospheric. At −40°C ethylene compressed to 200 psig may be condensed and this in turn may be evaporated at temperatures down to −100°C which is normally low enough for the demethanizer condenser. For lower temperatures it is possible to have a third refrigeration cycle based on liquid methane condensed by evaporating liquid ethylene at −100°C. With this temperatures down to −160°C may be obtained but such low temperatures are very rarely used.

In order to use the refrigeration available in both the process streams and the refrigerant gases efficiently, large numbers of condensers and heat exchangers are required and these entail a complicated system of pipework. Mild steels cannot be used at temperatures below about −20°C and stainless steels must be used for those parts of the plant exposed to temperatures below this level. This, together with the high power requirements imposed by the refrigeration load, makes low temperature distillation plants expensive to construct and operate. In order to get the output: capital ratio as high as possible, therefore, individual new plants are getting bigger as advancing technology permits the construction of bigger and bigger compressors and other equipment items. In the cracking section mild steel is satisfactory for most equipment items and piping but special high temperature resistant steels are required for the cracking tubes, and this, in turn, demands that a furnace fuel free from vanadium must be used. This rules out most petroleum residue fuels, which contain traces of vanadium, and distillate or gaseous fuels must be provided.

Cracking units are relatively cheap and there is not the same incentive to increase the size of individual units as in the case of low temperature distillation plants. It is usual, therefore, to limit the size of cracking units to a capacity of 10,000–20,000 t/a of ethylene and to provide a number of them for each low temperature distillation unit.

The first U.K. cracker for olefin production was built by British Celanese in 1942, using gas oil as a feedstock, and this remained the only example until the Customs and Excise regulations were amended in 1945 and 1946 to permit the use of light hydrocarbon oils on a duty free basis. There was then a spate of new construction, and, between 1949 and 1951, units were brought on stream by Petrochemicals Ltd., Shell, British Hydrocarbon Chemicals and I.C.I. These all used naphtha as feedstock except for the Shell unit which started up on gas oil and was later changed over to propane/ethane. A few years later Esso joined the ranks of olefin producers with a unit at Fawley, Shell took over Petrochemicals Ltd. and ultimately shut its own propane cracker down and British Celanese changed over to naphtha feedstock and were taken over by Courtaulds. There are thus five companies currently operating olefin crackers, all of which have considerably expanded capacity since the 1949–51 era and which are now expanding even further. The present capacity and planned expansion of these companies is shown in Table 4.

It has been customary, up to the present time, to measure the capacity of an olefin plant by its maximum ethylene output since propylene and the C_4 olefins have been freely available from refinery sources. Naphtha has become the common feedstock but not all of the plants have the same specification for their feed

TABLE 4. CAPACITY OF U.K. ETHYLENE PRODUCING INSTALLATIONS
(thousands of tons/annum)

	Present capacity	Under con-struction	Com-pletion date	Announced expansion	Total
British Hydro-carbon Chemicals					
Grangemouth	130	—	—	250	380
Baglan Bay	60	—	—	—	60
Courtaulds,					
Spondon	24	—	—	—	24
Esso Petroleum					
Co. Fawley	120	—	—	—	120
I.C.I., Wilton	140	200	1965	450	790
Shell Chemical					
Co. (Petro-chemicals Ltd.),					
Carrington	100	150	1966	—	250
Totals	574	350		700	1624

or produce the same yield of ethylene so that the naphtha input cannot be deduced from published ethylene capacities. There are signs that a change of outlook in the assessment of olefin plants may be on the way.

Firstly, the specification for modern gasolines calls for more catalytic reforming and less thermal reforming and catalytic cracking in refineries and this reduces the amount of refinery propylene available. Secondly, demands for propylene are growing very rapidly and, in the future, it is likely that olefin producers will need to look carefully at propylene as well as ethylene capacity when planning expansions. In parallel with these trends there has been an explosive increase in demand for naphtha as feedstock for town's gas production and, if this continues to grow at the present rate, the surplus of naphtha fractions in the refining pattern may disappear. The outcome of these trends is heavily dependent on the results of the oil and gas searches being made in the North Sea.

The use of light distillate for petroleum chemicals (including ammonia) and for town's gas manufacture is shown in Table 5.

In cracking for ethylene it has been shown that, for high yields, high cracking temperatures, short contact times and rapid quenching are necessary but, as shown in Table 3, even at high ethylene yields, the production of acetylene is still quite small. In order to produce a worthwhile yield of acetylene, cracking temperatures of about 1200°C and contact times of less than $\frac{1}{10}$ sec are necessary. These conditions cannot readily be obtained in externally heated cracking tubes due to limitations in materials of construction and in the rates of heat transfer which may be economically attained in practice. These difficulties were avoided by the process developed at Hüls, in Germany, in which methane from coal carbonization or natural gas from a nearby field was decomposed to a mixture of acetylene, carbon and hydrogen by being blown through an electric arc. This process is, however, costly in electric power and, more recently, alternative processes have been devised. These depend either on a regenerative process

TABLE 5. DELIVERIES OF LIGHT PETRO-
LEUM DISTILLATE TO PETROLEUM
CHEMICALS PLANTS AND GASWORKS
(thousand tons per annum)

	Petroleum chemicals	Gasworks
1952	365	—
1953	507	—
1954	607	—
1955	566	—
1956	666	—
1957	793	—
1958	831	41
1959	1067	225
1960	1562	400
1961	1578	497
1962	1949	715
1963	2706	900
1964	3150	1333

in which the hydrocarbon feed is brought momentarily into contact with hot refractory brickwork or on an internal combustion process in which part of the feed is burnt with oxygen.

The two best known of the regenerative processes are the Farbwerke Hoechst High Temperature Pyrolysis (HTP) process and the Wulff process. They are broadly similar in the method adopted. The preheated hydrocarbon feed is brought into brief contact with hot refractory brickwork at about 1200°C and immediately quenched. The brickwork has to supply the heat for the cracking reactions and is separately heated by combustion of the off gas after acetylene recovery; continuity is achieved by having two furnaces in parallel, one of which is heating while the other is cracking. Acetylene is recovered from the cracked gases by extraction with an organic solvent such as dimethyl formamide. These processes are especially suited to the simultaneous production of acetylene and ethylene, the proportions being varied by control of the cracking conditions. The Wulff Process Corporation has had a pilot plant operating in California for many years but the large-scale commercial application of these regenerative processes is only just beginning.

The best known version of the partial combustion processes is that developed by the Badische Anilin und Soda Fabrik (B.A.S.F.) which was first operated commercially in Milan in 1952 using natural gas as feedstock. Natural gas and oxygen are preheated separately, mixed and passed through a burner section to a water quench. Described in this way the operation sounds simple but, in order to achieve the accurate control over temperature and time of contact in the burner flame, which is required for high acetylene yield, and to prevent the burner flame striking back along the gas/oxygen stream, the composition of the mixture and its velocity must be very accurately controlled. The automatic control system is, in fact, the key to successful operation of the process. By-product carbon is removed, first in a water scrubber and finally in a coke filter, and the acetylene is recovered in a pure state by solution in an organic solvent; N-methyl pyrrolidone has been used for this purpose.

Typical analyses of the furnace effluent gas, when either naphtha or methane are used as feedstock, are shown in Table 6.

So far, acetylene manufacture from petroleum has not been established in the U.K., but three plants are at present (Dec. 1965) under construction and a fourth is planned. Two of these will be Wulff plants of about 30,000 t/a acetylene capacity; one is being erected by British Geon Ltd., the Distillers Co. associate, at Barry, Glam. to supply acetylene for its vinyl chloride plant and the other by British Oxygen at Maydown, Northern Ireland

TABLE 6. COMPOSITION OF FURNACE EFFLUENT FROM
B.A.S.F. ACETYLENE PROCESS

	Naphtha mol.%	Methane mol.%
C_2H_2	9·3	8·0
C_2H_4	0·2	0·2
CH_4	4·2	4·2
CO_2	3·9	3·4
CO	37·3	25·9
H_2	43·5	56·8
N_2	0·7	0·8
O_2	0·2	0·2
Higher hydrocarbons	0·7	0·5

to provide raw material for the adjoining "Neoprene" synthetic rubber plant of duPont. The latter will be a more economic alternative to the calcium carbide at present produced by British Oxygen at Maydown. A third Wulff plant of about 10,000 t/a capacity is planned at Hull by the new joint company, set up by Distillers Co. and Courtaulds for the manufacture of vinyl acetate, for which it will provide the raw material. Finally I.C.I. is building a plant of about 50,000 t/a capacity at Runcorn, Cheshire, which will use the B.A.S.F. process and will replace the large calcium carbide plant at present in operation there.

7. SYNTHESIS GAS

Synthesis gas is a rather loose term applied generally to mixtures of carbon monoxide and hydrogen, or even to mixtures of nitrogen and hydrogen, which were derived originally from the water-gas reaction between steam and coke.

$$C + H_2O \longrightarrow CO + H_2$$

If this reaction mixture is treated with more steam over an iron oxide catalyst, the carbon monoxide content may be reduced to less than 1% by the water-gas shift reaction.

$$CO + H_2O \longrightarrow CO_2 + H_2$$

The water-gas reaction is endothermic and the shift reaction exothermic: overall, heat has to be supplied to the process. The carbon dioxide in the gas from the shift reaction may be readily scrubbed out and it is thus possible to obtain any ratio of $H_2:CO$ from pure hydrogen to the $1:1$ ratio of the water gas reaction. The carbon dioxide may be easily recovered in a pure state from the scrubbing system if required. If pure carbon monoxide is needed, it may be separated from water gas by the usual methods such as low temperature distillation or selective absorption in cuprous salt solutions.

The water-gas reactions applied to coke are now virtually obsolete in this country as a means of producing synthesis gas and will not be further described. The basic reactions, adapted for application to petroleum feedstocks, remain of fundamental importance, however, and are the starting point for so many important chemical syntheses that synthesis gas production can rightly be regarded as a primary process.

Commercial synthesis gas processes of today fall broadly into two groups—steam reforming processes and partial oxidation processes. Many variants of each group are to be found which differ in the feed used, catalysts for various stages of the process and in the pressure and temperature conditions under which they operate. In general it may be said that steam reforming processes operate only on light hydrocarbon feedstocks up to, and including the naphtha fractions, while the partial oxidation processes are more versatile and can run on any hydrocarbon material including heavy fuel oil. It will, however, be obvious that, the higher the molecular weight of the hydrocarbon, the lower the yield of hydrogen per mole converted.

Steam Reforming Processes

The most widely used process employs methane as feedstock; the basic reactions are as follows:

$$CH_4 + H_2O \longrightarrow CO + 3H_2$$

This is then followed by the shift reaction which provides further hydrogen and gives an overall reaction which may be written:

$$CH_4 + 2H_2O \longrightarrow CO_2 + 4H_2$$

These reactions may be applied to higher paraffins which will give a higher $CO:H_2$ ratio in the first stage; this may be an advantage when the gas is to be used for syntheses involving carbon monoxide. Both stages of the process are promoted by catalysts and it is necessary for the gases to be free from sulphur.

In practice, equimolar mixtures of methane and steam are passed through a reactor packed with catalyst, usually nickel promoted with magnesia or alumina on an inert support, at a temperature of 800°–900°C; reaction is virtually complete and the product gases contain only a small proportion of unreacted methane. For some purposes this product may contain too much hydrogen and some adjustment may be necessary, either by partial removal of hydrogen or by use of higher hydrocarbons in the feed. When a pure hydrogen product is required, the product gases from the methane/steam reaction are reacted further with steam at about 450°C over a promoted iron oxide catalyst which achieves a high conversion of carbon monoxide to dioxide. The latter is removed by scrubbing the gases with a selective absorbent which may be regenerated and recycled. The "Girbotol" process uses an aqueous solution of monoethanolamine, and the same process may also be applied to removal of hydrogen sulphide from the feed gases. The "Vetrocoke" process employs aqueous potassium carbonate solution activated with a small quantity of potassium arsenite as an absorbent when the reaction cycle is as follows:

$$K_2CO_3 + CO_2 + H_2O \longrightarrow 2\ KHCO_3$$

$$2\ KHCO_3 \longrightarrow K_2CO_3 + CO_2 + H_2O$$

In both processes the first stage of absorption of carbon dioxide is carried out under pressure; the reagent is then injected into a pressure reduction tower when a large part of the carbon dioxide is released. Regeneration of the reagent may be completed by blowing with air or by heating. The carbon dioxide may be recovered and, after a simple purification, compressed and sold as liquid or solid carbon dioxide.

The methane/steam process is particularly attractive when supplies of natural gas are readily available and, as a starting point for ammonia and fertilizer manufacture, it has frequently been established in underdeveloped areas, with surplus natural gas, as a first venture into chemical manufacture. In the U.K. it has been in use for some thirty years by I.C.I. using methane from coal carbonization in the first instance and, later, the light gases from oil cracking as feedstock. Coal carbonization is declining and methane has come to have a high value as a component of town's gas and is, therefore, a relatively expensive raw material. This has favoured the use of higher hydrocarbons and the recently developed high-pressure reforming processes, using naphtha as feedstock, have become of major importance, both for the production of synthesis gas and as a means of converting light liquid hydrocarbons into town's gas.

Several high-pressure reforming processes have been developed in the last few years but the one due to I.C.I. is typical and was the first to be applied commercially, the first plant coming on

stream at Heysham in mid-1962. The basic reactions are similar to
those of the methane/steam process but, by operating under
pressure and using a liquid feedstock, advantage can be taken of
the large increase in volume which takes place through the
process to produce the product gases at high pressure and thus
save on compression costs when the synthesis gas is used in
subsequent processes. In effect, fuel is being used directly to
compress the gases instead of going through the normal stages
of steam and power generation and mechanical compression.

The preferred feed is a highly paraffinic straight run naphtha
with a final boiling point of about 180°C. The feed is vaporized
in steam heated evaporators, mixed with hydrogen, preheated by
heat exchange with product gases and passed over a catalyst in
the hydrodesulphurization tower. Elemental and combined
sulphur in the feed are converted to hydrogen sulphide which is
removed by passing the gases through an absorber packed with
zinc oxide. Steam is added after the absorption tower and the
mixture then passes into the tubes of the reforming furnace;
these are of chromium/nickel steel and are packed with a nickel-
bearing catalyst in the form of rings, specially developed by I.C.I.
The tubes are contained in a furnace chamber which may be
heated by gas or liquid fuel and which supplies the heat needed
for the endothermic reforming reactions; if liquid fuel is used, it
must be a distillate and free from vanadium which would attack
the nickel/chromium steel of the furnace tubes. The reforming
temperature is similar to that for the methane/steam reaction—
i.e. about 800°C—and the exit gases from the reforming tubes
are partially cooled in a waste heat boiler before going to the
shift reactor. Carbon dioxide is removed from the gases after
shift reaction by one of the conventional processes already
described.

This I.C.I. process is claimed to be very flexible; by a suitable
choice of operating conditions, the composition of the product can
be varied to suit the end use for which it is required. When it is
to be used for ammonia synthesis, the reforming step is operated
to leave some unchanged hydrocarbon, mainly methane, in the

gas from the primary reformer. By addition of the correct amount of air and further reaction over an oxidation catalyst, a gas mixture is obtained which, after shift reaction and removal of carbon dioxide, will contain the required 1:3 nitrogen : hydrogen ratio for ammonia synthesis.

Partial Oxidation Processes

When a hydrocarbon is reacted with a limited amount of air or oxygen under controlled conditions, it is converted to a mixture of carbon monoxide and hydrogen which may then be submitted to the shift reaction in the usual way; if air is used, the mixture will be contaminated with nitrogen which may be a disadvantage. For methane the equation might be written:

$$CH_4 + \tfrac{1}{2}O_2 \longrightarrow CO + 2H_2$$

The actual mechanism of the transformation is complex and proceeds through a number of distinct stages. The process may be applied to any petroleum fraction from natural gas to heavy fuel oil; its ability to use liquid feedstocks was one of the advantages claimed for the process when it was first developed. The appearance of the pressure reforming processes described above may have reduced this advantage quite considerably for U.K. conditions.

Two variants of the process, one developed by the Shell Group and the other by the Texas Development Co., have attained commercial importance. Shell Chemicals use the Shell process for the production of hydrogen for ammonia synthesis at Shell Haven, Essex and I.C.I. have a "Texaco" unit in their synthesis gas complex at Billingham, Co. Durham, although this may have been shut down after the development of their naphtha reforming process. In order to avoid excessive contamination of the product gases with nitrogen, both processes use pure oxygen for the partial oxidation step; this necessitates the construction of a large air separation plant which adds to the capital cost of the process. If the object is to produce pure hydrogen for ammonia synthesis, some of the by-product nitrogen from the air separation plant may be blended back into the product, and this is usually accomplished by using a liquid nitrogen wash to remove the last traces of carbon monoxide and hydrocarbons from the hydrogen product.

In the partial oxidation step oxygen and hydrocarbon, in proportions varying according to the carbon/hydrogen ratio of the feedstock, are preheated separately and mixed under pressure in an externally heated reaction chamber packed with a nickel based catalyst. Reaction takes place at about 1000°C and the reactor effluent gases consist of a mixture of some carbon monoxide and hydrogen with a few per cent of carbon dioxide, some carbon, and a very small quantity of unchanged hydrocarbon. After partial cooling this mixture is scrubbed to remove the carbon and then passed to the shift reaction in the usual way.

Choice of Process

The production of synthesis gas described above has three main stages—primary conversion, shift reaction and gas purification. There are alternative processes and plant designs available for each of these stages and the number of possible combinations is large; each of these will have its own characteristic balance of fuel and utility requirements and there may be substantial differences between the total energy needs for some of them. Finally the composition of the product varies according to the end use for which it is intended and this will also have an influence on the choice of process for the various stages. It is not possible to say, therefore, that one or other combination of processes has an overall economic advantage, and the optimum solution for each individual project must be worked out. It can, however, be generally stated that, while the present surplus of naphtha fractions continues, the pressure reforming processes for light hydrocarbon distillate feedstocks will be economically attractive in many applications. If, as in the case of I.C.I. at its factories at Heysham, Billingham and Severnside, a number of different processes requiring synthesis gas are being operated, there may be a number of possible process combinations differing little in economics and resulting in the use of several processes in the overall synthesis gas complex.

Oxidation

Many of the industrially important organic compounds contain only oxygen in addition to carbon and hydrogen. In order to introduce the oxygen into the paraffin molecule, however, two stages of reaction are generally necessary—first conversion of the paraffin to an olefin or halogen compound—followed by further reactions. It is clear that, if this could be reduced to a one-stage process by direct introduction of oxygen from the air into the hydrocarbon molecule, manufacture of many chemicals would be cheapened. Typical reactions might be:

$$CH_4 + \tfrac{1}{2}O_2 \longrightarrow CH_3OH$$

$$CH_4 + O_2 \longrightarrow HCHO + H_2O$$

$$C_2H_6 + \tfrac{1}{2}O_2 \longrightarrow CH_3CH_2OH$$

$$C_2H_6 + O_2 \longrightarrow CH_3CHO + H_2O$$

It has been shown by many workers that these reactions do, in fact, take place when paraffins are oxidized with air under carefully controlled conditions. The yield of useful products is not, however, high enough to form the basis of an economic industrial process and much of the hydrocarbon is lost as oxides of carbon and water. Moreover, when the higher paraffins are used as feed, a complex mixture of oxygenated compounds is obtained, which is difficult to separate and which contains the products in the wrong proportions for the market. Processes using propane and butane as feedstock have been developed and operated commercially in the U.S.A., where the gaseous paraffins are more readily available and cheaper than in this country, by the Celanese Corporation of America and others and a substantial part of U.S.

production of the simple aliphatics such as methanol, formaldehyde and acetic acid is produced in this way. The oxidation step is simple; a mixture of air with an excess of hydrocarbon is passed through a reaction chamber at a pressure of up to 20 atm and a temperature of about 400°C. The reaction gases are then cooled and sent to the separation plant, which may contain over a hundred interlinked fractionating columns, for purification of the multiple products which include methanol, formaldehyde, formic acid, ethanol, acetaldehyde and acetic acid together with some esters and other oxygenated derivatives of the butane and propane feed.

Chemical oxidation of the paraffins by strong oxidizing agents, such as nitric or chromic acids, may offer a better yield of the desired product but the advantages of a single-stage process are lost and, up to the present, no such process has achieved commercial operation in the U.K. Oxidation of aromatic hydrocarbons, either with air or chemical reagents, is more easily controlled and is widely practised for the production of specific chemicals such as phthalic and maleic anhydrides. These processes are described in Chapter 9.

In the U.K. the only commercial paraffin oxidation known to be operating is the one installed by the D.C.L. at Hull in 1962 for production of acetic acid by oxidation of naphtha, on which a limited amount of information has been published. Naphtha is oxidized in the liquid phase with air under pressure and at elevated temperature. Precise conditions are not known but temperatures are believed to be fairly low, around 200°C, and the pressure fairly high; an oil-soluble metal salt, e.g. manganese, cobalt or nickel naphthenate, is used as catalyst. The vent gas from the reactor is cooled in stages to below 0°C, for maximum recovery of volatile products and unoxidized hydrocarbons, expanded through a turbine which provides part of the power for the process, and finally vented to atmosphere; the vented gas consists almost entirely of nitrogen and carbon dioxide. The liquid reaction products are separated by distillation. The yield of useful products is about 70–75 lb per 100 lb of naphtha converted and consists of about 75% acetic acid, 17% formic acid and smaller amounts of propionic, butyric and succinic acids. The Hull plant has recently been enlarged to a capacity of around 90,000 t/a.

READING LIST

1. Modern Wood Distillation. *Chemistry & Industry*, Nov. 1958, pp. 1465–8.
2. *Forest Record* No. 19. *The Manufacture of Wood Charcoal in Great Britain*, by L. Reynolds. H.M. Stationery Office, 1961.
3. *Industrial Fermentations*, Vol. I, by L. A. Underkafler and R. J. Hickey. Chemical Publishing Co. 1954.
4. *British Fermentation Industries*, by J. W. Whitmarsh, Pitman, 1958.
5. *Soaps and Detergents*, by E. G. Thomsen and John McCutcheon. McNair, Dorland & Co., New York, 1949.
6. *Distillation Principles and Processes*, by Sidney Young. Macmillan, London, 1922.
7. *Elements of Fractional Distillation*, by C. S. Robinson and E. R. Gilliland. McGraw Hill, New York, 1950.
8. *Modern Petroleum Technology*. The Institute of Petroleum, London, 1962.
9. *Advances in Petroleum Chemistry and Refining*, by Kenneth Kobe and John J. McKetta Jr. Interscience Publishers, New York, 1958.
10. *Introduction to Petroleum Chemicals*, Edited by H. Steiner. Pergamon Press, London, 1961.

CHAPTER 3

Chemicals Produced from Synthesis Gas

THE largest single use in the chemical industry for the products of the synthesis gas reactions described in Chapter 2 is in the production of ammonia for which installed capacity in the U.K. is expected to exceed 1,000,000 t/a by 1970. The manufacture and uses of ammonia are, however, dealt with in another volume of this series and will not be further described here. An important use of ammonia is for the production of urea and this compound, the first synthetic organic chemical, can hardly be omitted from a book on organic chemical industry. Other important uses of synthesis gas are based on the reactions of olefins with carbon monoxide/hydrogen mixtures (the OXO reaction) and the reactions of these mixtures over various catalysts to produce either methanol or more complex hydrocarbons and oxygenated compounds (the Fischer–Tropsch reaction).

UREA MANUFACTURE

The raw materials for the production of urea are ammonia and carbon dioxide and, as the latter is a by-product of the synthesis gas reactions, it is usual to find urea plants adjacent to ammonia plants. The reaction between ammonia and carbon dioxide occur in two stages; the first stage is the formation of ammonium carbamate according to the equation:

$$2\ NH_3 + CO_2 \longrightarrow NH_2COONH_4$$

The carbamate then dehydrates under the conditions in the reactor to form urea and water:

$$NH_2COONH_4 \longrightarrow NH_2CONH_2 + H_2O$$

There are some difficulties in the practical application of the process since completion of the first reaction is only achieved by the use of high pressure and an excess of ammonia at moderate temperature while the second reaction does not go to completion but is favoured by high temperature; the ammonium carbamate is, moreover, highly corrosive and calls for special materials of construction in the reactor. When there are no alternative means of disposing of the unreacted carbamate, its decomposition into ammonia and carbon dioxide for recycle is a substantial charge on the process. Urea plants can, therefore, be divided into "once through" and "total recycle" types. In the U.S.A., where there is a large outlet for ammonia and urea in aqueous solution as liquid fertilizers, once through processes are largely used. For U.K. conditions, however, where urea is not much used as a fertilizer and there is, in any case, little application of fertilizers in liquid form, total recycle processes are almost obligatory, and a typical process of this type is described.

Purified carbon dioxide, recovered from synthesis gas manufacture, is compressed to reactor pressure which may vary from 1500 to 6000 psig according to process design; in modern total recycle plants reactor pressures of about 4000 psig are favoured. A mixture of fresh and recycle ammonia is compressed to the same pressure and the two reactants fed into a high-pressure reaction tower. This tower is subject to the full effect of carbamate corrosion and must have a specially resistant lining, which may be of lead, stainless steel, titanium or silver. The $NH_3:CO_2$ ratio in the feed may also vary but 4:1 is a good average figure compared with the stoichiometric requirement of 2:1. The reactor is maintained at a temperature of 190°C–200°C. Urea formation is exothermic and carbamate dehydration endothermic but, overall, heat has to be removed from the tower. This may be done by cooling coils but some designs avoid this by recycling ammonium carbamate from a later stage in the process back to the reactor.

The reactor effluent consists of urea, undecomposed ammonium carbamate, excess ammonia and water produced by the reaction and introduced with the carbamate recycle. The pressure is reduced to about 250 psig when most of the excess ammonia flashes off and is condensed and recycled to the reactor. The remaining solution contains mainly urea and ammonium carbamate. In non recycle processes it is possible, at this stage, to concentrate the solution by evaporation and to recover most of the urea by crystallization; the mother liquor, still containing urea together with undecomposed carbamate, is then used for production of liquid fertilizers. In total recycle processes, however, the solution left after flashing off excess ammonia is heated to decompose the carbamate into carbon dioxide and ammonia. The gases from the decomposer may be reabsorbed in aqueous ammonia solution to form ammonium carbamate, which is recycled to the reactor, or they may be recovered separately and recycled to the individual reactant feeds. Since carbon dioxide in urea plants is normally a by-product available at virtually nil cost, it is not usually worth recompressing the recovered material which is vented to atmosphere.

The urea solution may be further concentrated and the urea recovered by crystallization or, when the urea is required as a fertilizer, it may be evaporated to greater than 95% purity and then sprayed into the top of a tower, down which it falls against a rising current of cold air. The resulting product is in the form of small spherical granules, or prills, which are dried, graded for size, coated with a powder such as ground limestone or phosphate rock to prevent caking and sent to storage. Over and undersized material is remelted and sent back to the top of the prilling tower.

Great care has to be exercised when handling concentrated solutions or molten urea to minimize the production of biuret— a condensation product formed by elimination of ammonia from two molecules of urea:

$$NH_2CONH_2 + NH_2CONH_2 \longrightarrow NH_2CONHCONH_2 + NH_3$$

This compound is poisonous to plants and the usual limit set for agricultural urea is about $\frac{1}{2}$% of biuret. Every effort is made therefore, to limit the hold up time in the process of hot concentrated urea solutions and of molten urea. A simplified flow diagram for a recycle urea process is shown in Fig. 7.

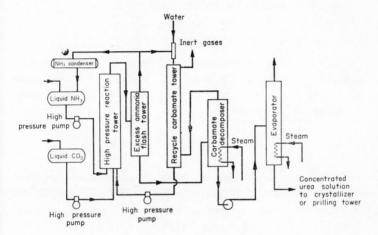

FIG. 7 Total Recycle Process for Urea.

I.C.I. is the only manufacturer of urea in the U.K. at the present time and is believed to have a number of plants in operation. A major new plant will be brought on stream at Billingham early in 1966 with a capacity of 1000 t/day; when this plant is ready the other units will probably be shut down. The new unit will use a version of the total recycle process developed by Toyo Koatsu in Japan; plants using this process world wide are estimated to have a total capacity of 1,500,000 t/a.

The chief chemical use for urea in this country is in the production of plastics and adhesives and is currently estimated to absorb about 25,000 tons annually. Other possible uses which may develop are for dewaxing of petroleum fractions and as a starting point for the synthesis of melamine (see Chapter 10). The greatest world wide tonnage use of urea, however, is for agricultural purposes and a substantial part of U.K. production is

C

exported for this market. Its high nitrogen content (pure urea contains 46·6%) makes it valuable as a fertilizer and it may also be used as a protein supplement in the feed of ruminants. Neither of these outlets has developed to any extent in the U.K. and, consequently, the market remains relatively small.

PRODUCTION AND USES OF METHANOL

Methyl alcohol, or methanol, is formed when synthesis gas containing $CO:H_2$ in the ratio $1:2$ is passed over zinc oxide based catalysts under pressure and at elevated temperature according to the equation:

$$CO + 2H_2 \longrightarrow CH_3OH$$

Because of its dependence on the same raw materials methanol manufacture, like urea manufacture, is usually carried out adjacent to synthetic ammonia plants. In the case of methanol there is an additional reason for this as the plant used for the high-pressure reaction is identical with that used for ammonia production so that the units may be used for either purpose according to market requirements.

Where by-product hydrogen is freely available from sources other than synthesis gas production, it may be mixed with carbon dioxide, and the reaction then proceeds as follows:

$$CO_2 + 3H_2 \longrightarrow CH_3OH + H_2O$$

The reaction based on carbon monoxide requires less hydrogen and is normally preferred.

In a typical plant a carbon monoxide/hydrogen mixture of approximately stoichiometric proportions is compressed to about 4000 psig, preheated by exchange with reactor product gases, and fed into a reactor packed with a catalyst consisting of zinc oxide with about 10% of chromium oxide. The reaction is exothermic and the reactor temperature is maintained constant at about 300°C by varying the space velocity through the reactor and the temperature of the inlet gases. The space velocity in the reactor controls the conversion per pass and, consequently the heat generated; when high conversion per pass is required, internal cooling coils must be provided. The reactor gases are first cooled by exchange with cold feed gases, then in a condenser under full operating pressure where crude methanol separates out and the unreacted gases are recycled to the reactor.

The crude methanol is let down to atmospheric pressure, when dissolved gases and some of the low boiling impurities flash off, and is then purified by distillation. The distillation train consists of a low boilers column in which the impurities boiling at a lower temperature than methanol, mainly dimethyl ether, are taken overhead and a methanol column in which the pure alcohol (99+ %) is taken overhead and water flows to waste from the base. A fraction is taken from near the bottom of this column which contains the high boiling alcohol by-products with some methanol. Ancillary distillation columns for the recovery of methanol from the low boiling and high boiling by-product fractions are also provided.

If small quantities of alkali are added to the catalyst in methanol synthesis the yield of the higher alcohols may be substantially increased. This process variant is no longer of commercial importance, however, since the isobutyl alcohol, which is produced in highest yield, may be made more cheaply when the OXO reaction is applied to propylene (see page 170).

There are two producers of methanol in this country of which the larger is I.C.I. with plants at Billingham and Heysham. Because of the interchangeability of ammonia and methanol plant it is not possible to give a figure for plant capacity but this is probably of the order of 150,000 t/a. The other producer is British Hydrocarbon Chemicals at Grangemouth whose plant is estimated to have a capacity of 60,000 t/a. These two manufacturers share the U.K. market which probably absorbs most of the capacity since I.C.I. has announced an expansion of its plant.

Roughly half of the total output is converted to formaldehyde by oxidation or dehydrogenation over silver or copper catalysts according to the equations:

$$CH_3OH + \tfrac{1}{2}O_2 \xrightarrow{\text{Ag.}} HCHO + H_2O$$

$$CH_3OH \xrightarrow{\text{Cu.}} HCHO + H_2$$

The most important use of formaldehyde is for production of phenol/formaldehyde, urea/formaldehyde and melamine/formaldehyde resins by the plastics industry and this absorbs more than half of the output. Other important uses are for manufacture of hexamethylene tetramine by reaction with ammonia and of penta-erythritol by condensation with acetaldehyde. A new outlet which may, in time, dwarf all other applications is for polymerization to the polyoxymethylene plastic recently produced by duPont in the U.S.A. and marketed under the trade name of "Delrin".

Pure formaldehyde has a boiling point of $-19°C$ and is normally sold as a 40% aqueous solution commonly called "formalin"; it tends to form polymers and its solutions are usually stabilized by the addition of some methanol. Its production from methanol is simple and some resin manufacturers prefer to buy methanol and convert it to formaldehyde on their own premises. I.C.I. has a large formaldehyde plant and also supplies methanol to other resin manufacturers. Synthite Ltd. is a large independent producer of formaldehyde and markets its output through the Barter Trading Corporation.

Another major outlet for methanol is for production of methylamines by reaction with ammonia. The first stage of the reaction is formation of the primary amine according to the equation:

$$CH_3OH + NH_3 \longrightarrow CH_3NH_2 + H_2O$$

This reaction is always accompanied by some de-amination of the primary amine to secondary and tertiary amines as follows:

$$2 \text{ CH}_3\text{NH}_2 \longrightarrow (\text{CH}_3)_2\text{NH} + \text{NH}_3$$

$$3 \text{ CH}_3\text{NH}_2 \longrightarrow (\text{CH}_3)_3\text{N} + 2 \text{ NH}_3$$

These reactions are reversible and an equilibrium is set up depending on the ratio of alcohol to total nitrogen present. The yield of the primary amine may, therefore, be increased by recycling the higher amines to the reactor. The reaction is carried out at about 400°C and 1500 psig and a molar ratio of ammonia: alcohol of 4:1; the resulting reaction mixture is separated into its components by distillation. This reaction is applicable to the production of other aliphatic amines but, as the molecular weight of the alcohol increases, so does the tendency for it to dehydrate to the olefin and this, together with decreasing volatility of the amines and consequent difficulty in purification, limits its application to alcohols up to C_4.

I.C.I. is the only U.K. producer of methylamines and is believed to manufacture about 7000 t/a of monomethylamine with smaller quantities of the secondary and tertiary amines. The amines have a variety of uses in the manufacture of rubber chemicals, dyestuffs, pharmaceuticals, photographic chemicals, pesticides and herbicides and the total consumption is increasing slowly.

Methanol has a number of miscellaneous uses as a solvent and in the production of esters such as methyl acetate, methyl methacrylate and dimethyl terephthalate. It is also the starting point for production of methyl chloride which is described, for convenience, with other alkyl halides in Chapter 4.

THE OXO REACTION

This is a most important general reaction of carbon monoxide/ hydrogen mixtures which has found application in a wide variety of syntheses. When equimolar mixtures of carbon monoxide and hydrogen are reacted with an olefin at about 170°C and 3000 psig in the presence of a cobalt catalyst, an aldehyde containing one more carbon atom than the original olefin is formed according to the reaction:

$$2RCH{=}CH_2 + 2CO + 2H_2 \longrightarrow RCH_2CH_2CHO + \underset{CH_3}{\overset{R}{\diagdown}}CHCHO$$

The normal aldehyde may constitute from 40 to 60% of the products. These aldehydes may be hydrogenated to alcohols or oxidized to acids as required.

The manufacture and use of individual chemicals made by this process will be described in the appropriate chapters but, because of the general nature of the process, a typical application will be described here.

When propylene and isobutylene are co-polymerized in the presence of phosphoric acid, a mixture of branched chain heptenes may be fractionated from the product in good yield. This mixture may be subjected to the OXO reaction to give a yield of up to 75% of iso-octyl alcohols for use in plasticizer manufacture (see Chapter 8). The catalyst consists of a cobalt salt on a pumice support packed into a high pressure reaction tower; an equimolar mixture of carbon monoxide and hydrogen is compressed to about 3000 psig and fed to the bottom of the tower while the olefin is fed in at the top. The reaction is exothermic and, after initial heating to start the reaction, the temperature in the tower is maintained constant at about 150°C by working at a low conversion and recycling unchanged olefin at a ratio of 4:1 to 5:1 of product. The effective catalyst is the volatile cobalt carbonyl and depletion of catalyst in the reactor is prevented by addition of cobalt naphthenate dissolved in the olefin feed.

The overhead product is cooled and scrubbed for recovery of carbonyl which is returned to the reactor with the olefin feed; the excess synthesis gas is recycled. The bottom product from the reactor is separated into unchanged olefin, which is returned to the reactor, and a product fraction which is let down to a lower pressure and fed to the cobalt recovery tower. The cobalt carbonyl is driven off by heating and decomposed; decomposition is promoted by bubbling hydrogen into the bottom of the tower, the cobalt being deposited as metal or oxide on a suitable packing. The aldehyde product is then hydrogenated at about 3000 psig and 200°C over a nickel based catalyst.

THE FISCHER–TROPSCH REACTION

This reaction was discovered in 1925 in Germany and was originally conceived as a route from coal to petrol and higher hydrocarbons, and it was, in fact, applied for this purpose on a very large scale in Germany during the last war. The reaction may be written:

$$nCO + 2nH_2 \longrightarrow (CH_2)_n + nH_2O$$

The reaction is carried out at normal or medium (150 psig) pressure in the presence of catalysts containing cobalt and iron; it is quite strongly exothermic and the temperature must be controlled within a narrow range or side reactions leading to the production of methane and carbon dioxide, with deposition of carbon on the catalyst, will take charge.

The reaction has never been applied to a commercial process in the U.K. and it is quite clearly uneconomic except in conditions where the supply of petroleum products is artificially restricted as in wartime, or where coal is exceptionally cheap and petroleum products relatively expensive. The last set of conditions does exist at one place in South Africa, near Johannesburg, and a large plant is still in operation there. Even this plant depends largely on the oxygenated products of the reaction to make it economic.

The reaction is particularly interesting, however, because it produces almost entirely straight chain carbon compounds and many variants of the basic reaction have been tried to improve the yield of straight chain acids, aldehydes, ketones and alcohols.

In the U.S.A. the Hydrocol Corporation built a large plant, using petroleum methane as the source of synthesis gas, to produce high octane petrol and a substantial proportion of oxygenated derivatives. The process has never achieved great economic success and it remains a technically interesting, but commercially unattractive, proposition under today's conditions.

Synthesis gas may also be a source of pure carbon monoxide by extraction with ammoniacal cuprous salt solutions. It has been found that carbon monoxide will react directly with olefins and with alcohols to form acids according to the equations:

$$RCH{=}CH_2 + CO + H_2O \longrightarrow \begin{array}{c} R \\ CH_3 \end{array}\hspace{-0.5em}\Big\rangle CHCOOH$$

$$ROH + CO \longrightarrow RCOOH$$

A number of processes using these reactions have been worked out in the U.S.A. and Germany and the possibility of producing straight chain acids and primary alcohols on a large scale makes the whole field of carbon monoxide chemistry of particular interest and may well lead to the development of commercial installations in the U.K. in the future.

READING LIST

1. *The Fischer–Tropsch and Related Syntheses*, by Henry H. Storch, Norma Golumbei and Robert R. Anderson. Chapman & Hall, London.

CHAPTER 4

Chemicals Derived from Acetylene

THE traditional method of producing acetylene is by reacting calcium carbide with water:

$$CaC_2 + 2H_2O \longrightarrow C_2H_2 + Ca(OH)_2$$

The readily transportable nature of calcium carbide and the ease, therefore, with which acetylene may be produced in simple apparatus at any desired place, together with its suitability for lighting and welding, has made the hydrocarbon familiar to every layman.

PRODUCTION OF CALCIUM CARBIDE

Calcium carbide was first made by Wohler in 1862 and its commercial manufacture in the electric furnace was established by T. L. Willson in North Carolina in 1892 by reaction of coke and lime at a temperature of about 2100°C. The same process is used today, although there has been considerable improvement in equipment since that time.

$$CaO + 3C \longrightarrow CaC_2 + CO$$

The furnace consists of a cylindrical steel vessel with conical bottom and domed top, the whole lined with refractory bricks. Three electrodes, set at the apices of an equilateral triangle, project into the furnace from the top and reach nearly to the bottom of the cylindrical section. Coke and limestone are crushed and graded to about $\frac{1}{2}$ in. in size, mixed in the proportion of about

40 : 60 parts by weight, and fed from hoppers through the top of the furnace. Feeding is done intermittently as the level of the material inside the furnace falls and the hoppers are sealed by a special valve to prevent escape of carbon monoxide from the furnace. The by-product carbon monoxide from the reaction is drawn off from the top of the furnace and may be used as raw material for chemical synthesis or as fuel. Molten carbide collects in the lower part of the furnace and is tapped off from time to time into steel vessels, mounted on bogies, in which it is left to solidify. The bogies are transferred to the crushing plant where the carbide is crushed and graded according to requirements.

The electrodes are gradually burned away in the hottest part of the furnace and their construction, and the methods provided for their continuous renewal, form an important part of the process. The most widely used system is the Soderberg electrode which consists of a carbon rod 2–3 ft in diameter contained in a metal cylinder. The cylinder, of thin gauge brass or copper, passes through a seal in the top of the furnace and extends upwards into a room above the furnace room. Guides and rollers are provided so that the electrode may move downwards into the furnace as the lower end is burned away. The cylinder is filled with electrode paste which consists of a mixture of specially calcined anthracite granules, finely divided coke and ash free pitch, usually of petroleum origin. As the electrode moves gradually into the hot zone of the furnace, the paste hardens until it forms, effectively, a homogeneous carbon rod which is consumed, together with its metal casing, in the reaction zone. At the top new metal sections are welded on and packed with paste as the electrode moves downwards. The current is supplied by continuous copper strips, brazed on to the sides of the cylinder casing, and carried down into the furnace with it.

A thermal process for calcium carbide manufacture has been devised in which the heat is supplied by mixing an excess of coke with lime and burning this excess in a stream of oxygen. Very large quantities of by-product carbon monoxide are produced by this method and the economics of the process are greatly improved if this can be used as raw material for a subsequent chemical synthesis; this variant of the process has not been used in the U.K.

The quality of commercial carbide is measured by the volume of acetylene evolved when a weighed quantity is reacted with water; good quality carbide will yield 4·5 ft³ per lb, equivalent to a calcium carbide content of about 80%. The electric furnace process is expensive in power and requires about 3000 kWh per ton of carbide or 9900 kWh per ton of acetylene; it is usually established, therefore, in areas where cheap off-peak power, usually from hydro-electric installations, is available. It is also important that supplies of lime and coke should be available at the plant at minimum transport cost. These considerations have made Canada and Norway important producers of calcium carbide although very large quantities were produced in Germany during the war, the power being supplied from thermal generating stations fuelled with brown coal.

In the U.K. the cost of transporting about 3·3 tons of carbide for every ton of acetylene required has tended to cancel out the disadvantage of high power cost and a number of attempts to establish carbide and acetylene manufacture in this country have been made. The installation of a carbide plant by the forerunners of British Celanese in 1918 has already been mentioned. This plant soon succumbed to competition from ethanol as a cheaper precursor of acetic anhydride than acetylene and was closed down. In order to meet its need for acetylene as a starting point for synthesis of trichloro- and perchloroethylene, however, I.C.I. built a carbide furnace at Runcorn in Cheshire, and the more recent growth of the market for polyvinyl chloride (PVC) for which acetylene is a convenient starting point, has caused the original facilities to be considerably enlarged. The outbreak of war in 1939 found Britain very short of calcium carbide and, for strategic reasons, the Government sponsored the construction of a plant with a capacity of about 70,000 t/a at Kenfig, near Port Talbot in South Wales. This plant was operated, on behalf of the Ministry of Supply, by the Distillers Company Ltd. and,

after the war, was bought by it to supply the acetylene requirements of its subsidiary company, British Geon Ltd., for PVC
manufacture at Barry, Glam.

The most recent development of all is the construction of a
50,000 t/a carbide plant by the British Oxygen Co. Ltd. near
Londonderry, in Northern Ireland, to provide acetylene for the
production of "Neoprene" synthetic rubber by the duPont company on an adjoining site. The total production of carbide in the
U.K. in 1963 is estimated at 330,000 tons split very roughly as
100,000 tons to Distillers, 180,000 tons to I.C.I. and 50,000 tons
to British Oxygen.

Acetylene may be generated from carbide by either the wet or
dry process. In the wet process the carbide is added to a relatively
large volume of water which releases the acetylene while the
calcium hydrate residue is discharged as a dilute slurry consisting
mainly of water. The disposal of this slurry may present problems
when large quantities of acetylene are generated since, even after
settling, the lime deposit will still contain some 50% of water.
In the Cologne area of Germany the brown coal pits were used
for the disposal of wet generator slurry and some pits were known
to contain nearly 2,000,000 tons of lime in the form of a paste
with 50% of water. For these reasons the so-called dry generator
is now more favoured; in this process carbide and water are
mixed in the proportion of 1:1 by weight under controlled
conditions. The heat of reaction is used to evaporate the water
in excess of the stoichiometrical equivalent, thus leaving a substantially dry calcium hydrate which may be used for other
purposes. The generator is a cylindrical tower with a number of
trays, each swept by a scraper arm attached to a central rotating
spindle. Carbide is added at the top of the tower and is swept
down from tray to tray by the scraper arms. Water is added in
stages to the trays as the material passes down the column, thus
avoiding an excessive temperature rise at any one point. Acetylene
is drawn off from the top of the tower and dry calcium hydrate
is discharged from the bottom. The crude gas contains traces of
ammonia, hydrogen sulphide and volatile phosphorus com-

pounds and is purified by scrubbing with water and caustic soda solution before being fed to the chemical synthesis plants.

Because of its importance for welding, the generation, handling and transport of acetylene has been well described in the literature. For chemical uses, however, the high costs of transport are avoided by siting the chemical plants adjacent to the carbide plant. Even under the most favourable conditions in this country the carbide process cannot now compete with the more recent processes, described on page 44 *et seq.*, for production of acetylene from petroleum and the three major companies producing calcium carbide are all changing to petroleum naphtha as raw material (see page 46).

REACTIONS OF ACETYLENE

Acetylene, with its triple bond, is one of the most reactive of the lower hydrocarbons and may form the starting point for a host of chemical syntheses, some of which are shown in Fig. 8.

Acetylene is, however, rather unstable and, in particular, is liable to explode when compressed so that its application to large-scale manufacture requires a special technology. The work of Reppe and his collaborators at Ludwigshaven has done much to extend our knowledge of the reactions of acetylene and to develop their practical applications to full scale processes, but the technical difficulties still limit the use of acetylene on the large scale. However, many of the products of acetylene reactions may equally well be produced from ethylene as a starting point and, up to the present, ethylene has been both cheaper to produce and easier to handle. As the petroleum based acetylene processes become more firmly established, the situation may change but it seems probable that acetylene will remain complementary to ethylene as a raw material for organic synthesis rather than become a substitute.

One of the earliest chemical uses of acetylene was for production of acetaldehyde by addition of water in the presence of mercuric sulphate as catalyst; the acetaldehyde may subsequently be converted to acetic acid and acetic anhydride as was done by British Celanese at Spondon (see page 8). The major chemical uses of acetylene in the U.K. at present are:

1. Chlorinated hydrocarbon solvents.
2. "Neoprene" synthetic rubber.
3. Acrylic esters.
4. Vinyl acetate.
5. Vinyl chloride.

The chlorinated solvents trichloroethylene and perchloroethylene are made only by I.C.I., mainly at their factories in the Merseyside area. Acetylene and chlorine are reacted together in tetrachloroethane solution, in the presence of an iron or antimony halide catalyst, at a temperature of 75–85°C. The solution must be efficiently agitated to avoid high local concentrations of chlorine or acetylene. Chlorination proceeds smoothly to produce 1.1.2.2-tetrachloroethane from which hydrochloric acid is then eliminated, either by boiling with a slurry of lime and water or by pyrolysis, with or without a catalyst, at temperatures up to 600°C. The reactions are:

$$CH \equiv CH + 2Cl_2 \longrightarrow CHCl_2 - CHCl_2$$
$$CHCl_2 - CHCl_2 \longrightarrow CCl_2 = CHCl + HCl$$

By reacting trichloroethylene from these reactions with a further quantity of chlorine, pentachloroethane is produced and this is converted to perchloroethylene by removal of hydrochloric acid with alkali.

$$CCl_2 = CHCl + Cl_2 \longrightarrow CCl_3 - CHCl_2$$
$$CCl_3 - CHCl_2 \longrightarrow CCl_2 = CCl_2 + HCl$$

The major uses for these solvents are for metal degreasing and for dry cleaning; production in the U.K. is running at about 10,000 t/a of each.

"NEOPRENE" SYNTHETIC RUBBER

It has been known for many years that acid cuprous chloride

will catalyse the linear polymerization of acetylene to di-vinyl acetylene according to the equation:

$$3 \text{ CH} \equiv \text{CH} \longrightarrow \text{CH}_2 = \text{CHC} \equiv \text{CCH} = \text{CH}_2$$

It was later shown that, by operating with small conversions of acetylene per pass, mono-vinyl acetylene could be obtained as the main product of the reaction; by operating continuously in reactors in which the catalyst circulates countercurrent to the gas, the process has now been adapted to commercial operation.

$$2 \text{ CH} \equiv \text{CH} \longrightarrow \text{CH} \equiv \text{CCH} = \text{CH}_2$$

When mono-vinyl acetylene and hydrochloric acid are introduced simultaneously into an aqueous solution of cuprous chloride containing free hydrochloric acid at a temperature of about 50°C, 2-chlorobutadiene is formed and is recovered from the gases emerging from the reactor by condensation. 2-chlorobutadiene, also known as chloroprene, may be polymerized to produce a range of oil resistant synthetic rubbers—the chloroprene rubbers. The process was originally developed in the U.S.A. by the duPont company, who applied their trade name "Neoprene" to the rubber, and is now carried out also in Northern Ireland. The factory is supplied with acetylene from an adjacent carbide plant specially erected for the purpose by the British Oxygen Co. and this plant will shortly be replaced by a Wulff process acetylene plant using naptha as feed stock. Current production of "Neoprene" is estimated to be about 15,000 t/a and this will require slightly more acetylene.

Chloroprene may also be made from chlorobutenes (see page 166) but the process is not yet applied in the U.K.

ACRYLATES

The esters of acrylic acid were originally made on a large scale from ethylene via ethylene oxide and ethylene cyanhydrin (see page 117) and this route is still used to some extent in the U.S.A. The presently favoured commercial processes, however, are based on Reppe's discovery that carbon monoxide could be added on to acetylene in the presence of water to form acrylic acid and that, if the water is replaced by an alcohol, the corresponding acrylate is produced.

$$CH \equiv CH + CO + H_2O \longrightarrow CH_2 = CHCOOH$$
$$CH \equiv CH + CO + C_2H_5OH \longrightarrow CH_2 = CHCOOC_2H_5$$

These reactions have been applied to the production of acrylic esters on a very large scale by the Rohm and Haas Co. in the U.S.A. and are now being similarly applied in the U.K. by their subsidiary company, Charles Lennig and Co. Ltd., at Jarrow on the Tyne. The process is carried out at substantially atmospheric pressure and a temperature of less than 50°C and yields of around 90% on acetylene used are obtainable.

VINYL ESTERS

As in the case of the acrylic esters, commercial manufacture of the esters of vinyl alcohol has, in the past, been based mainly on ethylene as raw material but, in contrast to the acrylics, it seems likely that ethylene will continue to be the most important starting point for vinyl compounds for some time to come; these compounds are, therefore, described more fully in the chapter on ethylene derivatives. The Distillers Company has, however, used the acetylene route to vinyl acetate for some time and has now joined with Courtaulds, which previously operated an ethylene based process, in a project to manufacture their combined requirements of vinyl acetate. The plant is currently under construction adjacent to the existing Distillers Co. factory at Hull. It will use acetic acid from the Distillers naphtha oxidation plant there and acetylene from a new 10,000 t/a Wulff plant specially built for the purpose (see page 46).

The process is a simple direct reaction between acetylene and acetic acid and may be carried out either in the liquid or in the vapour phase.

$$CH \equiv CH + CH_3COOH \longrightarrow CH_3COOCH = CH_2$$

In the liquid phase process, glacial acetic acid, oleum and mercuric oxide are mixed to give a catalyst concentration of about 2·5% as mercuric oxide; this mixture is then contacted with a large excess of acetylene at about 70°C. Vinyl acetate is recovered from the gases emerging from the reactor by condensation and the excess of acetylene is recycled. In the vapour phase process, a mixture of acetic acid vapour with a large excess of acetylene is passed over a catalyst containing cadmium or zinc salts at about 200°C. The ester recovery and acetylene recycle arrangements are similar to those for the liquid phase process.

VINYL CHLORIDE

Polyvinyl chloride was introduced as a thermoplastic before the Second World War and became of special importance in Germany in the drive to replace imported natural raw materials by indigenously produced synthetics. It is not yet clear whether acetylene or ethylene will emerge as the dominant raw material for vinyl chloride manufacture. On balance, it seems likely that ethylene will be favoured and, accordingly, vinyl chloride is mainly described under ethylene derivatives. In this case, however, it is reasonably certain that at least a part of U.K. vinyl chloride production will continue to be made from acetylene since the Distillers Co. is building an acetylene plant specifically for this purpose and I.C.I. is likely to have acetylene to spare from its new plant. The reaction is a direct combination of acetylene and hydrogen chloride:

$$CH \equiv CH + HCl \longrightarrow CH_2 = CHCl$$

A mixture of hydrogen chloride and purified acetylene is passed through a tubular reactor, packed with carbon pellets impregnated with mercuric chloride as catalyst, at a temperature of about 200°C. It is important that the reactants should be dry to minimize both corrosion by hydrogen chloride and hydration of acetylene to acetaldehyde. Vinyl chloride monomer is separated from the reaction mixture in a refrigerated condenser and purified by distillation.

OTHER REACTIONS OF ACETYLENE

Because it could be made from calcium carbide and from indigenous methane from coal or natural gas, acetylene was more easily available than ethylene in Germany during the war and this undoubtedly stimulated the great developments in commercial applications of acetylene chemistry which took place there. The most important application was the production of butadiene (see Fig. 8) as an intermediate for synthetic rubber manufacture. In comparison with Germany and the U.S.A., the development of acetylene chemistry in the U.K. has been slow and this has undoubtedly been due to the high cost of acetylene based on calcium carbide. Now that four major commercial plants producing acetylene from petroleum will shortly be in operation, it may be anticipated that some of the more specialized reactions of acetylene investigated by Reppe at Ludwigshaven may find commercial application in this country.

READING LIST

1. *Acetylene—Its Properties, Manufacture and Uses*, by S. A. Miller. Ernest Benn Ltd., London, 1965.
2. *Acetylene Chemistry*, by J. W. Reppe. P.B. Report 18852S. Charles A. Meyer & Co., New York, 1949. (This report may be difficult to find in libraries but it is the only full account of Reppe's work known to have been published.)

CHAPTER 5

Chemicals Derived from Ethylene and Ethane

ETHYLENE, or olefiant gas, was first made by Deiman in 1795 by dehydration of ethanol with concentrated sulphuric acid; modifications of this process remained the standard method of preparation until ethylene became available in large quantities as a by-product of petroleum refining in the early part of this century. The development of commercial production by this means is described in detail in Chapter 2.

The corresponding paraffin, ethane, may be prepared by the Würz reaction from methyl iodide:

$$2 \text{ CH}_3\text{I} + 2 \text{ Na} \longrightarrow \text{CH}_3 - \text{CH}_3 + 2 \text{ NaI}$$

This method, and the alternative of hydrogenation of ethylene prepared from ethanol, are expensive and ethane remained something of a laboratory curiosity until the development of low-temperature distillation made separation of the constituents of natural gas a simple matter. Even then, its stability made it less interesting than ethylene as a commercial raw material.

When available cheaply, it is the preferred raw material for cracking to ethylene but some direct chemical outlets have been developed. There is an economic incentive to by-pass the dehydrogenation step and produce chemicals at present made from ethylene direct from ethane but commercial successes in this field have been few.

Ethylene is present to the extent of about 2% in coke oven gas from which it may be separated by washing the gas with concentrated sulphuric acid. Alternatively, when coke oven gas is subjected to low temperature distillation for the recovery of hydrogen for ammonia synthesis, an ethylene rich fraction is obtained as a by-product from which pure ethylene may readily be recovered. About 100 tons of coal must be carbonized to give 1 ton of ethylene but the very large tonnages of coal carbonized in heavily industrialized countries, such as the U.S.A., Germany and Great Britain, represent a substantial tonnage of the olefin. Although some ethylene was recovered as ethanol from this source in Great Britain during the First World War, economic recovery on a large scale requires the simultaneous presence in one place of a large quantity of coke oven gas and a large user of hydrogen to provide enough ethylene for a viable recovery unit. These conditions existed in Germany with the great concentration of the coal, steel and chemical industries in the Ruhr valley, and large quantities of ethylene were recovered from coke oven gas before and during the Second World War to supply the synthetic rubber plant at Hüls. This ethylene was supplemented by additional quantities produced by hydrogenation of acetylene from the Hüls arc process. Even in Germany these methods cannot now compete with petroleum based ethylene and German chemical industry has largely gone over to naphtha cracking for its ethylene supply.

In the U.K. there was little chemical usage of ethylene before the Second World War. The first commercial production of polyethylene (polythene) by I.C.I. was based on ethylene from vapour phase dehydration of ethanol over a phosphoric acid catalyst at 300–400°C and this continued until the first cracking plant came on stream at Wilton in 1951. An early attempt by the D.C.L. about 1942 to establish a direct oxidation process for the manufacture of ethylene oxide, which was ultimately abandoned due to process difficulties, also depended on ethanol as its source of ethylene. Thus ethylene-based chemistry on a commercial scale in the U.K. may be said to begin with the establishment of the petroleum chemicals industry from 1949

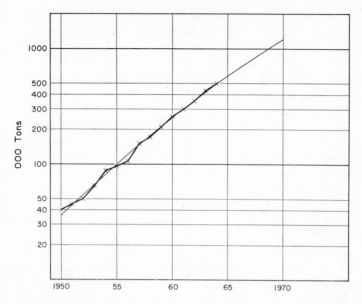

Fig. 9 U.K. Ethylene Consumption 1950-1964 with Trend Line Projection to 1970.

onwards. The growth of ethylene consumption since that time, however, has been remarkable and is shown in Fig. 9.

From this it can be seen that, over the past ten years, consumption has grown at an almost constant rate of 20%/annum and that, assuming that the growth rate falls towards 15%/annum over the next five to ten years, consumption will rise from its 1964 level of 500,000 t/a to about 1,200,000 t/a by 1970. It has already been noted (see page 43) that currently planned expansions will bring the total U.K. ethylene capacity to 1,624,000 t/a by about 1968 but it may be anticipated that capacity will be matched to demand by shutting down some of the older plants, either for scrapping or to be held in reserve. For comparison it may be noted that world capacity for ethylene, excluding the Communist countries, for which figures are not available, is currently estimated to be nearly 7,000,000 t/a and that this is expected to rise to more than 10,000,000 t/a in a few years time.

The double bond in the ethylene molecule makes it almost as reactive as acetylene and the fact that it is more stable, may be compressed and transported as a gas or as a liquid and is also cheaper to produce, has made it the preferred raw material for many processes. The principal reactions of ethylene are shown in Fig. 10.

In spite of the many interesting syntheses which may start from ethylene, it is as the precursor of three major thermoplastic materials that it finds its largest tonnage outlets. A full description of these will be found in another volume of this series and only a brief summary is given here.

POLYETHYLENE

Polyethylene, or polythene as it is more generally known, was discovered almost accidentally by workers at the I.C.I. Research Laboratories at Winnington, Cheshire, in the early thirties; this work has been well described by R. O. Gibson. Its remarkable dielectric properties made it of great interest in work on high-frequency communications and the fact that it was available, albeit in small quantities and at high cost, is said to have made the development of radar possible during the last war. While ethanol remained the source of ethylene, the cost was bound to be high and the advent of petroleum based ethylene in the fifties made progressive reductions in price and rises in consumption possible. The process was accelerated by the fact that the original I.C.I. patents began to run out in 1956 and other manufacturers entered the market which has now become highly competitive. Thus U.K. production capacity by 1966 is estimated to be about 350,000 t/a and a fair part of the growth in ethylene consumption shown in Fig. 9 is due to estimated growth in consumption of polythene.

The polythene referred to above is produced by polymerization of ethylene at pressures up to 2500 atm in the presence of traces of oxygen. It is an almost wholly amorphous material with a

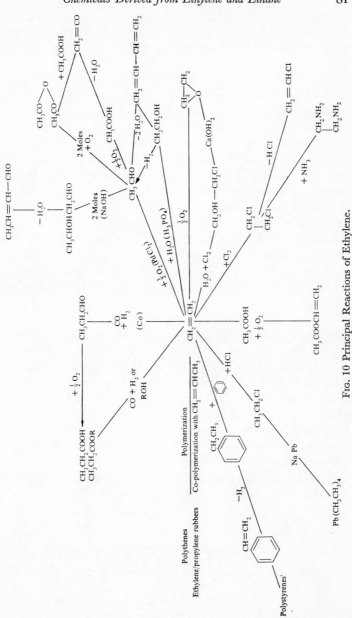

Fig. 10 Principal Reactions of Ethylene.

density varying from 0·92 to 0·94 according to polymerization conditions and is usually referred to as low density or conventional polythene. In the mid-fifties a new form of polythene began to appear in small quantities. This was high density or linear polythene, produced as a result of the discovery by Professor Karl Ziegler and his co-workers at the Kaiser Wilhelm Institut at Mülheim, that certain organo-metallic compounds in the presence of titanium chlorides would promote the polymerization of ethylene at substantially atmospheric pressure. The polymers were found to have a density of 0·98 and a high degree of crystallinity which gave them higher melting points and greater strength than were obtainable with the conventional material.

The work of Ziegler was extended by Professor Giulio Natta at Milan to higher olefins and to co-polymers where the steric regularity conferred on the polymers by the new catalysts is of especial interest. Since that time, other catalyst systems and methods for producing stereo-regular polymers, both thermoplastics and elastomers, have been developed and have attained commercial success.

As a thermoplastic, high density polythene aroused great interest but commercial development has been slow. There are two producers in the U.K. at present—Shell Chemicals with a process based on the Ziegler/Natta work and appropriate licences and B.H.C., which has taken a licence for a process developed by the Phillips Co. in the U.S.A. I.C.I. has announced plans to install substantial capacity at Wilton, using a process developed in its own laboratories. Actual U.K. consumption at present (1965) is almost certainly less than 50,000 t/a but, with planned expansions already announced by the existing producers and the I.C.I. plant to come, it is likely that more than 500,000 t/a of ethylene will be required for all grades of polythene by 1970.

POLYSTYRENE

The second of the trio of major thermoplastics, polystyrene, also made its first commercial appearance in the decade before the last war. It is produced from ethylene and benzene via ethyl benzene and monomeric styrene and, as the major raw material is benzene, it will be described with the aromatics in Chapter 9. It may be noted here, however, that it absorbs some 40,000 t/a of ethylene and production is still expanding.

POLYVINYL CHLORIDE

The third member of the thermoplastic trio, polyvinyl chloride (PVC), has already been mentioned (see page 75). In addition to the method of manufacture from acetylene there described, the monomer may readily be produced by dehydrochlorination of ethylene dichloride and this method does, in fact, give rise to considerably more than half of the total non-Communist world production, currently estimated at about 2,750,000 t/a. The monomer is gaseous under normal conditions (b.p.—13·8°C) and, therefore, requires special equipment for its storage and transport. For this reason manufacturing and polymerization facilities are usually part of one complex which is itself sited as close as possible to a source of ethylene and chlorine.

Ethylene dichloride (1.2-dichloroethane) is produced by direct reaction of ethylene and chlorine in the presence of an aluminium chloride catalyst at a temperature of about 50°C; the reaction is exothermic and the reactor temperature must be controlled by cooling. Ethylene dichloride is produced in high yield and is purified by distillation. Dehydrochlorination may be effected by the action of strong alkalis or by pyrolysis as follows:

$$CH_2Cl - CH_2Cl \longrightarrow CH_2 = CHCl + HCl$$

Ethylene dichloride vapour is passed over a contact catalyst, such as pumice or kaolin, at a temperature of about 500°C; the catalyst may be packed into a stainless steel tube heated directly in a furnace. The reaction gases are rapidly quenched with cold ethylene dichloride and passed on to a surface condenser to recover the remainder of the condensable materials. Hydrogen chloride is recovered from the uncondensed gases by water scrubbing and may be reconverted to chlorine by oxidation in the presence of a catalyst. Recovered chlorine is recycled to the ethylene dichloride plant. Alternatively, the recovered hydrogen chloride may be reacted with acetylene to give additional vinyl chloride.

The mixed reaction products from the quench tower and surface condenser are fractionated, either under pressure or with refrigeration, to give a pure vinyl chloride monomer product, ethylene dichloride for recycle to the pyrolysis furnace and some higher chlorinated compounds which are discarded. The yield of monomer on ethylene dichloride is better than 90% of theoretical.

A decision on whether to use the ethylene or the acetylene route to vinyl chloride depends on a number of factors of which the two most important are the costs of ethylene and acetylene. The availability of chlorine and hydrogen chloride, and the cost or value to be assigned to them may also exert a considerable influence on the decision. It is clearly advantageous if the direct production of hydrogen chloride from chlorine and hydrogen or the reconversion of by-product material to chlorine can be avoided. Finally, since all the primary raw materials and the finished product are gases which are relatively expensive to store and transport, plant location factors may have some influence. The importance of these economic factors will vary from company to company and little is known of their absolute magnitude. The tendency to date seems to be towards compromise solutions which will avoid the production of pure acetylene and which will leave ethylene as the major vinyl chloride precursor.

The most interesting of these recent developments is the combination of the ethylene chlorination, dehydrochlorination and hydrogen chloride conversion into one process, usually referred to as the oxychlorination process, for which the overall equation may be written:

$$2 \, CH_2 = CH_2 + Cl_2 + \tfrac{1}{2}O_2 \longrightarrow 2 \, CH_2 = CHCl + H_2O$$

This process is still undergoing commercial development and it is not possible, at present, to give more information about it. Clearly, however, it offers advantages since it requires only chlorine and ethylene as raw materials and avoids awkward process steps. Its economics must depend largely on the efficiency of conversion of the two major raw materials and, so far, no information has been published on this point.

Another method of solving the problem is to use some variant of the Wulff cracking process (see page 45) for the simultaneous production of ethylene and acetylene in the required proportions. It is now claimed that the gases need not be separated but that the two methods of preparation can be combined according to the overall equation:

$$C_2H_4 + C_2H_2 + Cl_2 \longrightarrow 2\ CH_2 = CHCl$$

The use of this process has been reported for some recent new capacity in Japan.

In the U.S.A., development appears to have been mainly along the ethylene route whereas, in Germany, the early manufacture was based mainly on acetylene and this has tended to continue. In this country there are only two manufacturers of vinyl chloride monomer—I.C.I. and D.C.L. through its subsidiary, British Geon Ltd. Both started by using acetylene from carbide and hydrogen chloride, produced by burning chlorine in hydrogen, as raw materials, although I.C.I. probably had some by-product hydrogen chloride from other chlorination processes as well. In 1961 B.H.C. started producing ethylene dichloride at Grangemouth for supply to the British Geon plant at Barry in South Wales. The quantity was sufficient to give, on pyrolysis, about half of the D.C.L. vinyl chloride requirements and the by-product hydrogen chloride was reacted with acetylene, based on carbide from the nearby D.C.L. plant at Kenfig, to supply the remainder. More recently the ethylene dichloride plant at Grangemouth has been replaced by a similar plant at the new B.H.C. ethylene complex at Baglan Bay, which is not far from Barry and must show a considerable saving on transport costs. D.C.L. has also announced

that the Kenfig carbide plant will close and acetylene requirements will be supplied by a 30,000 t/a Wulff acetylene plant,
now under construction. The economic factors which led to the
decision to make the Wulff an "acetylene only" plant rather than
a combined ethylene and acetylene unit are not clear.

I.C.I. production of vinyl chloride has been concentrated
mainly at Runcorn where it has facilities for both carbide and
chlorine production. For I.C.I., also, the carbide route appears to
have become uneconomic in modern conditions and the company
has announced its intention to build a large petroleum based
acetylene unit using the B.A.S.F. process (see page 45). It has
also announced that an 8 in. ethylene pipeline will be built to
link its large ethylene producing complex at Wilton with the
Merseyside area with a branch to Hillhouse, near Fleetwood,
Lancs., where its main polyvinyl chloride facilities are situated.
In addition the company has also announced that it will build
a large vinyl chloride unit using the oxychlorination process which
it has developed. It is clear, therefore, that I.C.I. intends to
provide considerable flexibility which will allow it to alter the
balance of the various vinyl chloride processes used in the future,
according to the prevailing economic climate.

Polyvinyl chloride is a very versatile plastic and the recent
developments in monomer production described above have made
its production possible at a price which compares more than
favourably with polyolefins and polystyrene. Growth of the
British market has been extremely rapid and consumption has
increased from insignificant amounts just after the last war to
some 200,000 tons during 1965; there is, as yet, no sign that the
market is saturated since demand still appears to be growing at
a rate of about 15% annually. For many applications the polymer
needs to be compounded with suitable plasticizers, usually esters
of higher alcohols, and some PVC products may contain up to
50% of plasticizer. This, in turn, has created a large demand for
these materials and their production has become an important
part of heavy organic chemicals industry (see Chapter 8).

A monomer, allied to vinyl chloride, which has attained considerable importance in the U.S.A. for the manufacture of fibre forming polymers, although not, as yet, produced on a large scale in this country, is vinylidene chloride. It may be made by the liquid phase chlorination of vinyl chloride to 1.1.2-trichloroethane and subsequent dehydrochlorination with caustic soda.

$$CH_2 = CHCl + Cl_2 \longrightarrow CH_2Cl - CHCl_2$$

$$CH_2Cl - CHCl_2 \longrightarrow CH_2 = CCl_2 + HCl$$

Alternatively the 1.1.2-trichloroethane may be made by liquid phase chlorination of ethylene dichloride.

HALOGENATED DERIVATIVES

A vast number of aliphatic halogen derivatives is known but few of them are of major importance commercially. Many of them do, however, have small-scale uses as intermediates in the production of fine chemicals and pharmaceuticals, as refrigerants, anaesthetics, fire extinguishing agents and so on; because of the general nature of halogenation reactions and the wide variety of uses to which the products are put, they do not fit readily into any system of classification based on end uses or raw material sources. It is convenient, therefore, to deal with all the halides of the lower hydrocarbons at this point and not only those of the C_2 group.

The most important compound commercially, ethylene dichloride, for which non-Communist world capacity currently exceeds 1,000,000 t/a has been described in the preceding section and two important solvents, trichloroethylene and perchloroethylene, have been dealt with in Chapter 4 together with 2-chlorobutadiene, since they represent important outlets for acetylene.

There are three common methods for making mono-halogen derivatives of paraffins:

1. Reaction of a hydrogen halide with an alcohol

$$CH_3CH_2OH + HI \longrightarrow CH_3CH_2I + H_2O$$

2. Addition of a hydrogen halide to an olefin

$$CH_2 = CH_2 + HBr \longrightarrow CH_3CH_2Br$$

3. Direct halogenation of the paraffin

$$CH_3 - CH_3 + Cl_2 \longrightarrow CH_3 - CH_2Cl + HCl$$

Polyhalogenated derivatives may be made by further direct halogenation of the monohalide or by addition of a halogen to an olefin or acetylene hydrocarbon. By ingenious combinations of halogenation and dehydrohalogenation, various symmetrical and unsymmetrical saturated and unsaturated derivatives may be made; the production of vinylidene chloride described above is a good example.

Monohalides have, in the past, been made mainly from the reaction of the appropriate hydrogen halide and alcohol; the reaction is specific for the compound required and high yields may normally be obtained. The growing availability of hydrocarbon raw materials has, however, focused increasing attention on the possibilities of direct halogenation, especially for chlorine compounds. The difficulty has always been that the reactions are not specific and a wide spectrum of halogen derivatives is obtained, especially with C_3 and higher hydrocarbons. For companies producing a range of halogen derivatives or for those with special large-scale applications, however, the lack of specificity may be offset by the economic advantages of large-scale continuous operation and cheap raw materials; the use of direct halogenation processes is increasing.

ETHYL CHLORIDE

Ethyl chloride is one of the most important monohalides in tonnage production. Its major use is as an intermediate in the production of lead tetraethyl but substantial quantities are used for manufacture of ethyl cellulose and it has other small-scale outlets as a refrigerant and local anaesthetic. Small quantities are still made from ethyl alcohol but the only large-scale U.K. plant, operated by the Associated Octel Co. at Ellesmere Port in Cheshire as part of their facilities for production of tetraethyl lead antiknock fluids, uses a combined ethane chlorination/ethylene hydrochlorination process devised by the Shell Development Co. in the U.S.A.; ethane and ethylene are supplied as separate streams by pipeline from the nearby plants of Shell Chemicals at Carrington and Stanlow.

Chlorine, ethane and the recycle gas stream containing ethylene are preheated and fed to the first reactor, where the main reaction of chlorination and formation of by-product hydrogen chloride takes place at about 400°C. The exit stream is cooled and sent to the first column where most of the ethyl chloride and higher chlorinated by-products are condensed and recovered as bottom products and sent to intermediate storage. The overhead from this column is blended with sufficient ethylene to bring the ethylene : hydrogen chloride molar ratio to 1:1, preheated to about 40°C and passed into the hydrochlorination column. Heat from the exothermic reaction is removed by circulating oil and hydrochlorination is about 80% complete. The product gases are cooled and fed to the second column where crude ethyl chloride is recovered as a bottom product to storage. The overhead consists of ethane, unreacted ethylene, hydrogen chloride and some inert gases and is recycled to the chlorinator. There is controlled venting at this point to prevent excessive build up of inert gases. Crude ethyl chloride from both columns is combined and purified by distillation. Appreciable quantities of higher chlorinated ethanes are produced as by-products; their disposal is sometimes difficult as there is little commercial demand for them.

The remainder of the lead tetraethyl process, about which only a limited amount of information has been published, may conveniently be described here. An alloy, containing about 9 parts of lead to 1 part of sodium by weight is contacted with a large excess of ethyl chloride at temperatures below 100°C. The use of aldehydes and ketones as catalysts is mentioned in the patent literature. The reaction is:

$$4 \text{ NaPb} + 4 \text{ C}_2\text{H}_5\text{Cl} \longrightarrow \text{Pb(C}_2\text{H}_5)_4 + 4 \text{ NaCl}$$

Only about 25% of the lead in the alloy is converted and the remainder is purified and recycled to lead/sodium alloy formation.

The lead tetraethyl is purified by distillation and blended with ethylene dibromide and/or ethylene dichloride and a dye to form the antiknock fluid of commerce. The process has a theoretical requirement of 4 moles of sodium per mole of lead tetraethyl, the actual requirement being somewhat greater. This is produced electrolytically and the by-product chlorine serves for the manufacture of the ethyl chloride and ethylene dichloride required in the process and for blending with the finished product. Tetraethyl lead is a highly toxic compound and is distributed and blended with gasoline under strictly controlled conditions. About 35,000 t/a of lead are used in the manufacture of anti-knock fluids.

The other monohalides of ethane are not made on a large scale in this country. Of the dihalides, ethylene dichloride has already been described. Ethylene dibromide is mainly used for blending with anti-knock fluid and is made by Associated Octel Ltd. from ethylene and bromine at Hayle in Cornwall and in Anglesey where the company has plants for the recovery of bromine from sea water. Other di- and polyhalides of the C_2 hydrocarbons are of minor importance with the exception of some fluorine compounds dealt with under "fluorocarbons" below.

METHYL HALIDES

Methyl halides are rarely made by direct halogenation of methane because of the difficulty of avoiding a mixture of products, which may not conform to the pattern of requirements, and because of the need to decompose, or otherwise dispose of, large quantities of by-product hydrogen halide. Plants for the chlorination of methane are in operation in the U.S.A. but, in this country, reaction between methanol and the appropriate hydrogen halide is the method of preparation of methyl chloride, bromide and iodide. Methyl chloride, the most important compound commercially, is produced when methanol vapour and hydrogen chloride react at about 350°C in the presence of a catalyst such as calcined alumina or zinc chloride on pumice:

$$CH_3OH + HCl \longrightarrow CH_3Cl + H_2O$$

Methyl chloride (b.p. $-24°C$) is recovered from the reactor effluent by refrigeration or condensation under pressure and purified by distillation. The product is used as a catalyst carrier in the polymerization of isobutylene to "Butyl" rubber, as a methylating agent, for example, in the production of methyl cellulose, as a starting point in the production of silicones and in a considerable number of other smaller outlets. I.C.I. is the most important producer but Midland Silicones Ltd. has its own methyl chloride plant to provide for its internal needs. Consumption, though not known exactly, probably lies between 10,000 and 20,000 t/a.

Methyl bromide, made in a similar way to methyl chloride, is used as a fire extinguisher in high tension electrical installations but is not known to have any other large scale applications. As a fire extinguisher it may be replaced by one of the fluorine compounds described below.

Of the higher halo-methanes, methylene dichloride and carbon tetrachloride are produced in large tonnages; chloroform, although not now much used as an anaesthetic, is still employed on a substantial scale as an extraction solvent. Methylene dichloride, CH_2Cl_2, is made by further chlorination of methyl chloride under controlled conditions. The compound is important as a spinning solvent for cellulose tri-acetate but its largest tonnage outlet is as a paint remover. It is the active solvent in many of the formulations widely sold for use by the professional and amateur decorator. Chloroform, the next compound in the series of chlorinated methanes, is made by treating acetone or ethanol with bleaching powder according to the equation:

$$2CH_3CO\ CH_3 + 6CaOCl_2.H_2O \longrightarrow 2CHCl_3 +$$
$$(CH_3COO)_2Ca + 2Ca(OH)_2 + 3CaCl_2 + 6H_2O$$

The acetone is run into a water suspension of the bleaching

D

powder in a cast iron still fitted with coils for heating and cooling and with an efficient stirrer. The temperature is held below 45°C until all of the acetone has been added when it is gradually raised until all the chloroform has distilled off. The crude product is refined by treatment with concentrated sulphuric and final distillation. As with methyl chloride, I.C.I. is the chief manufacturer of both methylene dichloride and chloroform but other manufacturers may make for their own needs.

CARBON TETRACHLORIDE

Carbon tetrachloride is probably produced on a larger scale than any of the other chlorinated methanes and is also one of the oldest organic chemicals in commercial production. Although it might be expected that, in this case, chlorination of methane would be the cheapest route and, in the U.S.A., now accounts for the lion's share of production, the method has not, so far, been adopted in this country; carbon disulphide is still the starting point for all commercial manufacture. The reactions are:

$$CS_2 + 3\ Cl_2 \longrightarrow S_2Cl_2 + CCl_4$$

$$CS_2 + 2\ S_2Cl_2 \longrightarrow 6\ S + CCl_4$$

A solution of carbon disulphide in carbon tetrachloride containing some sulphur monochloride is treated with an excess of chlorine in a lead-lined vessel containing iron turnings as a catalyst and fitted with cooling coils. The reaction is exothermic and the temperature is held at about 30°C by circulating cooling water. When conversion of the carbon disulphide is substantially complete, the reactor contents are passed to a distilling column where carbon tetrachloride containing traces of a sulphur monochloride is taken off overhead. The distillate is refined by treatment with alcoholic caustic soda or solid sodium carbonate, which also reduces the water content. If high purity is required, the material may be given a final distillation.

The residue from the first distillation column is agitated with carbon disulphide in a lead-lined reactor at about 60°C. At the end of the reaction the reactor contents are distilled to yield a mixture of carbon tetrachloride, sulphur monochloride and un-reacted carbon disulphide which forms the charge to the chlorinator. Residual sulphur is freed from sulphur monochloride by air blowing and is recycled to carbon disulphide manufacture. Recovered sulphur monochloride is returned to the reactor. The overall yield of carbon tetrachloride should be better than 90% based on carbon disulphide used.

An alternative to the process described above is first to prepare sulphur dichloride by reaction of sulphur and chlorine and then to react this with carbon disulphide:

$$CS_2 + 2 SCl_2 \longrightarrow CCl_4 + 4S$$

Yields are comparable with the direct chlorination process first described.

The major producer of carbon tetrachloride in this country is Albright and Wilson; Courtaulds also has substantial capacity at Trafford Park, near Manchester. I.C.I. would certainly have the facilities for its production and may produce some. Plant capacities have not been published but it is believed that total U.K. production is substantially in excess of 10,000 t/a. Important uses are for fire extinguishers and as a solvent for dry cleaning and degreasing but the largest outlet, which is still growing, is as the starting material for manufacture of the fluorocarbons described below.

FLUOROCARBONS

Mixed fluorine and chlorine derivatives of methane and ethane were first investigated commercially by duPont in the U.S.A. before the Second World War. They were found to have lower boiling points and to be much less toxic and more stable than the corresponding chlorine compounds. This made them particularly suitable for use as refrigerants and several compounds were marketed for this purpose under the trade name of "Freon". Since the war consumption has grown rapidly, helped by the huge increase in output of domestic refrigerators. Manufacture in this country has been developed by I.C.I. and Imperial Smelting Corporation who use the trade names "Arcton" and "Isceon" respectively. In recent years the production of vast numbers of aerosol packages offered a new application for the fluorocarbons since their stability and freedom from toxicity made them eminently suitable as propellants. Although it might be thought that an aerosol pack uses only a small quantity of propellant, the 130 millions of packages which are now sold annually in this country alone, add up to a substantial tonnage of fluorocarbons; this application accounts for the major part of the market for these compounds and is still growing rapidly.

The naming of the fluorocarbons has presented problems in the past since the chemical names are cumbersome and trade names may become confusing. The International Standards Organization (I.S.O.) has now proposed a systematic method of numbering refrigerants, based on their chemical structure, as follows: beginning from the right the first number is the number of fluorine atoms in the molecule, the second the number of hydrogen atoms plus one and the third the number of carbon atoms minus one. If this last number is zero it is omitted. Thus, to take the two compounds which probably account for well over 90% of the market, trichlorofluoromethane is 11 and dichlorodifluoromethane is 12. Of the ethane compounds the most commonly used is dichlorotetrafluoro ethane which is 114. These numbers are now commonly used in commerce preceded by the appropriate trade name as, for example, "Arcton" 11 or "Isceon" 12. In cases where the fluorine atoms may be distributed between two carbon atoms the symmetrical compound is denoted by the suffix a. Thus $CClF_2-CCl_2F$ is 113 and CF_3-CCl_3 is 113a. Finally the presence of bromine or iodine atoms instead of chlorine is denoted by the suffixes B or I followed by a number; thus CBr_2F_2 would be 12B2.

Production of fluorocarbons by direct fluorination or hydro-fluorination is not a practicable process and commercial production depends on halogen exchange through the action of hydrogen fluoride on a suitable chlorocarbon. For methane derivatives the starting point is carbon tetrachloride as follows:

$$CCl_4 + HF \longrightarrow CCl_3F + HCl$$

An autoclave, fitted with a fractionating column, is charged with some antimony trichloride and a little chlorine and carbon tetrachloride and anhydrous hydrogen fluoride are fed in. The pressure may be held at 150–450 psig and the temperature at about 100°C. Replacement of one chlorine atom by one fluorine atom lowers the boiling point by up to 50°C and the desired compound may be continuously fractionated off. By controlling the temperature and pressure one, two or three fluorine atoms may be introduced but complete fluorination does not appear to be possible. The products must be produced to a very rigid specification and are certainly among the purest chemicals in commercial production; water content, in particular must be kept down to 10–15 parts per million.

As noted above, 11 and 12 make up the bulk of commercial production and roughly 50:50 mixtures of these two are the most commonly used propellants but 114 is used where extra resistance to hydrolysis is required. A new and growing use for 11 is as a blowing agent for rigid polyurethane foams; the fluorocarbon is mixed with one of the constituents of the foam composition and expands during foaming so that the foam cells are filled with fluorocarbon vapour. This improves the stability of the foam and gives a significant increase in its insulating properties. CF_3Br (13B1) is finding application as a fire extinguisher in spite of its relatively high price; it is particularly useful where freedom from toxicity is important as in aircraft. Finally a small but interesting use for $CF_3CHBrCl$ (123aB1) is as an anaesthetic under the name of "Fluothane". Three possible routes to this compound are illustrated:

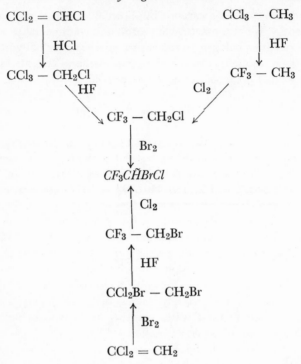

The total consumption of fluorocarbons in the outlets described above is not known with any certainty but 20,000 t/a may be taken as an order of magnitude figure which, if not attained yet, will almost certainly be reached in a few years. There is, however, an important use, which has not yet been mentioned, as plastics monomers for the fluorinated plastics. The best known of these is polytetrafluoroethylene (PTFE) made by polymerization of tetrafluoroethylene. This is formed when $CHClF_2$ is passed through a platinum tube at about 700°C.

$$2\ CHClF_2 \longrightarrow CF_2 = CF_2 + 2\ HCl$$

PTFE is not a true thermoplastic and is very difficult to fabricate. Improved thermoplasticity is obtained in polymers of

$CClF = CF_2$ or in copolymers of $CF_2 = CF_2$ and $CF_2 = CFCF_3$ and these are produced in America but not, so far as is known, in this country. For further details of this important group of chemicals the reader is referred to the reading list at the end of the chapter.

HALIDES OF HIGHER HYDROCARBONS

None of the higher hydrocarbon halides has major applications in British industry as yet but a number of halogenation reactions are of potential importance. One of the most interesting of these is the process for the production of allyl chloride by the hot chlorination of propylene developed by the Shell Development Co. in the U.S.A.

$$CH_2 = CHCH_3 + Cl_2 \longrightarrow CH_2 = CHCH_2Cl + HCl$$

Dry propylene is preheated to about 400°C and mixed with chlorine at about 20°C in a jet mixer; a 4:1 excess of propylene is used. The mixed gases pass into a steel tube reactor where the heat of reaction raises the temperature to about 500°C and the chlorine is almost completely reacted. There is some deposition of carbon and two reactors in parallel are used and run alternately to allow time for cleaning out. The reactor products are condensed by liquid propylene at −40°C to recover the organic chlorides. The uncondensed gases are scrubbed with water to recover hydrogen chloride which may be sold or reconverted to chlorine by oxidation. The excess propylene is scrubbed with aqueous caustic soda and recycled to the reactor with the fresh propylene feed.

Allyl chloride is recovered from the liquid condensate in a two column still. The first column removes the light ends, mainly 2-chloropropylene, pure allyl chloride is taken overhead from the second column and the higher chlorides, mainly dichloropropylenes, form the residue from this column; yield of allyl chloride is about 85% based on propylene. It has a number of potential uses and, as an important intermediate in the original Shell process for the manufacture of synthetic glycerol in the U.S.A., it will be referred to again in the next chapter. The by-product chloropropylenes may be used for the production of soil fumigants and nematocides for which there is a substantial demand.

Halogenation may be used as a means of introducing a reactive centre into the chemically inert paraffinic hydrocarbon chain since the halogen may readily be replaced by other groups such as OH, SH and NH_2; the halide may also be used as an alkylating agent for aromatic hydrocarbons. A process for the photosynthetic chlorination of Fischer–Tropsch kerosine was operated by the I.G. Farbenindustrie in Germany during the war and the resulting monohalides were then converted to alkyl sodium sulphonates by treatment, for example, with sodium sulphite to form the basis for synthetic surface-active agents. Benzene, alkylated by means of a chlorinated kerosine (keryl benzene), and subsequently sulphonated, formed the basis for the first commercial alkyl aryl sulphonate detergents.

Another useful general reaction is the dehydrochlorination of monochlorides to give olefins. This reaction, applied to the monochlorides of pure normal paraffins, may provide an alternative to wax cracking as a source of straight chain olefins for production of bio-degradable alkyl aryl sulphonates or of primary alcohols for detergent manufacture. An extreme case of this type of reaction is the new Shell process for production of butadiene by reaction between butane and iodine in the presence of catalysts and water vapour, which is being applied for the first time on a commercial scale by the Société des Elastomères de Synthèse in France.

ETHYLENE OXIDE AND ITS DERIVATIVES

Ethylene oxide was discovered more than a hundred years ago but it was not until 1925 that large-scale manufacture was initiated by Union Carbide in the U.S.A. The potential of ethylene oxide as a building block for a wide range of aliphatic chemicals was quickly realized and plants were erected in Europe, especially in Germany. Failure to understand or to observe the rather special conditions necessary for safe storage and handling of the material led to a number of accidents and growth of output in the period prior to World War II was relatively slow. Much valuable knowledge was gained during this period, however, which opened the way to the vast expansion in production and the world-wide proliferation of ethylene oxide plants which has taken place since the war. Total world manufacturing capacity, excluding the Communist countries, is currently estimated to be approaching 1·5 million t/a of which approximatedly 90% is by direct oxidation of ethylene with air or oxygen.

Commercial development of ethylene oxide may be regarded as being indirectly due to the growth of the motor car industry. It was production of the high octane gasolines required by modern cars which first opened up the possibility of producing ethylene cheaply on a large scale. Production line methods used in the industry demanded quick drying, durable paints which, in turn, required special solvents; some of the first ethylene oxide derivatives produced by Union Carbide were the monoalkyl ethers of ethylene glycol, marketed under the trade name of "Cellosolve", which were particularly suitable for this purpose. Finally the motor car needs a non-volatile freezing point depressant for its cooling system and this need is well met by ethylene glycol produced from ethylene oxide and water.

The first commercial process depended on the formation of ethylene chlorohydrin by reaction of ethylene with chlorine and water:

$$C_2H_4 + Cl_2 + H_2O \longrightarrow CH_2Cl - CH_2OH + HCl$$

The chlorohydrin was then decomposed with an alkali, usually calcium hydroxide, to give ethylene oxide and calcium chloride which was sent to waste.

$$CH_2OH - CH_2Cl + HCl + Ca(OH)_2 \longrightarrow$$

$$\begin{matrix} CH_2 \diagdown \\ | \qquad O + CaCl_2 + 2H_2O \\ CH_2 \diagup \end{matrix}$$

Ethylene dichloride is formed as a by-product of the process in amounts up to 20% by weight of the ethylene oxide produced and small quantities of $\beta'\beta'$ dichloro-diethyl ether are also produced.

The process may be conveniently divided into three stages—chlorohydrination, saponification and ethylene oxide distillation. In the first stage ethylene is reacted with a mixture of hydrochloric acid and hypochlorous acid produced by dissolving chlorine in water;

$$Cl_2 + H_2O \longrightarrow HOCl + HCl$$

Production of chlorinated by-products is minimized by working in dilute aqueous solution, in which chlorohydrin concentration is limited to 4–4·5%, and by designing the apparatus so that ethylene and free, undissolved chlorine do not come into contact. In the version of the process due to the Société Carbochimique, this is achieved by adding the chlorine and ethylene to the reactor system at widely separated points and by arranging for a rapid circulation of chlorohydrin solution round the system so that there is always sufficient flow past the point of chlorine addition to ensure that the gas is completely dissolved. The ethylene feed need not be pure, provided that any contaminants are inert in the reaction tower; the process will work well with ethylene/ethane mixtures containing as little as 35% of ethylene. The ethylene and chlorine feeds are controlled in the correct ratio by an automatic ratio flow controller. By controlling this ratio, together with the rates of water addition and chlorohydrin solution take off, a steady state may be attained with a chlorohydrin concentration of 4–4·5% and a tower temperature of about 60°C. Conversion of ethylene is not complete and the tower exit gas is cooled, scrubbed with aqueous caustic soda and blended with fresh ethylene for return to the chlorohydrin tower.

In order to prevent excessive build up of inert gases a certain amount of the scrubbed gas is bled off at this point and this may be varied according to the concentration of ethylene in the fresh feed. The bleed gas is passed through an active carbon adsorption system for recovery of any chlorinated by-products contained in it and may then be recycled to ethylene purification or sent to fuel.

The second stage of the process is the hydrolysis ("saponification") of ethylene chlorohydrin with milk of lime. In this stage, in order to minimize by-product formation, ethylene oxide must not remain in contact with ethylene chlorohydrin or with alkaline solutions; saponifier design is directed, therefore, to ensuring that it is removed from the solution as saponification proceeds. A number of designs has been tried for this purpose and a typical one is illustrated in Fig. 11, in which the saponifier is

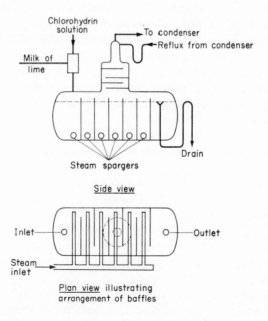

FIG. 11 Typical Saponifier for Decomposition of Ethylene Chlorohydrin.

divided into a number of chambers, each provided with a live steam distributor, through which the solution follows a serpentine path. The spent liquor, consisting essentially of an aqueous solution of calcium chloride, but containing some lime in suspension and traces of ethylene glycol and other by-products in solution, is passed to the drains via a settling system. Production of an effluent of acceptable quality for discharge into rivers or into municipal sewer systems is difficult and may be a substantial charge on the process.

In the third stage the crude ethylene oxide from the saponifiers is separated from light ends, mainly acetaldehyde, and from any chlorinated compounds in a distillation system which is operated under a pressure of about 20 psig. This is sufficient to raise the boiling point of ethylene oxide to about 34°C and to allow ordinary cooling water to be used. Pure ethylene oxide is passed to refrigerated storage and the whole distillation and storage system is pressurized with an inert gas, usually nitrogen, from which oxygen must be rigidly excluded. The chlorinated products from the distillation system are blended with those recovered from the tower effluent gas scrubbing system and batch distilled for the recovery of pure ethylene dichloride and $\beta\beta'$ dichlorodiethyl ether. A diagrammatic flow sheet for the complete process is given in Fig. 12.

Overall yields of ethylene oxide up to 80% of theory, based on ethylene feed, may be obtained, i.e. about 1·2 tons of oxide per ton of ethylene. More than two tons of chlorine per ton of oxide are required and this all goes to waste as calcium chloride or appears in by-products of low value. Even the ethylene dichloride may present a disposal problem unless it can be incorporated into a vinyl chloride manufacturing complex. There has always been, therefore, a strong incentive to avoid the chlorination step and to produce the oxide by direct oxidation of ethylene with air or oxygen.

The possibility that worthwhile yields of the oxide might be obtained directly by reaction of ethylene and air does not appear to have been known before 1931. In that year work carried out

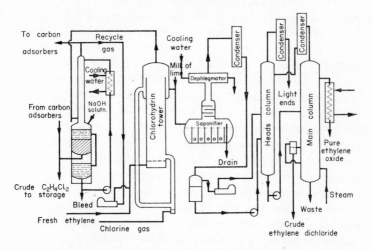

FIG. 12 Ethylene Oxide by the Chlorohydrin Process.

in Paris by the Société Française de Catalyse Généralisée had a successful outcome and a patent was granted to T. E. Lefort and the Société for a process using a metallic silver catalyst. All subsequent developments have depended on the use of metallic silver as a catalyst and may be regarded as stemming from the original discovery. The translation of the laboratory results into a successful commercial plant was an arduous business; control of the highly exothermic reaction proved difficult and a big step forward was the discovery that an addition of small quantities of a halogen compound, such as ethylene dibromide, to the reactor gases made control much easier. It was found necessary to work with dilute mixtures of air and ethylene but, at the same time, to keep outside the explosive limits of ethylene/air mixtures and to avoid excessive dilution which would make recovery of the product too expensive. A satisfactory compromise solution to these problems was eventually found and the first commercial plant was commissioned by Union Carbide in the U.S.A. before the war.

Other companies carried on with development and direct oxidation plants were erected in Germany during the war but were never, apparently, fully commissioned. In the U.S.A. many companies were known to be working on the process in the years immediately after the war and the Scientific Design Co., a firm of chemical engineering contractors, developed their own version of the process which has been the basis of a number of successful commercial plants throughout the world. The Shell Development Corporation discovered that oxygen could be used instead of air and this, by eliminating nitrogen from the circulating gases, lessens the amount of gas which must be bled off after each pass through the reactor, makes greater recycle of ethylene possible and reduces operating costs. At the same time it is possible to reduce the size and cost of the operating equipment at the expense of adding an air separation plant to the capital expenditure on the plant; it was found possible to demonstrate that, above a certain size of plant, the combined capital and operating savings of the oxygen process would more than offset the cost of the air separation equipment. The first two plants using the Shell Development process were built by Wyandotte Chemical Corporation in the U.S.A. and by Shell Chemicals in the U.K. about 1958. The increasing size of commercial plants has tended to favour the Shell Process and a number of plants has now been built under licence all over the world. The Shell Process is illustrated diagrammatically in Fig. 13.

A mixture of fresh ethylene and recycle gas is joined by a carefully controlled oxygen stream, preheated by exchange with reactor effluent and fed to the reactor. This is, in effect, a tubular heat exchanger of mild or stainless steel in which the tubes are packed with the specially prepared silver catalyst on a corundum support. The heat from the strongly exothermic reaction is removed by circulation of a coolant stream around the tubes and is recovered in a waste heat boiler; the reactor temperature is controlled at about 280°C and operating pressure may be as high as 300 psig. The reactor exit gases are cooled and scrubbed with water for the recovery of ethylene oxide. A small amount is

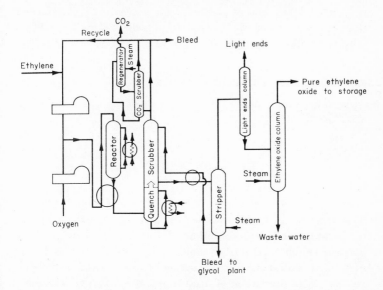

Fig. 13 The Shell Development Process for Ethylene Oxide.

bled off to prevent excessive build up of inert gases and the remainder is divided into two streams; one is recycled directly and the other passes through a carbon dioxide removal system before joining the recycle stream. When air is used as the oxidizing medium, the amount of nitrogen present necessitates a very large bleed from the reactor system and this is usually passed through a purge reactor for maximum recovery of ethylene oxide before being vented.

There are three manufacturers of ethylene oxide in the U.K., Shell Chemicals, I.C.I. and Union Carbide Chemical Co. and all three now operate the direct oxidation process. Shell Chemicals uses the Shell Development oxygen process, I.C.I. the Scientific Design Co. process and the Union Carbide plant is based on "know-how" from the parent company in the U.S.A. Present total capacity is estimated to be about 95,000 t/a; both Shell Chemicals and I.C.I. have announced expansions to their plants, without giving details of planned tonnages, but it is anticipated that completion of these expansions will bring total U.K. ethylene oxide capacity above 150,000 t/a.

REACTIONS OF ETHYLENE OXIDE

An important reaction of ethylene oxide is isomerization to acetaldehyde;

$$\begin{array}{c} CH_2 \\ | \\ CH_2 \end{array} \!\!\!\! \diagdown O \longrightarrow CH_3CHO$$

The reaction is highly exothermic and is favoured by high temperature and acid conditions. It may be accompanied by polymerization as described under polyethylene glycols below and, once initiated, these reactions proceed with increasing velocity and liberation of heat until they assume explosive violence. These reactions, initiated by unsuitable storage conditions, appear to have been the cause of most, if not all, of the accidents with ethylene oxide. Another fact of importance in the storage and handling of the oxide is that the explosive limits of ethylene oxide/air mixtures are very wide and storage and handling systems must be blanketed with an inert gas, usually nitrogen. Pure, neutral ethylene oxide may, however, be safely stored at normal temperatures although large storage installations are usually provided with some refrigeration. It may be transported in pressurized tank cars and cylinders and large quantities are moved around the country in this way, both by road and railway. The major producers issue detailed advice to customers on the safe storage and handling of the material and, provided these are adhered to, all risk can be eliminated.

Ethylene oxide is toxic; 10% mixtures with carbon dioxide are used for fumigation and are particularly useful for disinfestation of foodstuffs as there are no residues left after treatment. This outlet only absorbs very small quantities and the oxide finds its major use is as an intermediate for chemical synthesis. It reacts readily with compounds containing active hydrogen atoms to give 2-hydroxy ethyl derivatives:

$$\begin{array}{c} CH_2 \\ | \qquad \diagdown \\ | \qquad \qquad O + RH \longrightarrow RCH_2CH_2OH \\ | \qquad \diagup \\ CH_2 \end{array}$$

These may, in turn, react with more ethylene oxide to give polyoxyethylene derivatives.

$$\begin{aligned} RCH_2CH_2OH + nC_2H_4O \longrightarrow{} & RCH_2CH_2O\ CH_2CH_2OH\ + \\ & RCH_2CH_2O\ CH_2CH_2O\ CH_2CH_2OH\ + \\ & \cdots\cdots\cdots\ + \\ & RCH_2CH_2(OCH_2CH_2)_{n-2}OCH_2CH_2OH \end{aligned}$$

The simplest reaction of this type, which also accounts for more than half of the total consumption of the oxide, is the production of ethylene glycol by reaction with water:

$$\begin{array}{c} CH_2 \qquad\qquad\qquad CH_2OH \\ | \qquad \diagdown \qquad\qquad\qquad | \\ | \qquad \qquad O + H_2O \longrightarrow \qquad | \\ | \qquad \diagup \qquad\qquad\qquad | \\ CH_2 \qquad\qquad\qquad CH_2OH \end{array}$$

This reaction will take place in the presence of traces of acids at temperatures of 50–100°C but it is more usually carried out by heating ethylene oxide with a large excess of water to 150–200°C at a pressure of 300–350 psig. Some di-ethylene and tri-ethylene glycols are always formed by reaction between the monoglycol first formed and additional oxide, the quantity depending on the excess of water used. The greater the dilution, the higher is the proportion of monoglycol and the greater the cost of recovery from the solution. An economic balance is generally struck at about 15 moles of water per mole of oxide when di- and tri-glycol production is about 12% and 2% respectively of the total mixed glycols. The reaction is exothermic and may be carried out by circulating the solution of mixed glycols through a jacketed pipework system which acts as a steady state reactor to which ethylene oxide and water are added and from which crude mixed glycols solution is withdrawn continuously.

The aqueous mixed glycols are passed to a three column still where water is distilled off in the first column, pure ethylene glycol in the second and commercially pure di-ethylene glycol in the third. The water distilled from the first column, containing traces of glycol, is mixed with the fresh water feed to the reactor system. Tri-ethylene glycol is recovered by batchwise fractionation of the bottom product from the third column and a small amount of residue, consisting mainly of higher glycols, is run to waste. Overall yield of useful glycols should be better than 95% of theoretical on ethylene oxide used. Equipment may be of mild steel; the process is simple to operate and, in the U.S.A. where the glycol market is much larger than in this country, it is often applied directly to the aqueous solutions recovered from the first stage recovery systems of direct oxidation plants, thus avoiding the expense of oxide purification.

At this point it may be noted that ethylene glycol may be made by hydrogenation of esters of glycolic acid which, in turn, is produced by reacting formaldehyde with carbon monoxide in the presence of water. The equations are:

$$CH_2O + CO + H_2O \longrightarrow CH_2OHCOOH$$

$$CH_2OHCOOH + ROH \longrightarrow CH_2OHCOOR + H_2O$$

$$CH_2OHCOOR + 2H_2 \longrightarrow CH_2OHCH_2OH + ROH$$

The first stage reaction is carried out at about 200°C and 10,000 psig in the presence of excess carbon monoxide and water and a trace of sulphuric acid, to yield an aqueous solution of glycolic acid. This is purified by distillation and esterification and the ester is then hydrogenated over a chromite catalyst at about 200°C and 4500 psig. The glycol product is purified by distillation and the alcohol recycled to esterification. The process is not, at present, operated in this country but substantial quantities of glycol are believed to be made in the U.S.A. in this way. The overall yield of glycol approaches 80% on the formaldehyde used and formation of higher glycols, which sometimes present a disposal problem, is avoided.

Ethylene glycol, as a simple dihydric alcohol, has found some uses as a cheap substitute for the trihydric alcohol, glycerol. It is, however, toxic since it is metabolized to oxalic acid in the body and it must, therefore, be excluded from foodstuffs. Substantial quantities are used as a plasticizer in regenerated cellulose films, which are subsequently lacquered to prevent migration of the glycol; it can also partially replace glycerol in the production of alkyd resins for the paint industry and for some explosives. As a bi-functional alcohol it can form polyesters with dibasic acids; these have achieved large-scale commercial importance and are described in Chapter 9.

By far the largest tonnage outlet for ethylene glycol is for anti-freeze formulations for the protection of engine cooling systems; it is also used in aircraft de-icing fluids. Because of its high boiling point it does not evaporate from the open circulatory cooling systems commonly used in the past for private and commercial vehicle engines, which can thus be kept full by addition of water as required. The glycol is liable, however, to air oxidation to acidic products and anti-oxidants such as tri-ethanolamine phosphate, sodium mercapto-benzthiazole and sodium nitrite, borate or benzoate must be added; even these do not last indefinitely and annual cleaning out of cooling systems and replacement of the coolant has been the rule. This has undoubtedly played a part in maintaining the market for ethylene glycol. Some vehicles are now being sold with specially formulated glycol coolants in sealed systems which are claimed to last indefinitely; whether such systems will eventually become standard on all vehicles, and to what extent their general adoption would affect the market for glycol is not yet clear. Ethylene glycol for anti-freeze purposes is sold to a number of British Standard Specifications. These are B.S.S. 3150, 3151 and

3152. The glycol to be used for anti-freeze formulations must conform to B.S.S. 2537/1953 for pure ethylene glycol.

U.K. producers of ethylene glycol, as for ethylene oxide, are I.C.I., Shell Chemicals and Union Carbide but no reliable information on their manufacturing capacity has been published. The total U.K. market for the glycol is, however, certainly in excess of 50,000 t/a and most of this is supplied from home production.

The co-produced di- and tri-glycols from the ethylene glycol process are used in the formulation of hydraulic fluids and have many applications as solvents, plasticizers and humectants. Di-ethylene glycol is the solvent used in the "Udex" process for recovery of aromatic hydrocarbons from petroleum fractions and is also the standard tobacco humectant in many continental countries although it is not used in this country.

POLYETHYLENE GLYCOLS

The reaction leading to the co-production of di- and tri-glycols with ethylene glycol may be extended to the production of polyoxyethylene chains of almost any length; products with molecular weights up to 10,000,000 have been produced. The lower molecular weight compounds are liquids at ordinary temperatures but at molecular weights of about 600 they become waxy solids which increase slowly in melting point as more ethylene oxide molecules are added to the chain. They are all completely soluble in water and dilute solutions of the very high molecular weight materials have a high viscosity.

Above tri-glycol the production of specific compounds is no longer practicable and commercial polyglycols are characterized by their average molecular weight. Products of any desired molecular weight may be produced at will but those in common commercial use have molecular weights of 200, 300, 400, 600, 800, 1000, 1500, 4000 and 6000. As molecular weight increases, the change in properties brought about by further additions of ethylene oxide units is quite small; for example, the increase of molecular weight from 4000 to 6000 only increases the melting point from 54°C to 55°C. Above an average molecular weight of about 6000, there is little advantage in adding further ethylene oxide units until molecular weights approaching 1,000,000 are reached. The properties of the polymers are then so changed that they become capable of forming filaments and films which are of potential interest since they are water soluble.

Polyglycol manufacture usually starts with ethylene glycol or diglycol; a weighed quantity of the chosen starting material mixed with a catalyst, such as an alkali metal carbonate, is placed in a vessel fitted with a stirrer and provided with means for heating or cooling. Equipment is usually of stainless steel. Ethylene oxide is measured in at a controlled rate while the temperature is held steady at about 100°C. The reaction is exothermic and the polymerization must be rigidly controlled, especially in the early stages, by the rate of ethylene oxide addition and by cooling. Heating is only required to bring the starting material to reaction temperature and, perhaps, at the end of a long reaction for high molecular weight materials when the reaction rate has slowed down seriously. The molecular weight of the finished product is roughly controlled by the total weight of ethylene oxide added, with physical checks on samples as the end of oxide addition approaches; efforts are made to control conditions so that the spread of molecular weight on either side of the average is as small as possible. This spread tends to widen as molecular weight increases.

The polymerization proceeds by a chain lengthening reaction in which new ethylene units add on to the ends of the polymer chains already formed; this means that, in production of materials with a molecular weight of 4000 or 6000 for example, there is very little glycol or diglycol starting material and the product is almost entirely ethylene oxide polymer, leading to a large increase in volume during the reaction and great dilution of the catalyst. Production of the very high molecular weight materials, therefore, calls for a different technique about which virtually nothing has been published. It is believed that the very high molecular weights are obtained by the use of special catalysts which consist essentially of alkali metals activated with carbon dioxide and water. These high molecular weight materials are not made in this country; in the U.S.A., Union Carbide have marketed a conventional high molecular weight polyethylene glycol of molecular weight around 20,000 under the name "Carbowax" 20M and a number of higher polymers with molecular weights from 700,000 to 9,000,000 under the name of "Polyox". These polymers are highly crystalline, thermoplastic and resistant to biological attack. They would appear to have a number of potentially large scale outlets but, so far, do not appear to have made much commercial headway. In this country Shell Chemicals are the major producers of polyglycols and Union Carbide also produce substantial quantities. Other manufacturers may produce relatively small quantities from purchased ethylene oxide. Copolymers of ethylene and propylene oxide are dealt with in the next chapter.

OUTLETS FOR POLYETHYLENE GLYCOLS

The polyethylene glycols have an astonishing diversity of uses, no one of which amounts to a very large tonnage but which, in total, add up to many thousands of tons of ethylene oxide annually. These uses depend, in general, on their water solubility, their stability and freedom from toxicity, their lubricating properties and their great solvent power for many drugs and dyestuffs. In the pharmaceutical and cosmetic industries they act as solvents and dispersing agents in the formulation of liquid compositions and as solid base materials in the preparation of creams, ointments and pills; in the production of tablets they may act both as binders and lubricants. In the engineering and metal working industries they are used as water-soluble lubricants in many operations and the solid compounds may be employed in the "lost wax process" casting technique. They may be used in resin production for the surface coating industries and in the formulation of printing inks; in the rubber industry they are mould release agents in the production of rubber moulded products and lubricants in the manufacture of articles from rubber latex. In paper and packaging industries they are plasticizers for cellulose tapes and binders in the production of corks; the textile industry uses many grades of polyethylene glycols in spinning, finishing, dyeing and printing operations. Of other outlets too numerous to mention, the use of solid polyethylene glycol for impregnation and preservation of archaeological timber specimens has been publicized although this does not appear likely to call for large tonnages.

The polyglycol chains are terminated by hydroxyl groups and esters or ethers may be made by starting with acids or alcohols respectively. The products are employed as emulsifiers and anti-static agents; the fatty acid esters, in particular, are useful emulsifiers in the large scale production of food products.

GLYCOL ETHERS

It has been noted above that, when the polyoxyethylene chain is built on to an alcohol base, a mono-ether results. Thus the first product from ethyl alcohol and ethylene oxide is ethylene glycol monoethyl ether. As in the case of ethylene glycol manufacture, it is not possible to restrict the reaction to one mole of ethylene oxide per mole of alcohol and some mono-ethers of di- and tri-glycol are always produced at the same time.

$$C_2H_5OH + C_2H_4O \longrightarrow C_2H_5O\ CH_2CH_2OH$$
$$C_2H_5OH + 2\ C_2H_4O \longrightarrow C_2H_5O\ CH_2CH_2O\ CH_2CH_2OH$$
$$C_2H_5OH + 3\ C_2H_4O \longrightarrow C_2H_5O\ CH_2CH_2O\ CH_2CH_2O$$
$$CH_2CH_2OH$$

The reactions are carried out commercially in the presence of alkaline catalysts such as caustic soda or acid catalysts such as boron tri-fluoride. The relative yields of the mono-, di- and tri-glycol ethers may be varied within limits by varying the proportions of alcohol and oxide in the reaction mixture and by a suitable choice of catalyst. With secondary alcohols, such as isopropanol, an acid catalyst is essential.

The mono-ethers of ethylene glycol are excellent solvents and are widely used in formulation of paints and lacquers; the boiling point may be varied by a suitable choice of alcohol, those most commonly used being methyl, ethyl and n-butyl. The di- and tri-glycol ethers are high boiling solvents and also find applications as plasticizers and in the formulation of hydraulic fluids. Further changes in solvent power and vapour pressure characteristics may be obtained by esterifying the terminal hydroxyl group with a carboxylic acid; it is possible, therefore, by suitable combinations of the ether group and of the esterifying acid to produce a whole range of solvents with properties, to some extent, "tailor made" to requirements.

The major U.K. producers of ethylene glycol ethers are Shell Chemicals and Union Carbide but several other companies manufacture glycol ethers and ether esters for special purposes. Total production is not known but is certainly on a scale of thousands of tons annually.

SURFACE-ACTIVE AGENTS

When a water soluble poly-oxyethylene chain is built on to a water insoluble hydroxy compound, a molecule is formed with hydrophobic groups at one end and hydrophilic groups at the other, which has the typical structure required for detergent action. The length of the poly-oxyethylene chain required to confer complete water solubiliity on the final product depends on the nature of the starting material and is generally related to the size of the hydrocarbon groups it contains within its structure. Thus p-octylphenol gives a completely soluble product when about eight molecules of ethylene oxide have been added on to its hydroxyl group, whereas nonyl phenol would require rather more to confer complete solubility. By this reaction a hydrophilic group may be introduced into any compound having a replaceable hydrogen atom and surface-active agents may be produced in which the ampholytic balance may be varied amost at will.

These compounds are not dissociated in solution and are thus usually referred to as non-ionic detergents and/or surface-active agents. They are described more fully in the volume of this series on surface-active agents. As they are relatively expensive compared with the more usual domestic and industrial detergents, the total tonnage consumed is not large but will account for some thousands of tons of ethylene oxide annually. I.C.I. was probably the first producer in this country with "Lissapol"; the two other producers of ethylene oxide also manufacture products of this kind. Detergent producers, such as Marchon Products or Prices (Bromborough) Ltd. (a member of the Unilever Group), purchase ethylene oxide for production of their own specialities and, because of the ease with which products designed for a specific use may be made, many companies produce specialities for the textile, leather, lubricating oil and similar industries. In its versatility ethylene oxide is an ideal raw material for the small-scale chemical manufacturer.

AMINO COMPOUNDS

Ethylene oxide reacts with ammonia to form a series of hydroxy-ethylamines—the ethanolamines.

$$NH_3 + C_2H_4O \longrightarrow NH_2CH_2CH_2OH$$

$$NH_2CH_2CH_2OH + C_2H_4O \longrightarrow NH(CH_2CH_2OH)_2$$

$$NH(CH_2CH_2OH)_2 + C_2H_4O \longrightarrow N(CH_2CH_2OH)_3$$

Finally the tri-ethanolamine will add on yet another molecule of the oxide to form a highly basic compound, tetra-(2-hydroxy ethyl) ammonium hydroxide.

$$N(CH_2CH_2OH)_3 + C_2H_4O \longrightarrow N(CH_2CH_2OH)_4OH$$

The reaction is carried out continuously by mixing ethylene oxide with an excess of ammonia in a coil reactor under high pressure and with a short time of contact. The reactor effluent is stripped of excess ammonia and the ethanolamines separated by fractionation under vacuum.

All three ethanolamines have a wide variety of uses in many industries, especially in detergents and cosmetics. They all form amine salts with fatty acids which have detergent properties; salts of mono- and di-ethanolamines have been used in substantial quantities as foam promoters in domestic powder detergents and those of tri-ethanolamine are embodied in shampoos and other toilet and cosmetic preparations.

Aqueous solutions of mono- or di-ethanolamine are used as absorption agents in the Girbotol process for removal of carbon dioxide or hydrogen sulphide from gas streams (see page 49). Di-ethanolamine has a substantial application as a neutralizing agent for selective weed killers such as 2.4–D, 2.4.5T and D.N.C. (see Chapter 9); it is preferred for this purpose to the alkylamines because of its milder odour. Dehydration of mono-ethanolamine gives ethylene imine and of di-ethanolamine, morpholine; ethylene imine polymerizes readily and is usually sold in polymeric form. Both of these compounds have a number of interesting outlets in improving the wet strength of paper and in the manufacture of rubber additives but they are not made in this country as yet.

$$NH_2 CH_2 CH_2 OH \xrightarrow{-H_2O}$$

$$NH (CH_2CH_2 OH)_2 \xrightarrow{-H_2O}$$

Ethylene oxide reacts with alkylamines to give N substituted ethanolamines; for example, with di-ethylamine it gives di-ethylamino ethanol, an intermediate in the synthesis of anti-malarial drugs, in high yield.

MISCELLANEOUS REACTIONS

With hydrogen cyanide, ethylene oxide forms ethylene cyan-hydrin which may be dehydrated to acrylonitrile or hydrolysed in the presence of an alcohol to give the esters of acrylic acid. This was, at one time, an important commercial method for producing these materials in the U.S.A. but it has now been largely superseded (see pages 73 and 153.) With cellulose and methyl cellulose, hydroxy-ethyl derivatives are formed; this reaction is believed to be the route used by Courtaulds for the manufacture of these materials.

The cyclic ether, dioxan, may be prepared by first reacting ethylene oxide in the presence of a small quantity of dilute sulphuric acid to form mixed low molecular weight polyglycols, followed by dehydration with more concentrated acid. Vapour phase catalytic dimerization of the oxide is another possible route to dioxan.

Dioxan boils at 101°C and is an exceptionally good solvent. Unfortunately it is insidiously toxic and has a great tendency to form peroxides; these properties have undoubtedly prevented its large-scale commercial development. By addition to aldehydes in the presence of a stannic chloride catalyst, ethylene oxide forms dioxolans:

Dioxolan itself and 2-methyl dioxolan, shown above, are both potentially interesting solvents.

Equimolar proportions of ethylene oxide and hydrogen sulphide react to form monothiothylene glycol

$$C_2H_4O + H_2S \longrightarrow HOCH_2CH_2SH$$

This compound is an intermediate in the synthesis of an important animal food additive, methionine, but a newer route from acrolein is now preferred. Thiodiglycol, produced when two molecules of ethylene oxide react with one of hydrogen sulphide, is more important since it may readily be chlorinated to $\beta\beta'$ dichloro-diethyl sulphide, better known as mustard gas.

Some indication has been given of the many potential reactions of ethylene oxide, of which only a few are commercially exploited on a large scale in this country so far. The rapid growth in ethylene oxide output, and the expansion plans announced by two of the major producers, suggest that more of them may become commercially important in the future.

ETHYL ALCOHOL OR ETHANOL

As the first aliphatic chemical produced on a large scale in a pure state, a number of references to ethanol have already been made and its production by the classical fermentation route has been described on pages 18–21. Although the fermentation route is still used to some extent, in most industrialized countries a synthetic process starting from ethylene is preferred. The fact that ethylene will react with strong (95–96%) sulphuric acid to produce a mixture of ethyl hydrogen sulphate and di-ethyl sulphate and that these compounds could be hydrolysed to ethanol and sulphuric acid has been known for many years. In fact, attempts to apply this process for the recovery of ethylene contained in coke oven gas were made in the early part of the century but did not prove economic. When more concentrated ethylene streams became available from refinery gas, further attempts to exploit the process were made and the first large commercial plant was erected by the Standard Oil Co. of New Jersey in the U.S.A. in the mid-1920's. The same process was used for ethanol production when the first British petrochemical cracker was established in 1942 by British Celanese at Spondon, near Derby; this plant is still in operation. The process has the advantage that relatively dilute mixtures of ethylene with inert gases such as ethane may be used as feedstock; it suffers from the disadvantage that the hydrolysis yields large quantities of dilute sulphuric acid which has to be reconcentrated to 95–96% strength before it can be used again and from the general high maintenance costs which beset most processes involving the handling of large amounts of strong acids. Further, when it is the main process for ethanol manufacture, the amounts of by-product di-ethyl ether produced are far in excess of the market demands for it.

Many efforts were made, therefore, to avoid the formation and hydrolysis of ethyl sulphates and the Shell Development Corporation devised a direct hydration process in which water is added directly to ethylene in the presence of a phosphoric acid catalyst; this was first applied on a commercial scale at the Shell Plant at Houston, Texas shortly after the last war. The process is now carried out in this country by B.H.C. at Grangemouth under licence from Shell and has virtually replaced the fermentation route. A diagrammatic flow sheet of the process is given in Fig. 14.

Pure ethylene and distilled water (1 : 0·6 molar ratio) are preheated by exchange with reactor products and finally heated to about 300°C in a furnace. The reactants are then passed at a pressure of about 1000 psig in to the reactor which is a stainless steel vessel packed with catalyst, consisting of phosphoric acid absorbed on an inert support. After cooling, the reaction products are neutralized and passed through a condenser followed by a water scrubber; the condensate plus the scrubber liquor constitute the crude ethanol which goes forward to purification. A small bleed stream is taken from the scrubbed gas to control the build up of inert gases in the system and the remainder is recycled to reactor feed; a small amount of phosphoric acid is added to replace that volatilized and removed from the reactor with the product stream.

The purification train consists of a stripper in which the crude alcohol is partially concentrated by distillation with open steam, a hydrogenation tower for removal of unsaturated

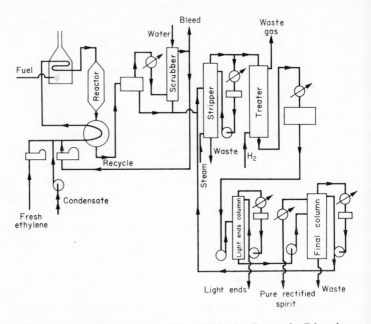

FIG. 14 The Shell Development Direct Hydration Process for Ethanol.

materials, a light ends column for removal of ether and a main column from which pure rectified spirits are taken a few trays below the top. The bottoms from this column, together with a small stream from the overhead condenser, are returned to the stripper. The rectified spirit product, being the binary azeotrope of ethanol and water, cannot be further purified directly by distillation and, if anhydrous alcohol is required, it is produced by a process of azeotropic distillation. When a mixture of rectified spirit and benzene is fractionated, a ternary azeotrope of benzene, ethanol and water first distils off. When this azeotrope is condensed it separates into two layers, the upper layer containing most of the alcohol and benzene and the lower layer consisting mainly of water with a little ethanol. The water layer is separated, stripped of its alcohol content and run to waste while the benzene layer is returned to the top of the column. In this way water is continuously removed from the system and a dry ethanol product may be taken off some plates below the feed point of the azeotroping column. When the system has reached equilibrium the benzene remains in the upper part of the column and only a small amount of make up to replace losses through the condenser is required.

The D.C.L. is traditionally the major producer of industrial alcohol in this country and still produces some fermentation material. Now, however, it draws most of its supplies from petroleum sources through its joint company with B.P., B.H.C. at Grangemouth, where the total installed capacity has been announced as 84,000 t/a. The only other producer is Courtaulds whose output is mainly for captive use, any surplus apparently being marketed through the D.C.L. organization. The Spondon plant probably has a capacity of 35,000–40,000 t/a. Apart from a small quantity imported, these two producers supply the whole of the British market.

The use of synthetic alcohol for potable purposes is not favoured in this country; these requirements are met entirely by fermentation and are not dealt with here. Because of the high rate of excise duty on potable spirit (currently about £25 per gallon of 100% alcohol), the temptation for unscrupulous persons to divert duty free industrial spirit to more interesting and, while undetected, more profitable outlets is obvious; its uses have therefore, always been hedged about with restrictions, many of them antiquated and long out of date. In recent years, however, the Commissioners of Customs and Excise, possibly encouraged by their experience with the Hydrocarbon Oil Duties which began in 1928 without a century or more of tradition behind them and which dealt with much larger volumes of material at relatively low rates of duty, have greatly changed and modernized their regulations and operating methods to the great benefit of industrial users of alcohol.

Pure ethanol must still be kept strictly in bond and it can only be moved freely when heavily "denatured" by addition of wood naphtha, bone oil, pyridine or similar compounds to render it undrinkable. There are two general denaturing formulae—the heavily denatured and violet dyed methylated spirit of the retail shops and the less heavily denatured and colourless industrial methylated spirit (IMS) used for many industrial purposes under limited Excise control. There are, however, many special denaturing formulae permitted by the Commissioners for ethanol used in chemical processes but, in these cases, there is usually some direct Excise supervision of the operations.

Ethanol of very high purity is used as a solvent for essences and flavourings, in perfumery, in many cosmetics and in pharmaceutical preparations. These applications require only relatively small quantities and the major outlet is as a general industrial solvent, either alone or in the form of one of its esters with carboxylic acids. The best known and most widely used of these is ethyl acetate, prepared by reaction of ethanol and acetic acid in what may be regarded as a typical esterification procedure.

ESTERIFICATION

A mixture of acetic acid, which may vary in strength between 10% and 80% in different versions of the process, with an excess of 95% ethanol and about 1% of concentrated sulphuric acid is passed through a preheater to an esterification/distillation column. The column is under heavy reflux and a controlled amount of distillate is withdrawn from the top which is maintained at about 80°C. The distillate contains about 20% of ester with ethanol and a little water and is sent to a separating column where the ternary azeotrope containing 83% ethyl acetate, 9% ethanol and 8% water is distilled off. This homogeneous distillate is washed with an equal volume of water and sent to a separator where it settles into two layers. The lower layer, containing water with small amounts of ethanol and ester, is returned to the separating column where the ester and alcohol are recovered in the ternary azeotrope. The upper layer from the separator, consisting mainly of ethyl acetate, is run to the drying column where sufficient distillate is taken off to remove all the water and alcohol present. This distillate is also returned to the separating column for recovery of the ester and alcohol; recovered ethanol thus accumulates in the lower sections of the separating column from which it is returned continuously to the esterification column. Water containing some sulphuric acid accumulates at the bottom of the esterification column and is discharged to waste after neutralization. The bottom product from the drying column consists of substantially pure ester which may be redistilled when a high purity product is required. The equipment for this process is usually of copper; the yield on acetic acid used is nearly quantitative. A process flow diagram is shown in Fig. 15.

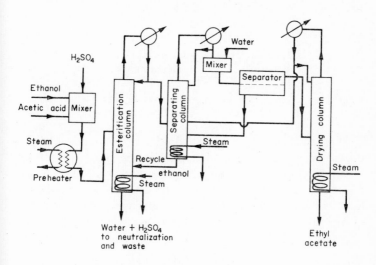

FIG. 15 Esterification Process for Ethyl Acetate.

Ethyl acetate is a colourless liquid with a fragrant odour; it boils at 77·1°C and is only partially soluble in water. It is widely used as a low boiling solvent, especially in nitrocellulose finishes; growth in this field, although still at a rate of over 10% annually, has been restricted in recent years by competition from methyl

ethyl ketone. The largest producer is D.C.L. which produces a wide range of ester solvents as well as ethyl acetate. The process is, however, simple and may well be carried out on general purpose chemical plant so that other traditional ester manufacturers such as Boake Roberts and W. J. Bush, both now part of the Albright and Wilson Group, or Howards of Ilford, now part of the Laporte Group, may produce as required.

Ethanol has, in the past, been an important starting point for chemical synthesis but has now been almost entirely replaced by ethylene and other olefins. Ethanol from fermentation, however, is always potentially available should economic conditions change; a brief description of the reactions employed is worth while.

(a) *Butadiene*

$$CH_3CH_2OH \xrightarrow{\text{Cu.}} CH_3CHO + H_2$$
Ethanol   Acetaldehyde

$$CH_3CHO + CH_3CH_2OH \longrightarrow CH_2{=}CHCH{=}CH_2 + 2H_2O$$
Acetaldehyde   Ethanol   1·3-Butadiene

Alternative routes are by dehydration of 1·3-butane diol produced by hydrogenation of acetaldol (see below) or of 1·4-butane diol produced from acetylene and formaldehyde (see Fig. 8, Chapter 4). All of these routes are uneconomic when C_4 hydrocarbons are cheap but the acetaldehyde process was used in America and the butane diol processes in Germany during the last war.

(b) *n-Butanol and n-Butyraldehyde*

$$2CH_3CHO \xrightarrow{\text{NaOH}} CH_3CHOHCH_2CHO$$
Acetaldehyde   Acetaldol

$$CH_3CHOHCH_2CHO \xrightarrow{-H_2O} CH_3CH{=}CHCHO$$
Acetaldol   Crotonaldehyde

$$\text{CH}_3\text{CH} = \text{CHCHO} \xrightarrow{+\text{H}_2} \text{CH}_3\text{CH}_2\text{CH}_2\text{CHO}$$

Crotonaldehyde   n. Butyraldehyde

$$\text{CH}_3\text{CH}_2\text{CH}_2\text{CHO} \xrightarrow{+\text{H}_2} \text{CH}_3\text{CH}_2\text{CH}_2\text{CH}_2\text{OH}$$

n. Butyraldehyde   n. Butanol

This route is still used to a small extent and is further described in Chapter 7. It has been largely replaced by application of the OXO process to propylene.

(c) *Acetic Acid and Anhydride*

$$\text{CH}_3\text{CH}_2\text{OH} + \tfrac{1}{2}\text{O}_2 \xrightarrow{\text{Ag.}} \text{CH}_3\text{CHO} + \text{H}_2\text{O}$$

Ethanol   Acetaldehyde

$$\text{CH}_3\text{CHO} + \tfrac{1}{2}\text{O}_2 \xrightarrow{\text{Mn. salt.}} \text{CH}_3\text{COOH}$$

Acetaldehyde   Acetic Acid

$$\text{CH}_3\text{COOH} \xrightarrow{\text{pyrolysis}} \text{CH}_2 = \text{CO} + \text{H}_2\text{O}$$

Acetic Acid   Keten

$$\text{CH}_2 = \text{CO} + \text{CH}_3\text{COOH} \longrightarrow (\text{CH}_3\text{CO})_2\text{O}$$

Keten   Acetic Acid   Acetic Anhydride

The primary conversion of ethanol to acetaldehyde is likely to be replaced by oxidation of ethylene, described later in the chapter, but is still used by both D.C.L. and Courtaulds. D.C.L., however, now makes its acetic acid by direct oxidation of hydrocarbons (see page 54) and its acetic anhydride by oxidation of acetaldehyde. Courtaulds still uses the keten route to acetic anhydride and obtains some of its keten by pyrolysis of acetone as an alternative to acetic acid. These processes are useful to Courtaulds since they provide an outlet for by-product acetic acid from cellulose acetylation and for any excess acetone from their chemical cracking complex. The pyrolysis process is described on page 129.

(d) *Acetone*

$$2CH_3CH_2OH + H_2O \xrightarrow{\text{Fe.}} CH_3COCH_3 + 4H_2 + CO_2$$
Ethanol   Acetone

A large plant for carrying out this process was erected by British Industrial Solvents Ltd., then a partly owned subsidiary of the D.C.L. in 1929 (see page 10) and operated until after the outbreak of war in 1939. The need to economize in imports led to a shortage of molasses for ethanol production and the plant was switched to dehydrogenation of isopropanol; this is now the standard process for acetone production and is described in Chapter 6. By-product hydrogen from the original process was used for n-butanol manufacture as described under (b) above.

ACETALDEHYDE

Conversion of ethanol to acetaldehyde is the first step in a number of chemical syntheses, some of which have been described above. It may be carried out with yields of about 95% by passing a mixture of ethanol vapour and air over a silver gauze catalyst at about 500°C. Once started the exothermic reaction is self sustaining but, for high yields, the temperature must be no higher than the bare minimum necessary to keep the reaction going. This is achieved by controlling the composition of the ethanol/air mixture. An alternative to partial oxidation is dehydrogenation of ethanol over a copper catalyst. These processes are still used in many parts of the world but are likely to be replaced by a new process for direct oxidation of ethylene developed by the Konsortium für Electrochemie G.m.b.H., a subsidiary of the Hoechst group in Germany. It has been known for many years that, when ethylene is passed into an aqueous solution of palladium chloride, it is converted into acetaldehyde and metallic palladium is precipitated.

$$CH_2 = CH_2 + PdCl_2 + H_2O \longrightarrow CH_3CHO + Pd. + 2HCl$$

The new invention consists in carrying out the reaction in the presence of sufficient cupric chloride in solution with the palladium chloride to prevent the precipitation of metallic palladium, while it is itself reduced to cuprous chloride which may, in turn, be reoxidized to the cupric state. In the two-stage process ethylene is passed into an equilibrium mixture of palladium chloride, cupric chloride and cuprous chloride at moderate super-atmospheric pressure and temperature so that acetaldehyde distils off. Solution is continuously withdrawn, oxidized with air in a separate reactor and recycled at such a rate that the cupric/cuprous chloride concentration remains at the desired figure. Alternatively, the reaction may be carried out in one stage by feeding ethylene and air simultaneously into the solution of mixed chlorides. It is claimed that the process may be applied to other olefins—for example acetone may be produced directly from propylene in this way. The chloride solution is highly corrosive and equipment in contact with it should preferably be made of titanium.

The process is undoubtedly cheaper than the earlier route through ethanol and, although not yet applied in this country, plants have already been built, or are under construction, in many parts of the world; it is likely to increase in importance and may well permit acetaldehyde to be used economically for syntheses at present carried out in other ways. The aldehyde is reactive and has applications in the manufacture of dyestuffs, fine chemicals and pharmaceuticals as well as in large tonnage outlets such as conversion to acetic anhydride and pentaerythritol.

Acetaldehyde is usually used in the factory where it is made since its low boiling point (20·9°C), wide explosive limits in air and ready reaction with any oxygen present call for special conditions of storage and transport. It may, however, be transported in heavy gauge aluminium drums or pressure tank cars under a nitrogen blanket; substantial quantities are moved in this way. The two major producers, D.C.L. and Courtaulds, manufacture mainly for conversion to acetic anhydride in their own plants but D.C.L. does market part of its output.

ACETIC ANHYDRIDE

There are several variants of the process for oxidation of acetaldehyde to acetic anhydride in commercial use. The reaction may be regarded as taking place in two stages—first conversion of the acetaldehyde to peracetic acid followed by reduction of this with more acetaldehyde to give acetic anhydride and water.

$$CH_3CHO + O \longrightarrow CH_3CO\text{-}O\text{-}OH$$
Acetaldehyde   Peracetic acid

$$CH_3CO\text{-}O\text{-}OH + CH_3CHO \longrightarrow (CH_3CO)_2O + H_2O$$
Peracetic acid   Acetaldehyde   Acetic Anhydride

Air is bubbled into liquid acetaldehyde, containing about 2% by weight of a catalyst such as manganese acetate, at a temperature of about 60°C and a pressure of about 60 psig. An excess of acetic acid is also present and benzene may be added, both as a diluent and to assist in the removal of water in the subsequent vacuum distillation and thus minimize reconversion of produced anhydride to acetic acid. The reactor attains a steady state into which a mixture of fresh and recovered acetaldehyde with acetic acid, benzene and catalyst from the recovery system is fed continuously and a mixture of anhydride, acid, aldehyde, benzene, water and catalyst is withdrawn; this is fed immediately to a crude vacuum column which removes the water with benzene and excess acetaldehyde overhead and gives a dry mixture of acetic acid and anhydride, still containing the catalyst, at the bottom. The overhead distillate is fractionated to give acetaldehyde as an overhead product and a benzene water mixture at the bottom; the aldehyde is mixed with fresh aldehyde feed, the benzene separated and returned to the reactor and the water sent to drain. The acid/anhydride mixture is fed to a separation column which gives acetic acid as a top product, acetic anhydride from a plate near the bottom and recovered catalyst as a bottom product. The anhydride may be further purified by vacuum distillation.

The reactor is usually fabricated of stainless steel: care is needed to select the correct grade for the reaction conditions chosen if serious corrosion is to be avoided. Other acid and anhydride handling plant may be of stainless steel or copper. The yield on acetaldehyde used may approach 95% of theoretical. So far as is known, D.C.L. is the only British company using the process for large-scale production of acetic anhydride.

Acetic anhydride reacts readily with carboxy groups to yield esters.

$$ROH + (CH_3CO)_2O \longrightarrow CH_3COOR + CH_3COOH$$

Its major commercial use is in acetylation of cellulose for production of cellulose acetate fibres and plastics and generally as an acetylating agent.

When carrying out oxidation of acetaldehyde in the past, it has always been considered essential to avoid accumulations of peracetic acid which is believed to have been the cause of a number of explosions. More recently it has been found that, under the proper conditions, peracetic acid may be stable enough to become the major product of the reaction. The process has been developed commercially by Union Carbide in the U.S.A. and a 10,000 t/a plant has been built. A variant of the method has been developed in this country by Courtaulds and peracetic acid is made on a moderate scale at their plant at Spondon.

Peracetic acid may be used industrially as a cheaper substitute for hydrogen peroxide, for example in the production of epoxidized oils, and yields acetic acid as by-product.

The keten route to acetic anhydride involves the preliminary conversion of acetaldehyde to acetic acid which is then subjected to pyrolysis.

$$CH_3COOH \longrightarrow CH_2 = CO + H_2O$$
$$CH_2 = CO + CH_3COOH \longrightarrow (CH_3CO)_2O$$

Acetic acid is vaporized at about 100 mm absolute pressure, mixed with about 0·3% by weight of triethyl phosphate as catalyst, and passed through an externally heated pyrolysis tube at about 700°C. Immediately on leaving the furnace the vapours are treated with enough ammonia to kill the catalyst, cooled rapidly in surface condensers to condense out water of reaction and unchanged acid and the uncondensed keten is absorbed in 100% acetic acid. The resulting mixture of acetic acid and anhydride is separated as in the oxidation process described above. The product from the surface condensers is aqueous acetic acid of about 35% strength and may be distilled to give 100% acid for recycle.

The pyrolysis of acetone to keten is carried out in a similar manner.

$$CH_3CO\ CH_3 \longrightarrow CH_2 = CO + CH_4$$

Keten itself is of potential interest as a chemical reagent but is unstable in the free state. It dimerizes readily and di-keten, a liquid boiling at 127°C, which is fairly stable, is produced by Courtaulds.

PENTAERYTHRITOL

Acetaldehyde will react with formaldehyde under strongly alkaline conditions to form pentaerythritol and a salt of formic acid as a by-product.

$$4\ HCHO + CH_3CHO + NaOH \longrightarrow \underset{\text{Pentaerythritol}}{C(CH_2OH)_4}$$
$$+ HCOONa$$

An aqueous solution containing about 25% by weight of formaldehyde is made strongly alkaline with caustic soda or with lime slurry and liquid acetaldehyde is added slowly below the surface with good agitation; the reaction is exothermic and cooling is necessary. A mole ratio of about 4·5 moles of formaldehyde to one of acetaldehyde is used. Reaction is complete after an hour or two at a temperature of 20°C when the solution is removed to the neutralizing tank and sufficient acid is added to leave the solution faintly alkaline. If caustic soda has been used in the first place, then formic acid is usually used for neutralization, and the sodium formate stays in solution but, if lime was the alkali used, then sulphuric acid is employed and the calcium ion is precipitated as sulphate and filtered off. The solution is then evaporated in vacuum and pentaerythritol allowed to crystallize out. The crude product may be used for some purposes but is purified by recrystallization when high purity is required, as in explosives manufacture. The mother liquor is recycled, after recovery of sodium formate if caustic soda has been the alkali used.

Pentaerythritol competes with other polyhydric alcohols such as glycerol, ethylene glycol and sorbitol; it is used extensively in combination with drying oils in the production of alkyd resins for the paint industry; the tetranitrate was an important explosive in war time. The most important U.K. producer is I.C.I.

VINYL COMPOUNDS

Ethylene may be regarded as the precursor of vinyl alcohol, $CH_2 = CHOH$. The alcohol itself is not known in the free state but it can exist in the form of its esters and as polyvinyl alcohol. The most important ester is the acetate which may be produced directly from acetylene and acetic acid. An alternative is the reaction of acetaldehyde and acetic anhydride to form ethylidene diacetate which yields vinyl acetate on pyrolysis in the presence of strong acids:

$$(CH_3CO)_2O + CH_3CHO \longrightarrow CH_3CH(OCOCH_3)_2$$
$$CH_3CH(OCOCH_3)_2 \longrightarrow CH_3COOCH = CH_2 + CH_3COOH$$

Isolation of the ethylidene di-acetate is not necessary and the two reactions may be combined into one operation. This route is being used by Courtaulds at Spondon but is being abandoned in favour of a joint venture with Distillers Co. based on acetylene and acetic acid (see page 74).

Another new process which may well find favour depends on oxidation of ethylene in the presence of acetic acid:

$$CH_2 = CH_2 + CH_3COOH + \tfrac{1}{2}O_2 \longrightarrow CH_3COOCH = CH_2 + H_2O$$

I.C.I., too, has announced that it will build a 30,000 t/a vinyl acetate plant using an ethylene oxidation process developed in its own laboratories. No details of this process are known at present but I.C.I. has claimed that it avoids the use of acetic acid. Thus, with the D.C.L./Courtaulds operation based on a 10,000 t/a acetylene plant, total capacity for vinyl acetate will be around 60,000 t/a within a year or two.

Vinyl acetate is an important monomer for production of homopolymers and co-polymers, especially with vinyl chloride. It is also the starting point for production of polyvinyl alcohol by hydrolysis. Emulsions of polyvinyl alcohol in water are used as the basis for emulsion paints and are also employed in manufacture of adhesives and textile finished. The acetals and butyrals, produced by reaction of the alcohol with the appropriate aldehyde, are increasing in importance in the plastics industry. Polyvinyl butyral, in particular, is the most satisfactory material known for the inter-layer in the manufacture of laminated safety glass. Total U.K. consumption of polyvinyl alcohol is currently around 1500 t/a.

NITROGEN COMPOUNDS FROM ETHYLENE

A very large number of nitrogen compounds may be derived from ethylene but they belong more to the field of fine chemicals and pharmaceuticals and none of them has achieved really large-scale bulk production, with the exception of the ethanolamines which have already been described as ethylene oxide derivatives. Two other groups, the ethylamines and the ethylene diamines are perhaps produced on a sufficiently large scale to be included here.

Ethylamine may be made by reaction of ethyl chloride with ammonia but the usual route is from ethanol and ammonia in the same way as for methylamine described on page 62. Di- and tri-ethylamines are always formed and, in this case there is some production of ethylene which is partly suppressed by working under pressure. The reaction may be applied to the production of propyl and butyl amines but there is a growing tendency for the alcohol to revert to the corresponding olefin as the carbon chain lengthens. For this reason, and because of decreasing volatility of the alcohol, other means must be devised for the production of the higher alkylamines which are described in Chapter 8.

The ethylamines, like the corresponding methyl compounds, are used mainly as intermediates in the manufacture of rubber chemicals, dyestuffs, pharmaceuticals, photographic chemicals, pesticides and herbicides. I.C.I. is the only major producer in this country; the scale of production is believed to be lower than for the methylamines but still to amount to a substantial tonnage.

When ethylene dichloride is reacted with ammonia under pressure at temperatures above 100°C, a mixture of ethylene diamine and the polyethylene polyamines such as tri-ethylene tetramine and tetra-ethylene pentamine is formed. Ethylene diamine has some uses as a solvent and is an intermediate in the preparation of ethylene diamine tetra-acetic acid. This may be made by reaction of the diamine with formaldehyde and hydrogen cyanide followed by hydrolysis.

$$4 \ HCN + 4 \ HCHO$$
$$+ \ H_2N \ CH_2CH_2NH_2 \longrightarrow (CNCH_2)_2N \ CH_2CH_2N \ (CH_2CN)_2$$

This compound acts as a sequestering agent for calcium ions and has a wide variety of uses. Two manufacturers are Whiffens, a subsidiary of Fisons, and Norman, Evans and Rais, recently taken over by Associated British Maltsters.

The amounts of the polyethylene polyamines co-produced with ethylene diamine may be varied within limits by varying the reaction conditions. They have a number of uses, particularly in the manufacture of specialized detergents and surface-active agents but the tonnage required is quite small although higher than for ethylene diamine. Total U.K. requirements of the ethylene amines are probably not much over 2000 t/a.

CONCLUSION

This description of the commercial applications of ethylene chemistry is generally confined to one or two reaction stages from the original raw material. It is by no means exhaustive and necessarily omits many interesting reactions and many important chemicals which have not yet attained large tonnage production. Enough has been said, however, to indicate the vast possibilities of ethylene as a starting point for chemical synthesis; many new possibilities will undoubtedly be exploited in the years to come. An important trend, which can already be discerned, is likely to become more marked; the constant drive for lower cost will lead to further elimination of intermediate steps and to more direct conversions of ethylene to the final product on the lines of the new I.C.I. process for production of vinyl acetate which has been referred to.

Greater dependence on ethylene may tend to concentrate developments in the neighbourhood of the large ethylene producing centres but a start has already been made on the distribution of ethylene by pipeline and further pipelines are planned. As the pipeline system is extended, it will counteract the tendency for manufacture to be concentrated round the ethylene crackers and will favour the setting up of ethylene conversion plants near the markets for the finished products.

READING LIST

1. *The Discovery of Polythene*, by R. O. Gibson. Royal Institute of Chemistry Lecture Series, 1964, No. 1.
2. The Manufacture and Use of Tetra-ethyl Lead, by Graham Edgar. *Ind. & Eng. Chem.* **31**, 1439–46, 1939

3. *Manufacture and Use of Fluorine and Its Compounds*, by A. J. Rudge, Oxford University Press, London, 1962.

4. *Castner Memorial Lecture 1965*, by H. M. Stanley. *Chemistry & Industry*, No. 27, pp. 1192–1199, 1965.

5. Symposium on Petrochemicals. Special Publication with Chemistry & Industry, pp. S. 1–68. (Contains also papers on raw materials and on light olefin recovery for reading in conjunction with Chapter 2, on C₄'s dealt with in Chapter 7 and on styrene and synthetic phenol dealt with in Chapter 9.)

6. Symposium on Petroleum Chemicals. *J. Inst. Pet.* **46**, 337–46, 1960. Also suitable for reading in conjunction with Chapters 2, 6 and 7.

7. *Polyethers*, Part I. Edited by Norman Gaylord. Volume XIII of the series on *High Polymers*. Interscience Publishers, London, 1963.

8. *Alcohol—Its Production, Properties and Applications*, by Charles Simmonds. Macmillan, London, 1919. (Very old but an excellent book.)

9. Acetaldehyde by Ethylene Oxidation, by J. Schmidt. *Chemistry & Industry*, No. 2, pp. 54–61, 1962.

10. Peracetic Acid, by J. A. John and F. Weymouth. *Chemistry & Industry*, No. 2, pp. 62–69, 1962.

CHAPTER 6

Chemicals Derived from Propylene and Propane

PROPYLENE, like ethylene, has been known for many years but did not become freely and cheaply available until cracking processes for octane improvement of gasoline became part of oil refinery practice. The erection of a plant for conversion of refinery propylene to isopropyl alcohol is generally regarded as marking the foundation of the petroleum chemicals industry. Propane did not become common until the development of low-temperature distillation processes made its separation from natural gas a simple matter. Unlike propylene, it is not widely used in chemical synthesis and is mainly sold as a liquid in pressurized containers for use in metal cutting and as a fuel. It may be used as a cracking feedstock to produce ethylene.

Production of propylene as a by-product of both refinery and specialized chemical cracking operations has been described in Chapter 2 and the possibility that by-product material may not be sufficient for all future requirements was envisaged. So long as excess by-product propylene has been available and has been diverted to fuel use, it has been logical to charge propylene into chemical processes at fuel value. If, however, it becomes necessary to crack for propylene as well as ethylene, it must become a cost bearer in the process; at the same time cracking for propylene requires milder conditions than for ethylene, leading to lower octane number gasoline fractions and decreased by-product credits, thus further increasing the total cost of production of the desired olefins. In total, the cost of such specially produced propylene is likely to be from 100 to 150% higher than the fuel cost assigned to it at present. This could have a profound effect on the economics of chemical uses of propylene.

Total production of propylene in this country, calculated as 100% olefin, is probably of the same order as the current half million tons annual ethylene production; it is, however, more dispersed, being produced in refineries from catalytic crackers and thermal reformers as well as from "chemical" crackers. Refinery C_3 streams usually contain about 50% propylene mixed with propane while chemical plant material may contain from 80–95% of the olefin according to the severity of the cracking operation. Chemical plant propylene is usually contaminated with some propadiene and acetylenic hydrocarbons and these may have to be removed by partial hydrogenation before the material can be used for chemical synthesis. So far propane has found little direct chemical use other than as a cracking feedstock for production of ethylene and propylene but the olefin has a large number of commercial applications and is second only to ethylene as a chemical raw material.

PLASTICS

The success of polythene as a plastic naturally invited consideration of propylene as a plastics monomer; the first efforts, however, produced only low molecular weight polymers of a rubbery consistency which were quite useless as thermoplastics and it was not until the Ziegler work on polythene was extended to stereo-specific polymerization of propylene by Natta in the mid-1950's that real progress was possible.

Polypropylene differs from polyethylene in having a methyl group which may lie on either side of the polymer chain. When the methyl groups are all on the same side, the polymer is said to be iso-tactic; when they occur on alternate sides it is syndio-tactic and, when the methyl groups have a random distribution, atactic. The early attempts to produce polypropylene yielded only atactic polymers and it was then discovered by Professor

Natta in Italy that, when polymerizing propylene with Ziegler-type catalysts, if the titanium tetrachloride of the Ziegler catalyst system was replaced by titanium trichloride iso-tactic polymers could be produced which had a crystalline structure and high melting point. This discovery paved the way for the commercial production of polypropylene, first by Montecatini in Italy and then in many other parts of the world; it also focused attention on the possibility that stereo-specific polymerization of other monomers such as butadiene and isoprene would be practicable. A fuller account of these developments will be found in books on the plastics industry.

The future growth of polypropylene, and hence of the demands which it will make on propylene supplies, is still somewhat uncertain. After being hailed some years ago as the wonder plastic of the future, large scale commercial plants for its production were erected in a number of countries, especially in the U.S.A. As commercial applications were extended, some disadvantages began to appear which slowed up development. These are now being gradually eliminated and a growing market for polypropylene, largely complementary to, rather than competitive with, polyethylene, may be confidently predicted for the future. Whether it will ever attain to the same tonnage as the polythenes cannot at present be stated. I.C.I. and Shell Chemicals are the only two producers in this country at present and both have announced increases in their capacity without stating the tonnages to be reached.

Co-polymers of propylene with other olefins are possible, some of which are elastomers and may be used as synthetic rubbers. Much development work has been done in Italy by Montecatini on ethylene/propylene rubbers and a product is now being manufactured and marketed commercially by the joint Shell/Montecatini company under the trade name of "Dutral". Ethylene/Propylene rubbers are also being produced by Hüls in Germany and by Esso and dupont in the U.S.A.; they are not yet manufactured in this country but small quantities are being imported. The raw materials, ethylene and propylene, are significantly cheaper than other synthetic rubber monomers so that development of a truly competitive product could lead to a substantial increase in the demands for the olefins.

ISOPROPANOL

When propylene is reacted with sulphuric acid of 70–80% strength isopropyl hydrogen sulphate and di-isopropyl sulphate are formed.

$$\begin{array}{c} CH_3 \\ | \\ CH = CH_2 + H_2SO_4 \longrightarrow CH_3 - \overset{\overset{\displaystyle CH_3}{|}}{CH} - HSO_4 \end{array}$$

$$CH_3 - \overset{\overset{\displaystyle CH_3}{|}}{CH} - HSO_4 + \overset{\overset{\displaystyle CH_3}{|}}{CH} = CH_2 \longrightarrow (CH_3 - \overset{\overset{\displaystyle CH_3}{|}}{CH})_2SO_4$$

Either of these compounds may readily be hydrolysed to form isopropanol and regenerate sulphuric acid. Small quantities of di-isopropyl ether and of hydrocarbon polymers are also produced.

$$(CH_3\overset{\overset{\displaystyle CH_3}{|}}{CH})_2SO_4 + 2\ H_2O \longrightarrow 2\ CH_3CHOH\ CH_3 + H_2SO_4$$

The acid absorption may be carried out in the liquid or in the vapour phase; the propylene feed need not be pure and a refinery C_3 stream from catalytic cracking or thermal reforming containing roughly 50% of propylene may be used. The C_3 stream from naphtha crackers may contain up to 95% of propylene and, because of the severe cracking conditions, it may also contain significant quantities of acetylenic hydrocarbons and propadiene which would lead to excessive polymer formation in the acid absorption and cause difficulty in purifying the final product; these may be removed by selective hydrogenation.

The absorption plant may consist of a series of stirred pot reactors through which the feed gas flows counter-current to

70–80% sulphuric acid or a tower absorber may be used, also with counter-current flow. Pressure assists the absorption and may be high enough for the propylene phase to be liquid; in both liquid and vapour phase processes, intimate contact between the hydrocarbon phase and the absorbing acid must be obtained. The reaction is exothermic and heat is removed, either by circulating cooling water through coils or, in the case of liquid phase processes, by refluxing part of the hydrocarbon in order to hold the temperature in the absorber to about 35°C. Conditions in the absorption system are corrosive and high quality lead lined equipment is generally employed.

The "fat" acid from the absorbers is diluted with water and fed into the hydrolysis tower where the crude isopropanol is stripped off with steam. The water addition and steam stripping are controlled to ensure complete hydrolysis, no loss of isopropanol from the bottom of the tower and minimum dilution of the acid. Dilute acid from the hydrolysis, commonly of about 40% strength, is concentrated in conventional equipment to 70–80% and recycled to the process. There is some formation of polymers and tar and carbonaceous material tends to accumulate in the circulating acid; sufficient acid is withdrawn and replaced by new acid to maintain this contamination at an acceptable level; the spent acid may be disposed of to low-grade uses such as the descaling of steel plates or, if this is not possible, it may be concentrated to 95–96% strength in a pot concentrator when all of the carbonaceous material is oxidized and a clean acid, which may be returned to the process, is produced.

The distillate from the hydrolysis tower contains about 50% of isopropanol, up to 10% of di-isopropyl ether and small quantities of propylene polymers; it is fed first to an ether column where a crude ether fraction is taken overhead and the bottom product passes on to the alcohol column. Isopropanol forms an azeotrope with water containing 87·7% of the alcohol and the commercial product produced from the alcohol column averages about 87%. Water is discharged to waste from the bottom of the column. The hydrocarbon polymers tend to collect at a point low down in the alcohol column and are removed by with-drawing liquid from a tray at this point, passing it through a separator, and returning the de-oiled liquid to the column.

The alcohol/water azeotrope is suitable for many commercial purposes but, if the anhydrous alcohol is required, it may be produced from the constant boiling mixture by azeotropic dis-tillation with benzene or di-isopropyl ether in the same way as anhydrous ethanol (see page 120). The yield from the process depends to a considerable extent on the concentration of pro-pylene in the feed gas and on the value assigned to it. Yields of well over 90% of theory on propylene used are possible if the value of the feedstock justifies the effort.

The main outlet for isopropanol is as raw material for con-version to acetone by dehydrogenation; demand for it is, therefore, strongly related to the acetone supply/demand situ-ation. This has been disturbed in recent years by increased use of the cumene route to phenol which yields about 0·6 ton of acetone per ton of phenol. In the U.S.A. a Shell process, not yet applied in this country, for production of hydrogen peroxide by oxidation of isopropanol is another source of by-product acetone which can affect the supply situation.

$$CH_3CHOH\ CH_3 + O_2 \longrightarrow CH_3CO\ CH_3 + H_2O_2$$

Finally, as noted on page 127, the Konsortium process for the direct oxidation of ethylene to acetaldehyde may also be applied to the direct production of acetone from propylene. The medium term outlook for isopropanol as a raw material for acetone manufacture is, therefore, somewhat uncertain although a change to other sources of acetone would not affect the overall propylene demand.

About 1% of the anhydrous alcohol is added to some gasolines in winter to prevent carburettor icing and this outlet absorbs many thousands of tons annually, especially in Germany. Both the azeotrope and the anhydrous alcohol are widely used as solvents. Their solvent properties are similar to those of industrial methylated spirits but they are somewhat cheaper and less subject to Customs and Excise control. Relatively small quantities of very pure anhydrous isopropanol are used as a solvent for essences and flavourings and in perfumery and cosmetics. This material was originally made by Howards of Ilford (now part of the Laporte Group) by hydrogenation of specially purified acetone; it has now been found possible to produce a satisfactory product from petroleum-based isopropanol by extractive distillation of the commercial azeotrope with water followed by rectification and dehydration by azeotropic distillation.

Major producers are Shell Chemicals, B.H.C., Courtaulds and I.C.I., the last two for their own captive uses. I.C.I. do not use the sulphuric acid process but have a direct hydration process of their own design which is somewhat similar to the direct hydration process for ethanol described on page 119. Plant capacities have not been officially stated but the total must be well in excess of 100,000 t/a.

The by-product di-isopropyl ether may be purified by distillation and finds a number of small-scale outlets as a solvent and as a water removal agent in azeotropic distillation. It readily forms peroxides in contact with air and these may be explosive; distillation of the dry material, therefore, needs care especially when distilling down to low residues. Any excess of ether over market requirements may be returned to the absorbers where it suppresses the formation of ether from the fresh feed.

n–Propyl alcohol is not produced at all from the sulphation process and is not, in any case, an important chemical. Small quantities can be separated from the fusel oil from ethanol fermentation; larger quantities could readily be made by application of the OXO process to ethylene. Some propionic acid is now available as a by-product from the D.C.L. production of acetic acid by oxidation of naphtha and this could be hydrogenated to the alcohol if required.

ACETONE

Acetone (dimethyl ketone) has, for many years, been one of the most important industrial solvents. Also, as it appears to be the only satisfactory solvent for nitro-cellulose in the preparation of propellant explosives, its availability, or lack of it, has assumed great importance in two world wars. It was originally made by calcination of calcium acetate produced by reaction of lime with acetic acid from wood distillation or from ethanol oxidation. This method then gave way to production by the Weizmann fermentation (see page 8) and from ethanol (see page 126). When isopropanol became freely available in the U.S.A. from 1926 onwards, it soon became the major feedstock for acetone manufacture and most of the world's supplies are now made in this way. As already noted, however, by-product acetone and direct oxidation of propylene may supersede the isopropanol route in the future.

In a typical dehydrogenation process, isopropanol vapour is pre-heated by exchange with reactor product and passed into a reactor packed with a copper or brass catalyst. The reaction is endothermic and the temperature is maintained at about 500°C by enclosing the reactor in a suitable furnace. Alternatively a zinc oxide catalyst at about 400°C may be used.

$$CH_3CHOH\ CH_3 \longrightarrow CH_3CO\ CH_3 + H_2$$

The reactor effluent is passed through a condenser to a water scrubber to remove the last traces of acetone from the non-condensable hydrogen which may then be used for hydrogenation reactions. The scrubber liquor is combined with the condensate and fractionated to give a pure acetone product and dilute isopropanol solution. This latter, in turn, is distilled to yield the isopropanol/water azeotrope for recycle and water which is reused in the scrubber. The process is very simple and corrosion problems are virtually absent so that mainly mild steel plant may be used. Yield on isopropanol is over 90%.

Producers of acetone are the same as for isopropanol except that D.C.L. processes the isopropanol produced by B.H.C. Figures for plant capacities have not been given and, as all four producers use a large part of their output for their own captive uses, it is difficult to estimate total consumption which certainly runs into tens of thousands of tons annually. The free market for acetone is mainly for solvent applications; it is largely used as a solvent for nitro-cellulose, as a spinning solvent in the synthetic fibre industry and is a constituent of many surface coating formulations. These uses probably take up less than half of the total output and it is for use as a chemical intermediate that most of the acetone is required.

Two molecules of acetone will condense together at low temperatures and in the presence of alkali to form diacetone alcohol which may then be further processed to yield successively mesityl oxide, methyl isobutyl ketone and methyl isobutyl carbinol according to the following series of equations:

$$2 \text{ CH}_3\text{CO CH}_3 \xrightarrow{\text{NaOH}} (\text{CH}_3)_2\text{COHCH}_2\text{CO CH}_3$$
Acetone — Diacetone Alcohol

$$(\text{CH}_3)_2\text{C(OH)CH}_2\text{CO CH}_3 \xrightarrow{\text{Acid}} (\text{CH}_3)_2\text{C} = \text{CH CO CH}_3$$
Diacetone Alcohol — Mesityl Oxide
$$+ \text{ H}_2\text{O}$$

$$(\text{CH}_3)_2\text{C} = \text{CH CO CH}_3 \xrightarrow{\text{H}_2} (\text{CH}_3)_2\text{CH CH}_2\text{CO CH}_3$$
Mesityl Oxide — Methyl Isobutyl Ketone

$$(\text{CH}_3)_2\text{CH CH}_2\text{CO CH}_3 \xrightarrow{\text{H}_2} (\text{CH}_3)_2\text{CH CH}_2\text{CHOH CH}_3$$
Methyl Isobutyl Ketone — Methyl Isobutyl Carbinol

In practice acetone is agitated with a small quantity of alcoholic potash at 0 to $-20°\text{C}$ when about 20% conversion to diacetone alcohol takes place. The reaction mixture is carefully neutralized with sulphuric acid to pH 7·5. The unconverted acetone is distilled off and the resulting crude diacetone alcohol may be purified by vacuum distillation. Control of pH during distillation is of fundamental importance since alkaline conditions cause reversion to acetone while, in the presence of acid, the alcohol dehydrates to mesityl oxide. Pure diacetone alcohol has many uses as a solvent and as a constituent of hydraulic fluids although its instability under other than neutral conditions limits

its applications. On hydrogenation over Raney nickel, it is converted to 2-methyl-2 : 4-pentane diol(hexylene glycol) which has uses as a solvent and as a base for ester plasticizers.

When mesityl oxide is the desired product, the crude diacetone alcohol is distilled with a trace of sulphuric acid to give a good yield of the unsaturated ketone. Mesityl oxide itself is an excellent solvent but its applications are limited by its powerful and unpleasant odour. By mild hydrogenation in the presence of a nickel or copper catalyst, it is converted to methyl iso-butyl ketone; the hydrogen from isopropanol dehydrogenation is generally used for this purpose. There is always some formation of the carbinol and this may be increased, if required, but can not be completely suppressed. The ketone and carbinol are separated and purified by distillation. Methyl iso-butyl ketone is a particularly valuable medium boiling constituent of lacquers in which it has, to some extent, replaced n-butyl acetate because of its higher solvent power. The carbinol has limited applications as a solvent. High yields are obtainable at each stage and the overall yield of ketone/carbinol in commercial plants is probably above 70%, which implies a better than 90% yield in the individual reactions.

D.C.L. have been producers of diacetone alcohol for many years. Other companies such as Boake Roberts have produced diacetone alcohol but have not gone farther along the reaction sequence. Shell Chemicals is the only company to operate the complete series of processes on a large scale and to market the complete range of products. Markets for mesityl oxide and methyl iso-butyl carbinol are relatively small but those for diacetone alcohol and methyl iso-butyl ketone require the conversion of many thousands of tons of acetone annually.

Acetone reacts readily with hydrogen cyanide to form the cyanhydrin.

The cyanhydrin reacts with 98% sulphuric acid to give methacrylamide sulphate which is decomposed with methanol to methyl methacrylate and ammonium hydrogen sulphate with an overall yield on acetone of about 80%.

$$\underset{CH_3}{\overset{CH_3}{>}}C\underset{CN}{\overset{OH}{<}} + H_2SO_4 \longrightarrow CH_2 = \overset{CH_3}{\underset{|}{C}}.CO.NH_2H_2SO_4$$

$$CH_3OH \diagup$$

$$CH_2 = \overset{CH_3}{\underset{|}{C}}\text{-}COOCH_3 + NH_4HSO_4$$

Methyl methacrylate is the monomer for a series of transparent polymers sold under various trade names of which the I.C.I. "Perspex" is the best known in this country. Other routes to methacrylic acid appear commercially possible such as oxidation of isobutylene or by the OXO reaction from allyl alcohol via 2-hydroxy-isobutyric acid but the acetone cyanhydrin route is still generally preferred.

I.C.I. is the only British producer of methyl methacrylate although both D.C.L. and Charles Lennig produce other acrylic esters (see page 74). Charles Lennig would be well placed to produce methyl methacrylate polymers for the British market since they would be able to obtain "know-how" from their U.S. parent, the Rohm and Haas Co.

BISPHENOL A

Acetone will react with phenol (mole ratio 1:2) in the presence of strong sulphuric acid to form di-2-(*p*-hydroxy phenyl) propane, commonly known commercially as diphenylol propane or bis-phenol A.

$$2 \; C_6H_4OH + CH_3CO\,CH_3 \longrightarrow HO\,C_6H_4 - \underset{\underset{CH_3}{|}}{\overset{\overset{CH_3}{|}}{C}} - C_6H_4OH + H_2O$$

This compound, first discovered by Dianin in 1891, has become a major organic chemical in the past fifteen years and world wide production probably now exceeds 50,000 t/a. Process details are not available but, in general, the acetone, phenol and sulphuric acid mixture is intimately mixed at a controlled temperature until reaction is complete; the bisphenol A is precipitated by the addition of a light hydrocarbon with which it forms a slurry. The lower acid layer is run off and the product separated from the slurry in a centrifuge in which it is washed with further hydrocarbon. It is known to be difficult to obtain a pure product of good colour and each manufacturer has his own tricks in the process and purification stages. The compound is an important component of epoxy resins, referred to in greater detail in the section of this chapter on glycerol, and has other uses as a bifunctional dihydroxy compound. The most important producers are Shell Chemicals at Stanlow, who produce mainly for their own captive use but supply some quantities to the general market, and R. Graesser and Co. at Chester, who sell their output for general use. There are also substantial imports from Western Europe.

MISCELLANEOUS USES OF ACETONE

Acetone is the starting point for synthesis of a number of chemicals, at present produced on a small scale, of which the future growth is uncertain and which may never become of major importance. Of these phorone and isophorone are good examples. In presence of alkali three molecules of acetone will link up to form the cyclic ketone, isophorone. Appreciable quantities of the open chain isomer, phorone, are produced as a by-product and this is the main product when the self-condensation takes place under acid conditions.

Isophorone boils at 215°C and is a useful high boiling solvent for vinyl resins and in paint formulations. It may be hydrogenated to 3:3:5-trimethyl hexanol which has some small industrial uses. Phorone may be hydrogenated to di-isobutyl ketone and then to di-isobutyl carbinol, both of which may be used as slow evaporating solvents. Isophorone is made on a small scale by D.C.L. and has not developed much in this country; in the U.S.A. about 10,000 t/a of acetone are absorbed in the manufacture of phorone and isophorone.

GLYCEROL AND RELATED COMPOUNDS

There is no synthetic glycerol production in this country and all home produced material is obtained from the sweet water by-product from fat splitting and soap manufacture. Technically, production of glycerol by this route is an exercise in minimizing the cost of concentrating dilute aqueous solutions and avoiding losses of product. The methods have been well described in the literature.

Commercial manufacture of synthetic glycerol was first established by Shell in the U.S.A. in 1948 and depended on the discovery by their research chemists before the war of the process for hot chlorination of propylene to allyl chloride which has been described on page 97. When allyl chloride is agitated with aqueous hypochlorous acid, produced by dissolving chlorine in water, at temperatures below 40°C a mixture of 1:2 and 1:3-dichlorohydrins is obtained in high yield.

$$CH_2 = CHCH_2Cl + HOCl \longrightarrow \begin{cases} CH_2OHCHClCH_2Cl \\ CH_2Cl\ CHOH\ CH_2Cl \end{cases}$$

Treatment of the mixed dichlorohydrins with milk of lime gives a virtually theoretical yield of epichlorohydrin which may be purified by distillation.

$$\begin{rcases} CH_2OH\ CHCl\ CH_2Cl \\ CH_2Cl\ CHOH\ CH_2Cl \end{rcases} \longrightarrow CH_2 - CH\ CH_2Cl \underset{O}{\diagdown\diagup}$$

Epichlorohydrin is hydrolysed to glycerol by treatment in a stirred autoclave with 10% caustic soda at about 150°C; glycerol is recovered from the resulting aqueous solution containing sodium chloride by conventional distillation. Overall yield from propylene is about 80% of theoretical. Shell has also established synthetic glycerol manufacture by the above route at Pernis, near Rotterdam, while, at the same time in the U.S.A., Shell Development has established a new synthesis via acrolein which will be described later in this chapter.

In addition to its use as an intermediate in glycerol synthesis, epichlorohydrin has become of major importance in the manufacture of a series of epoxy resins produced by condensation with bisphenol A.

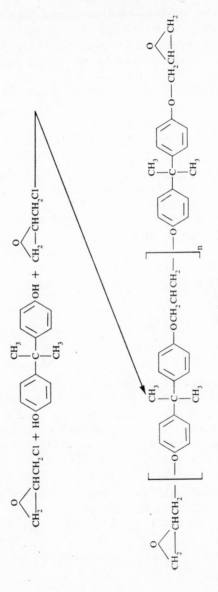

Epoxy Resin.

According to the value of n(p. 150), the resins may vary from viscous liquids to high melting point solids. Although development of the resins has been somewhat hindered by their high cost, their outstanding physical and chemical properties have opened up many uses for them in the surface coating, adhesive and electrical industries. Other hydroxy compounds may be used instead of bisphenol A and a whole series of resins of varying properties may be prepared which has been well described in the literature.

As well as its well known application as a base for nitro-glycerine explosives, glycerol has a very wide range of industrial uses based on its physical as well as its chemical properties. It is a viscous liquid with a sweet taste, somewhat hygroscopic and completely miscible with water. It is largely used for softening and lubricating purposes and as a humectant. It is entirely non-toxic and is therefore particularly suitable for use in connection with foods and drugs. As a polyhydric alcohol, its major chemical application is in production of alkyd resins for the paint industry. A number of its esters have industrial uses and it is also the base compound for some polyethers used in production of polyurethane foams.

The total consumption of glycerol in this country is estimated at about 30,000 t/a and consists almost entirely of by-product material produced by the soap companies; relatively small quantities of synthetic material are imported. In recent years glycerol has become subject to severe competition from other polyhydric alcohols such as ethylene glycol, pentaerythritol and sorbitol; the availability of these relatively cheap alternatives has probably avoided the necessity for a synthetic glycerol plant in this country. While fat splitting and soap manufacture persist there will always be some by-product glycerol available and it may be some time before the market grows sufficiently to justify the high capital expenditure required for a synthetic plant.

Allyl chloride is a very reactive compound and undergoes all the usual reactions of an alkyl halide and of an olefinic compound. It may readily be converted to allyl alcohol by treatment with 10% aqueous caustic soda at about 150°C and 200 psig.

The reaction mixture must be kept alkaline to avoid excess formation of di-allyl ether.

$$CH_2 = CHCH_2Cl + NaOH \longrightarrow CH_2 = CHCH_2OH$$
$$+ NaCl$$
$$2\ CH_2 = CHCH_2OH \xrightarrow{-H_2O} CH_2 = CHCH_2 - O - CH_2CH$$
$$= CH_2$$

Allyl alcohol may be converted to esters, of which the best known is di-allyl phthalate, which have a number of uses in the manufacture of pharmaceuticals and fine chemicals; polyallyl compounds are also becoming of increasing importance in the plastics industry. Allyl compounds are not made on a large scale in this country although D.C.L. have some production of di-allyl phthalate from imported alcohol.

Acrolein is the aldehyde of allyl alcohol and is an intermediate in the most recent synthetic glycerol process developed by Shell in the U.S.A. It was originally produced by dehydration of glycerol but is now made by direct oxidation of propylene with air in the presence of a cuprous oxide catalyst.

$$CH_2 = CHCH_3 + O_2 \longrightarrow CH_2 = CHCHO + H_2O$$

It may be converted to allyl alcohol by reduction with, for example, isopropyl alcohol giving acetone as a by-product; the alcohol may, in turn, be converted to glycerol by treatment with hydrogen peroxide.

$$CH_2 = CHHO + CH_3CHOHCH_3 \longrightarrow CH_2 = CHCH_2OH$$
$$+ CH_3CO\ CH_3$$

$$CH_2 = CHCH_2OH + H_2O_2 \longrightarrow CH_2OHCHOHCH_2OH$$

Alternatively, acrolein may be oxidized with hydrogen peroxide to glyceraldehyde which is then hydrogenated to glycerine.

$$CH_2 = CHCHO + H_2O_2 \longrightarrow CH_2OHCHOHCHO$$

In either case hydrogen peroxide is required and it is made by oxidation of isopropanol with air, giving acetone as a by-product (see page 141).

If cheap enough, acrolein could be an intermediate for the manufacture of acrylic esters and there are many other potential large-scale uses for it. Although it is not yet made on a large scale in this country, it can only be a matter of time before a plant is established.

ACRYLONITRILE

As a vinyl compound, acrylonitrile or vinyl cyanide, might have been expected to appear as an acetylene or ethylene derivative; it was, in fact, first made on a large scale by dehydration of ethylene cyanhydrin produced by the action of hydrogen cyanide on ethylene oxide.

$$\begin{array}{c} CH_2 \\ | \\ CH_2 \end{array}\!\!\!\!\searrow\!\!O + HCN \longrightarrow \begin{array}{c} CH_2OH \\ | \\ CH_2CN \end{array} \longrightarrow CH_2 = CHCN + H_2O$$

This process was superseded by one based on direct addition of hydrogen cyanide to acetylene.

$$CH \equiv CH + HCN \longrightarrow CH_2 = CHCN$$

A plant using this process was set up some years ago by I.C.I. and subsequently abandoned, presumably because it was un-economic under British conditions. The process is still used on a large scale in the U.S.A., however, and it is not certain that the ethylene oxide route has been entirely abandoned.

Both processes, however, have the disadvantage that hydrogen cyanide is needed; the latest route via propylene and ammonia, which avoids this complication, will almost certainly supplant the earlier processes completely as existing plants fall due for replacement. The conversion of acrolein to the nitrile by oxidation with air in the presence of ammonia has been known for some time.

$$CH_2 = CHCHO + NH_3 + \tfrac{1}{2}O_2 \longrightarrow CH_2 = CHCN + 2\,H_2O$$

This reaction and the oxidation of propylene to acrolein have now been combined into a one-stage "ammoxidation" process in which propylene is oxidized in the presence of ammonia to give the nitrile directly; this is analogous to the ammoxidation of methane to hydrogen cyanide described on page 233. One of the first commercially viable versions was developed by the Standard Oil Co. of Ohio in the U.S.A. and has been licensed to a number of producers. In this country the D.C.L. is known to have been actively working in this field and has now joined with I.C.I. and B.P. to form Border Chemicals Ltd. This company has a 40,000 t/a plant at Grangemouth which has recently come on stream.

Acrylonitrile is growing rapidly in importance as a monomer for production of synthetic fibres, plastics and elastomers. The acrylonitrile based fibres "Acrilan" and "Courtelle", produced by Chemstrand and Courtaulds respectively, are becoming almost as much household words as nylon and co-polymers of the nitrile with 1.3-butadiene and styrene in varying proportions have many applications as speciality synthetic rubbers and high strength plastics. Acrylonitrile is a highly reactive compound and may also find many outlets as a chemical intermediate when it becomes freely available in this country.

PROPYLENE OXIDE

Propylene oxide may be made by reaction of propylene with chlorine water and hydrolysis of the resulting propylene chlorohydrin in exactly the same way as described for ethylene oxide (see page 99).

$$CH_2 = CHCH_3 + Cl_2$$

$$+ H_2O \longrightarrow \begin{array}{c} CH_2ClCHOHCH_3 \\ \\ CH_2OHCHClCH_3 \end{array} + HCl$$

$$Ca(OH)_2$$

$$CH_2 - CHCH_3 + CaCl_2 + 2\ H_2O$$
$$\diagdown O \diagup$$

As in the case of ethylene oxide, some chlorinated by-products, mainly 1.2-dichloropropane, are produced.

There are, at present, three manufacturers, Shell Chemicals, I.C.I. and Pfizer Ltd. The material was first made in this country by Petrochemicals Ltd. using an ethylene chlorohydrin tower for the purpose. With the take over of Petrochemicals Ltd. by Shell and the installation of a direct oxidation process for ethylene oxide, still more of the chlorohydrin plant was converted to propylene oxide manufacture and I.C.I. followed this example on its plant at Wilton. Both companies have now entirely converted their ethylene chlorohydrin plants to production of propylene oxide and Pfizer has entered the field recently with a plant at Baglan Bay which draws its propylene from the nearby B.H.C. cracker.

Much research has been carried out in all industrialized countries in an attempt to develop a direct oxidation process for propylene oxide but, so far, no economic method has emerged. As noted in the previous section, the tendency is for the methyl group to be attacked, thus producing acrolein instead of the oxide. Claims that a successful process has been achieved have been made from time to time and it is likely that commercial development of one or more of these will be tried in the near future.

Consumption of propylene oxide has grown very rapidly in the past ten years and is probably in the region of 40,000 to 50,000 tons annually. It is a liquid boiling at 34°C and, although it still needs careful treatment, it is easier to store than the ethylene

G

derivative. Its reactions are very similar to those of ethylene oxide and most of its derivatives are made by similar processes. The most obvious of these is propylene glycol, made by reaction with water.

$$
\begin{array}{ccc}
CH_3CH & & CH_3CHOH \\
\Big\rangle O + H_2O \longrightarrow & & \Big| \\
CH_2 & & CH_2OH
\end{array}
$$

Like ethylene glycol it has found a number of uses in which glycerine was formerly employed but, unlike ethylene glycol, it is non-toxic and may therefore be used in contact with foodstuffs. It is in the British Pharmacopœia and the B.P. grade is used as a solvent for essences and flavourings and in the compounding of pharmaceutical preparations. It boils at 188°C, 9°C lower than ethylene glycol, and, when used as a plasticizer, more of it tends to be lost by migration. As a dihydric alcohol its reactions are similar to those of ethylene glycol and large tonnages are used in the manufacture of polyesters and similar materials. The diglycol and triglycol appear as by-products in manufacture of the monoglycol and have small-scale outlets as solvents and plasticizers.

The propylene glycol ethers may be produced by reaction of the oxide with alcohols using boron trifluoride as a catalyst. They have not attained commercial importance although Shell Chemicals produce and market small quantities of propylene glycol mono-ethyl ether under the trade name of "Proxitol".

$$
\begin{array}{ccc}
CH_3CH & & CH_3CHOH \\
\Big\rangle O + C_2H_5OH \longrightarrow & & \Big| \\
CH_2 & & CH_2O\ C_2H_5
\end{array}
$$

The isopropanolamines result from the reaction of propylene oxide with ammonia and are produced on a substantial scale by Shell Chemicals. They are similar to the ethanolamines and find similar uses; the fatty acid soaps of tri-isopropanolamine, unlike those of tri-ethanolamine are soluble in hydrocarbons.

Propylene oxide will undergo the same kind of polycondensation reactions as ethylene oxide and forms polypropylene glycols of the general formula:

$$\underset{\displaystyle \text{HO(CH}_2\overset{\displaystyle \overset{\text{CH}_3}{|}}{\text{CHO)}}_n\text{CH}_2\overset{\displaystyle \overset{\text{CH}_3}{|}}{\text{CHOH}}}{}$$

Ethers and esters may be obtained by starting the polycondensation with an alcohol or an acid. The polypropylene glycols are insoluble in water and, if the molecular weight is high enough, they are excellent lubricants with a high viscosity index. They were first made in the U.S.A. by Union Carbide and sold as synthetic lubricants under the trade name of "UCON".

Mixed polycondensates of propylene and ethylene oxides may be prepared, either directly or in the presence of an alcohol or an acid, and hydroxyl end groups may be esterified with fatty acids. This gives the possibility of producing water soluble lubricants; a number of the materials have inverted solubility coefficients and may be completely soluble in cold water but come out of solution when the temperature is raised. The possible variants are almost endless and some of them have substantial uses as speciality lubricants for gas turbine engines and for metal forming, but little detailed information is available.

When a water soluble polyethylene glycol is formed on the end of a water insoluble polypropylene glycol chain, the requirements for surface activity of both hydrophilic and hydrophobic centres in the molecule are satisfied. By varying the relative lengths of the polyoxypropylene and polyoxyethylene chains, the relative strengths of these may be varied. Surface-active agents of this type have been produced and marketed in the U.S.A. by the Wyandotte Chemical Co. under the trade name of "Pluronics" but they do not appear to have gained large-scale commercial acceptance

The largest tonnage use for polypropylene glycol derivatives, which has only become of major importance in this country in the last seven years or so, is in the manufacture of polyurethane foams. Urethanes are formed by the reaction of a hydroxy compound and an isocyanate; for the formation of high molecular weight compounds, bi- or poly-functional isocyanates and hydroxy compounds are required as starting materials. The chemistry of the polyurethanes is complex and a detailed treatment here would be inappropriate; much information has been published to which the student is referred in the reading list at the end of the chapter.

Some of the early development work on polyurethanes was done with polyethylene glycol polyesters as the dihydroxy compounds but polypropylene glycols were found to be more satisfactory, especially when the polyoxypropylene chains are formed on the hydroxyl groups of a polyhydric alcohol such as glycerol:—

$$
\begin{array}{l}
\mathrm{CH_2OH} \\
| \\
\mathrm{CHOH} \quad + \quad (3n + 3)\ \mathrm{HC} - \mathrm{CH_2} \\
| \qquad\qquad\qquad\qquad\ \ \underset{O}{\diagdown\!\diagup} \quad \mathrm{CH_3} \\
\mathrm{CH_2\,OH}
\end{array}
$$

$$
\begin{array}{l}
\qquad\qquad\qquad\qquad \overset{\mathrm{CH_3}}{\underset{|}{}} \qquad \overset{\mathrm{CH_3}}{\underset{|}{}} \\
\qquad\qquad \mathrm{CH_2O(CH_2CHO)_nCH_2CHOH} \\
\qquad\qquad\qquad\quad \overset{\mathrm{CH_3}}{\underset{|}{}} \qquad \overset{\mathrm{CH_3}}{\underset{|}{}} \\
\longrightarrow \mathrm{CHO\ (CH_2CHO)_nCH_2CHOH} \\
\qquad\qquad\qquad\ \overset{\mathrm{CH_3}}{\underset{|}{}} \qquad \overset{\mathrm{CH_3}}{\underset{|}{}} \\
\qquad\qquad \mathrm{CH_2O(CH_2CHO)_nCH_2CHOH}
\end{array}
$$

These compounds are described collectively as polyethers and a considerable range of them is now available, almost all of them based on propylene oxide as the provider of chain length. The foams may be rigid or flexible; unfoamed elastomers and resins for use in the surface coating field may also be produced by a suitable choice of raw materials. Much research work on the manufacture and use of polyurethanes is still going on and the whole field offers scope for extensive further development.

Of the three producers of propylene oxide mentioned above, Shell Chemicals manufacture almost a complete range of derivatives, including mixed ethylene oxide/propylene oxide polymers sold under the trade name of "Oxilube". I.C.I. has concentrated more on propylene glycol and the polyethers while Pfizer has confined its activities almost entirely to the polyethers. There are several independent manufacturers of polyethers who buy their propylene oxide from the major producers. One of the largest is Lankro Chemicals Ltd. at Eccles, near Manchester. This company has played a large part in the development of alkylene oxide chemistry in this country and was responsible, with Petrochemicals Ltd , for initiating manufacture of the ethylene glycol ethers in the early 1950's

The total market for propylene oxide in polyethers is not known and, in any case, it is growing so fast that estimates are out of date almost as soon as they are made. It is still probably counted in thousands rather than in tens of thousands of tons per annum but it will almost certainly attain the higher levels in the near future.

CONCLUSION

The total tonnage of propylene used for chemical manufacture is probably lower than that for ethylene but the applications are much more diverse. Ethylene utilization is dominated by the demand for polythene while there are several major outlets for propylene; some of these, such as the manufacture of cumene, butyl alcohols and detergent alkylates are described in later chapters. Some of the applications of propylene are growing so rapidly that it may soon overtake ethylene as the most important olefin for chemical synthesis.

READING LIST

1. *Polyurethanes*, by L. N. Phillips and D. B. V. Parker. Iliffe Books Ltd., London, 1964.

2. *Proceedings of the Symposium on Polyurethane Foams.* Edited by T. T. Healey. Iliffe Books Ltd.. London, 1963.

3. *Epoxy Resins,* by Henry Lee and Kris Neville. McGraw Hill, London, 1957.

4. *Allylic Resins and Monomers,* by Harry Raech Jr. Reinhold Publishing Coporation, New York, 1962.

5. *Synthetic Lubricants.* Edited by Ralph C. Gunderson and Andrew W. Hart. Reinhold Publishing Corporation, New York, 1962. See also the reading list for Chapter 5.

CHAPTER 7

Chemicals Derived from C_4 Hydrocarbons

WITH the C_4 hydrocarbons, isomerism becomes possible and two paraffins, three olefins and two diolefins are all known and are produced in petroleum refining operations. They are all gases at normal temperatures; their boiling points are shown in Table 7.

TABLE 7. Boiling Points of C_4 Hydrocarbon/somers

	B.P. °C
n-Butane	− 0.5
iso-Butane	− 6.9
n-Butene-1	− 6.3
cis-n-Butene-2	+ 3.7
trans-n-Butene-2	+ 0.9
Isobutene	− 0.9
Butadiene-1.3	− 4.4
Butadiene-1.2	+10.3

The boiling points show that, while some separation of individual hydrocarbons is possible by efficient distillation processes, isolation of pure single compounds is not easy. In practice, many chemical syntheses can be carried out with mixtures of C_4's and, when separation is necessary, it is effected by various ingenious extractive distillation methods, some of which will be described later.

As raw materials for chemical manufacture, the C_4 hydrocarbons have lagged behind the lower members of the series, with the exception of butadiene-1.3 for which the use in synthetic rubber manufacture dwarfs all other chemical uses of the C_4's.

The C_4 paraffins, n-butane and isobutane, occur in the natural gas associated with some crude oils; they are valuable constituents of gasoline since they provide volatility for easy starting and isobutane has a high octane rating. It is customary to incorporate as much of the C_4's in gasoline blends as vapour pressure considerations will allow. Normal butane may be isomerized to isobutane by passing its vapour over an aluminium chloride catalyst and this process is used to improve the octane rating of the volatile end of the gasoline.

Substantial quantities of C_4's can be, and are, incorporated in crude oil transported in tankers without incurring serious losses by evaporation. In consequence about 600,000 t/a of n-butane and isobutane are potentially available from U.K. refineries. Most of this is recovered and much of it blended with gasoline, especially in winter; any excess finds a ready sale as liquefied petroleum gas (LPG) for town's gas enrichment and for general industrial and domestic use. It is familiar to most people under trade names such as "Calor gas" and "Botto gas". In these outlets a relatively high price is obtainable and the C_4 paraffins, therefore, start by being expensive as chemical feedstock.

Another source of C_4's is refinery cracking and reforming operations; these C_4 streams contain substantial amounts of the C_4 olefins as well as the paraffins. All possible isomers are present; a typical refinery butane/butene (B/B) product would contain n-butane 30%, isobutane 22%, isobutene 14% and n-butenes 1 and 2 34%; traces of the dienes might also be present. The mixtures are valued in refineries for production of polymer gasoline, which contains low polymers of the C_4 olefins or copolymers of them with propylene, and of aviation alkylate which results from the reaction between isobutane and n-butene and consists of a mixture of iso-octanes. Any excess refinery B/B is blended with the paraffins for sale as LPG and, for this reason, the butenes too are relatively expensive as chemical feedstock.

Finally, the naphtha crackers for ethylene provide some by-product C_4; these are almost entirely unsaturated and contain olefins, diolefins, traces of C_4 acetylenes and only small amounts of the paraffins. The actual composition varies with the cracking process but a typical composition might be: 1.3-butadiene 30%, isobutene 33%, n-butene-1 21%, n-butene-2 12·5%, n-butane and isobutane 3·5% and traces of 1.2-butadiene and acetylenic hydrocarbons. Such highly unsaturated C_4 streams are not suitable for direct use in refinery operations or as LPG but are valuable sources of C_4 unsaturates for chemical purposes.

BUTADIENE

Two butadiene isomers are theoretically possible with the double bonds in the 1.2 and 1.3 positions. 1.2-butadiene is produced in small quantities under severe cracking conditions but is of no commercial importance; it is the conjugated compound, 1.3-butadiene, which is of major importance for chemical purposes. It may be separated from the other C_4 hydrocarbons by chemical absorption or by extractive distillation processes.

In a typical chemical absorption process the C_4 stream from a naphtha cracker, freed from acetylenes if necessary by partial hydrogenation, is contacted in a packed tower with an aqueous solution of ammoniacal cuprous acetate. As well as butadiene, this solution dissolves some butenes and these are first removed by passing the hydrocarbon rich solution down a tower countercurrent to a stream of pure butadiene. The solution then goes to a desorber where it is heated for the recovery of butadiene which is purified by further distillation; after addition of make-up ammonia the solution is returned to the absorption tower. Ammonia is recovered from the butadiene during distillation and from the stripped C_4 stream and is recycled. A system of this type is operated by B.H.C. at Grangemouth for the recovery of some 20,000 t/a of butadiene.

The cuprous salt process, although widely used, is not easy to operate and extractive distillation processes are gaining in favour. A number of extractive distillation solvents has been tried, one of the first being liquid ammonia; furfuraldehyde was also used on a large scale in the U.S.A. during the Second World War. Shell Development in the U.S.A. have a process based on acetonitrile (CH_3CN), originally devised for separation of butenes from butanes but adapted for butadiene separation, which has been licensed for a number of commercial plants in the U.S.A., Canada and Europe. Another process using N-methyl pyrrolidone as extractive solvent has been developed by B.A.S.F. in Germany.

In North America, which does not depend on naphtha cracking for ethylene, butadiene is made by dehydrogenation of n-butane or n-butenes. With n-butenes, this is in effect a steam cracking operation giving a yield of up to 75% of butadiene on butane feed. A compound catalyst is used, containing magnesium, iron, copper and potassium oxides, at a temperature of about 650°C. For n-butane feed, the Houdry process employs a regenerative type of operation. The reactors are of steel, lined with refractory brick and packed with a chromium oxide catalyst on an alumina support; they operate at about 6 mm absolute pressure. Butane vapour is preheated and fed into a reactor which has already been brought to reaction temperature at about 625°C until the endothermic reaction has caused the temperature to fall by about 10°C. The feed is then diverted to a second reactor while the deposited carbon is burned off the catalyst in the first reactor with air. This brings the contents back to reaction temperature; the reactor is then purged with high temperature steam and brought back on line. For a complete sequence of operations, three reactors are required—one reacting, one oxidizing and one purging. Butadiene is recovered from the reactor gases as described above for mixed C_4 streams from naphtha crackers.

Thermal and catalytic dehydrogenation of n-butane and n-butenes is a relatively expensive way of making butadiene and there is a constant search for a cheaper method. A new contender is the Shell Development Co.'s oxidative dehydrogenation process for n-butane or n-butene using iodine and air. The reaction may be regarded as taking place in stages—first iodine substitution, then removal of hydrogen iodide followed by oxidation of the hydrogen iodide to water and iodine which is recycled. This process is employed at the new plant of the Société des Elastomères de Synthèse in France. Other versions of the process using chlorine or bromine are believed to be feasible.

Three of the four major ethylene producers, Esso, I.C.I. and B.H.C. all operate butadiene recovery plants and the fourth, Shell Chemicals, has one coming on stream in 1966/7. Courtaulds subsidiary, British Celanese, whose naphtha cracker is smaller, is believed to dispose of its C$_4$ fraction to one of the major butadiene producers. Esso supplements its by-product butadiene with direct production from n-butene dehydrogenation. Total capacity will probably be about 100,000 to 120,000 t/a when the Shell Chemicals plant is completed. For the future the Houdry process in its present form is unlikely to be economic in this country since it is costly in fuel. More by-product butadiene is likely to become available as ethylene output increases and any additional requirements will probably be met by a new process similar to the Shell iodine method.

The largest single outlet for butadiene is for manufacture of styrene/butadiene synthetic rubber (SBR) by the International Synthetic Rubber Co. at Fawley; this plant draws its butadiene from the adjacent Esso refinery and petrochemical plant. The company is a consortium of tyre manufacturers with Dunlop as the major shareholder; it now has a second plant at Grange-mouth for production of polybutadiene rubber which draws its butadiene from British Hydrocarbon Chemicals. Other uses are for acrylonitrile/butadiene ("Hycar") rubber made by British Resin Products at Barry and for styrene/ butadiene co-polymers with a much higher styrene content than SBR. These co-polymers may be produced as emulsions (latices) with water or as solid resins; the latices have a diversity of uses in paper coating and impregnation, leather and wall paper finishes, carpet backing and similar applications and compete to some extent with polyvinyl alcohol and polyvinyl acetate emulsions; the solid resins are used for shoe soling materials, floor tiles and similar products. Major manufacturers are Monsanto, Dunlop and I.C.I. and the total output must be well over 20,000 t/a; the I.C.I. capacity alone has been given as 12,500 t/a and is currently being expanded to 20,000 t/a.

As a chemical intermediate, butadiene is not used as widely as might be expected; 1:4 addition to other olefins, the well known Diels-Alder reaction, offers many interesting possibilities for chemical synthesis which have not, so far, found large-scale commercial development. If the drive for a cheaper manufacturing process is successful, some of these possibilities could become economically attractive. Initial addition of halogen is predominantly in the 1:4 positions to give 1:4 di-halobutenes. These react with sodium cyanide to form 1:4 di-nitriles and dupont in the U.S.A. use this route for production of the nylon intermediate, adiponitrile, from 1:4 dichlorobutene-2. dupont is believed also to have developed a process for production of adiponitrile by direct addition of hydrogen cyanide to butadiene followed by hydrogenation; and either of these methods should be attractive alternatives to those described in Chapter 9. Production of mixed dichlorobutenes is the first step in a new process for manufacture of chloroprene (see page 73) developed by D.C.L. and currently being exploited in France in a joint venture by D.C.L. and a number of French concerns.

The cyclic oligomers, cyclo-octadiene and cyclo-dodecatriene, may be produced by polymerization with Ziegler type catalysts; they are potentially interesting since, by ring opening and oxidation, they can yield C_8 and C_{12} dibasic acids as alternatives to adipic acid for nylon manufacture. Small quantities of cyclo-octadiene incorporated in ethylene/propylene rubbers are said to make them susceptible to vulcanization by sulphur.

The only purely chemical synthesis known to be operated on a substantial scale in this country at present is the production by Shell Chemicals at Stanlow of the sulphone, 1.1-thiophan dioxide, commonly called sulpholane. This is made by reaction of butadiene with sulphur dioxide to form the unsaturated compound sulpholene which is then hydrogenated to sulpholane.

$$CH_2 = CHCH = CH_2 + SO_2 \longrightarrow$$

Sulpholane is a valuable extraction solvent for recovery of aromatics from petroleum (see page 32) and production is expanding.

ISOBUTENE

After recovery of butadiene from naphtha cracker C_4 streams, the residue is a mixture of about 50% isobutene with the isomeric n-butenes and about 7% of butanes. Large amounts of isobutene are also potentially available from refinery B/B streams from catalytic crackers and thermal reformers.

Isobutene is recovered from mixed B/B streams by absorption in sulphuric acid of about 60% strength at temperatures below 20°C. The first reaction is conversion of the isobutene to tertiary butyl alcohol which may be recovered by solvent extraction or by dilution with water followed by distillation.

$$(CH_3)_2C = CH_2 + H_2O \longrightarrow (CH_3)_3COH$$

If the acid solution is heated to 80–100°C a mixture, consisting mainly of di-isobutene with up to 20% of tri-isobutene and small amounts of higher polymers, separates as an upper layer and may be run off, washed with water and purified by distillation.

The dimer consists mainly of 2.4.4-trimethyl 1-pentene with some 2.4.4-trimethyl 2-pentene

$$CH_3$$
$$|$$
$$CH_3CCH_2C = CH_2$$
$$|\quad\quad|$$
$$CH_3\quad CH_3$$

$$2\ (CH_3)_2C = CH_2$$

$$CH_3$$
$$|$$
$$CH_3CCH = CCH_3$$
$$|\quad\quad\quad|$$
$$CH_3\quad\quad CH_3$$

Di-isobutenes form iso-octanes on hydrogenation and this reaction, followed by isomerization, was at one time a commercial route to these valuable gasoline components which has since been replaced by alkylation as described on page 162. The hydrocarbon has a number of uses as an intermediate for manufacture of plasticizer alcohols and detergents which are described in Chapter 8. On mild pyrolysis the dimers and trimers are re-converted to monomeric iso-butene which may be condensed and stored under pressure or in insulated refrigerated vessels at atmospheric pressure.

The largest tonnage use of isobutene is for manufacture of "Butyl" synthetic rubber by co-polymerization with small quantities of isoprene. This rubber is especially valuable for inner tubes on account of its low permeability to air and is made in large quantities in the U.S.A. Esso is the only producer in this country and has a substantial commercial plant at Fawley.

Lower molecular weight polymers are viscous liquids and are produced by low temperature polymerization of isobutene in the presence of a hydrogen fluoride catalyst. They are used as viscosity index improvers for lubricating oils and in the formulation of sealing compounds. The chief manufacturer in this country is W. R. Grace and Co. whose plant is adjacent to the B.H.C. plant at Baglan Bay from which it draws its isobutene supplies.

Di-isobutene may be produced in any oil refinery with a catalytic cracker and may be reconverted to isobutene if required. B.H.C., I.C.I. and Esso make the monomer on a substantial scale for the applications described above and B.H.C. exports isobutene in bulk from its Grangemouth plant. Shell Chemicals produces di-isobutene and supplies some to I.C.I. as part of a joint operation in the production of plasticizer alcohols but the main purpose is the preparation of a n-butene stream for chemical synthesis. Any isobutene polymers boiling in the gasoline range may usually be blended with the regular gasoline if there is no chemical outlet for them.

n-BUTENES

The n-butene stream left after removal of butadiene and isobutene from C_4 fractions from naphtha cracking is a mixture of n-butene-1, both geometrical isomers of n-butene-2 and any butanes present in the original C_4 fraction. All the n-butene isomers are converted to sec.-butyl alcohol when hydrated with dilute sulphuric acid in the same way as has been described for the hydration of propylene to isopropanol (see page 139). For n-butene hydration mild conditions are essential to avoid excessive polymer formation and sulphation at 35°C with 70% sulphuric acid is adequate.

$$CH_3CH_2CH = CH_2 \atop CH_3CH = CH\ CH_3 \Big\} \xrightarrow{+H_2O} CH_3CH_2CHOHCH_3$$

Sec.-butyl alcohol and its esters are used on a small scale as solvents but the main use for the alcohol is as an intermediate for conversion to methyl ethyl ketone (MEK)

$$CH_3CH_2CHOHCH_3 \longrightarrow CH_3CH_2COCH_3 + H_2$$

The dehydrogenation process is similar to that for the conversion of isopropanol to acetone which has already been described. MEK is used on a large scale as a solvent; it boils at 80°C and, due to its higher solvent power, it has replaced ethyl acetate in many applications.

Shell Chemicals is the only large-scale manufacturer of sec.-butyl alcohol and MEK in Britain and has a plant at Stanlow using refinery B/B as feedstock; the D.C.L. also produce some MEK as a by-product of their acetone manufacture. The solvent is produced in large quantities in the U.S.A. and in continental Europe; U.S.A. production is approaching 100,000 t/a.

BUTYL ALCOHOLS

Of the four possible isomeric butyl alcohols, two have already been described above. The tertiary alcohol is of small commercial importance and the secondary alcohol is only of importance as an intermediate in the synthesis of MEK. The two primary alcohols, normal and iso-butanol, are not made from C_4 hydrocarbons but are co-produced by the application of the OXO reaction to propylene.

$$CH_2 = CHCH_3 + CO + 2H_2 \longrightarrow \begin{cases} CH_3CH_2CH_2CH_2OH \\ \\ \begin{array}{c} CH_3 \\ \diagdown CHCH_2OH \\ CH_3 \end{array} \end{cases}$$

Normal butyl alcohol was first made in large quantities as a by-product of the Weizmann fermentation of carbohydrates, which was carried out on a very large scale for the production of acetone during the 1914–18 war. The n-butyl alcohol was regarded as an undesirable by-product and large quantities accumulated in storage while research went on to develop uses for it; this led to its use as a solvent for nitrocellulose and to the production of its esters, which are now widely used as solvents and plasticizers. Consumption developed rapidly in the inter-war years while other methods of making acetone were found; thus, availability of n-butanol declined and it became necessary to find other methods of making it. The chosen route was from ethyl alcohol via acetaldehyde and crotonaldehyde as described in Chapter 5. Although this process is still used by the D.C.L. at its Hull works, it has been largely replaced elsewhere by synthesis from propylene and it is now iso-butyl alcohol which is the by-product for which it is difficult to find sufficient uses. Normal butyraldehyde is an important intermediate in the OXO synthesis and some of it is recovered for sale. It will undergo an aldol condensation and dehydration to form 2-ethyl hexenal which may, in turn, be completely hydrogenated to produce 2-ethyl hexanol. This is an important plasticizer alcohol and is referred to again in Chapter 8.

$$2CH_3CH_2CH_2CHO \xrightarrow{\text{NaOH}} CH_3CH_2CH_2CHOHCHCHO$$
$$| $$
$$CH_3CH_2$$

$$-H_2O$$

$$CH_3CH_2CH_2CH=CCHO \xrightarrow{+2H_2} CH_3CH_2CH_2CH_2CHCH_2OH$$
$$| \qquad\qquad\qquad\qquad\qquad |$$
$$CH_3CH_2 \qquad\qquad\qquad\qquad\qquad CH_3CH_2$$

I.C.I. uses part of its OXO capacity at Billingham for normal and iso-butyl alcohols and most of the country's requirements are met from that source.

DEVELOPMENT POTENTIAL OF C₄'s

The use of the C₄ olefins and diolefins for chemical synthesis has been made difficult by the fact that they occur in mixtures, sometimes dilute, and the separation of an individual olefin is expensive. As more uses for them are developed, the cost of separation may be more widely spread and this will facilitate the commercial application of other syntheses for which the economics have previously been marginal. Some possibilities for butadiene have already been mentioned. Another interesting reaction is the catalytic oxidation of butadiene to the cyclic oxide, furan.

Isobutene may be oxidized to methyl acrolein and thence to methacrylic acid and is, therefore, a possible alternative to acetone as an intermediate for manufacture of methyl methacrylate.

The normal butenes may be converted to the corresponding oxides by the chlorohydrin route in the same way as for ethylene and propylene oxides. Both the 1.2 and the 2.3 oxides are known but, so far, they have not been commercially exploited. n-Butene-2 may be oxidized to maleic anhydride by a carefully controlled reaction with air over special vanadium oxide catalysts. This method has now been applied on a commercial scale and may well replace the standard benzene oxidation process which is currently most widely used.

These are but a few of the many possible reactions of the C_4 olefins and diolefins and it is unlikely that raw material of such potential for chemical synthesis will continue to be used for fuel in the future as it has been in the past.

CHAPTER 8

Chemicals Derived from C_5 and Higher Hydrocarbons

As THE basic carbon chain of organic chemicals becomes longer, it is increasingly difficult to prepare pure compounds cheaply on a commercial scale. Many commercial organic chemicals with a basic carbon chain of five or more carbon atoms are mixtures. This is the field of what are generally called "performance chemicals" where physical properties are more important than chemical purity; many of these chemicals are used in large tonnages but details of their application fall outside the scope of this work so that only the preparation of the basic chemical products is described in this chapter.

C_5 PARAFFINS

There are three possible isomeric pentanes but 2.2-di-methyl propane is little known; normal and isopentanes occur in natural gasoline. Isopentane (2-methyl butane), like isobutane, is a highly valued gasoline component because it gives volatility for easy starting and has also a high octane rating. n-Pentane may be isomerized to isopentane by heating over suitable catalysts and this reaction is employed in the oil refining industry to increase the availability of isopentane for gasoline blending. The C_5 paraffins have not been used in this country for large-scale chemical manufacture; there is one plant in the U.S.A. which produces amyl alcohols by chlorination of mixed pentanes from natural gasoline, followed by hydrolysis of the monochlorides with caustic soda.

174 *Heavy Organic Chemicals*

C$_5$ OLEFINS

There are six possible isomeric pentenes including the geometric isomers of n-pentene-2. These are produced in oil cracking operations. They may be regarded as potential precursors of the various amyl alcohols but production of the alcohols by hydration of pentenes with dilute sulphuric requires very mild conditions to avoid excessive formation of hydrocarbon polymers. Amyl alcohols are not widely used and the traditional source of the material is the fusel oil by-product from fermentation ethanol manufacture, from which a mixed amyl alcohol may be separated by fractional distillation, and this has, so far proved adequate for British requirements. The fermentation product consists mainly of isoamyl alcohol (3-methyl 1-butanol) and active amyl alcohol (2-methyl 1-butanol). The mixed alcohols may be esterified with acetic acid to produce the amyl acetate of commerce, of which D.C.L. is the only manufacturer in this country.

Amyl acetate was, at one time, an important high boiling lacquer solvent but its importance has declined; it is still used extensively as an extraction solvent, especially in the manufacture of penicillin, and in the formulation of cosmetics and toiletries.

C$_5$ DIENES

The two best known C$_5$ dienes are piperylene (1.3-pentadiene) and isoprene (2-methyl 1.3-butadiene). Piperylene is not produced by pyrolysis of 1- or 2-pentene but may be formed by catalytic dehydrogenation of n-pentane; it has not yet found any important commercial applications. Isoprene, on the other hand, has become of great importance in recent years. The isoprene molecule is the basic unit of the natural rubber molecule and the hydrocarbon has, therefore, been of great interest for many years as a possible precursor of a synthetic "natural" rubber. All efforts to produce isoprene polymers to match natural rubber failed, however, until the work of Natta on polypropylene showed that stereo-specific polymerization was possible. The latest commercial high *cis* polyisoprenes are now a very close match to natural rubber and competition between the two is a matter of economics. Isoprene is relatively expensive to produce and great progress has been made in recent years in the breeding of high yielding rubber trees and in putting the production of natural rubber on to an efficient commercial basis so that competition is likely to be keen; in any case the existence of a competitive synthetic process is likely to have a great stabilizing influence on natural rubber prices.

There are several routes to isoprene which have been used commercially in the U.S.A. although, so far, there has been no large scale development in this country. The simplest route is by dehydrogenation of the isoamylenes, 2-methyl 1-butene and 2-methyl 2-butene.

$$CH_2 = \overset{\overset{\displaystyle CH_3}{\displaystyle |}}{C}CH_2CH_3$$
$$CH_3\overset{\overset{\displaystyle }{\displaystyle |}}{C} = CHCH_3 \quad \xrightarrow{-H_2} \quad CH_2 = \overset{\overset{\displaystyle CH_3}{\displaystyle |}}{C}CH = CH_2$$
$$\overset{\displaystyle |}{CH_3}$$

These hydrocarbons are produced in cracking operations for gasoline production and may be recovered from the crude gasoline fraction. A C_5 fraction is first separated by distillation and the amylenes are recovered from this as amyl alcohols by washing with dilute sulphuric acid followed by solvent extraction. The mixed amyl alcohols dehydrate readily to give the hydrocarbons which may then be dehydrogenated. A similar method is catalytic dehydrogenation of isopentane which may be separated from the C_5 fraction from straight run gasoline.

$$\overset{\overset{\displaystyle CH_3}{\displaystyle |}}{CH_3CHCH_2CH_2} \xrightarrow{-2H_2} CH_2 = \overset{\overset{\displaystyle CH_3}{\displaystyle |}}{C}CH = CH_2$$

The supply of by-product amylenes from cracking is limited and cracking specifically for amylene production is uneconomic since the yield is small. An alternative route is demethanation of the isohexene, 2-methyl 2-pentene; this may be produced by dimerization of propylene to 2-methyl 1-pentene followed by isomerization.

Propylene is dimerized in the liquid phase at a pressure of about 3,000 psig and a temperature of 200°C in the presence of the Ziegler catalyst, tri-isopropyl aluminium. 2-Methyl 1-pentene is formed in about 95% yield and is isomerized over an acidic catalyst at temperatures of 150–300°C; the yield approaches the theoretical. The demethanation is carried out at 650–800°C with steam dilution and in the presence of hydrogen bromide.

$$2\ CH_2 = CHCH_3 \longrightarrow CH_2 = \underset{\underset{CH_3}{|}}{C}CH_2CH_2CH_3$$
2-methyl 1-pentene

$$CH_2 = \underset{\underset{CH_3}{|}}{C}CH_2CH_2CH_3 \longrightarrow CH_3\underset{\underset{CH_3}{|}}{C} = CHCH_2CH_3$$
2-methyl 2-pentene

$$CH_3\underset{\underset{CH_3}{|}}{C} = CHCH_2CH_3 \longrightarrow CH_2 = \underset{\underset{CH_3}{|}}{C}CH = CH_2 + CH_4$$
Isoprene

Yet another synthesis, which could be competitive if cheap formaldehyde is available, is the addition of formaldehyde to isobutene at about 120°C to give 4.4-dimethyl 1.3-dioxan which may be decomposed by pyrolysis to isoprene, formaldehyde and water.

Esso are believed to make small quantities of isoprene at Fawley from isoamylenes recovered from cracked distillate to supply the needs of their "Butyl" rubber plant. Although *cis*-polyisoprene is produced on a substantial scale in the U.S.A., it is not yet made in this country.

By modifying the reaction conditions it is also possible to produce a substantially pure *trans*-polyisoprene, equivalent to the natural product, gutta-percha. Supplies of the natural material, which is particularly required for the covers of golf balls, have become scarce and *trans*-polyisoprene is produced synthetically by Dunlop for their own requirements.

CYCLOPENTADIENE

This cyclic diene has been known for many years and is found in the fore-runnings from crude benzole recovered from coal carbonization. It is produced in the vapour phase cracking of naphtha for ethylene production and this is the source of most of the cyclopentadiene of commerce. The hydrocarbon boils at 42·5°C and readily condenses at normal temperatures to form a stable dimer—dicyclopentadiene.

Dicyclopentadiene melts at 32·9°C and boils at 170°C with reversion to the monomer. The hydrocarbon is separated by allowing a C₅ cut from freshly distilled cracked gasoline to remain in holding tanks long enough for the dimer to form; it is then redistilled, avoiding temperatures high enough to decompose the dimer. The material may be purified by heating to reform the monomer followed by a second dimerization and distillation to remove impurities. The dimer is stable under normal temperature conditions and forms a convenient means of transporting and storing cyclopentadiene. Both Shell Chemicals and B.H.C. produce some dicyclopentadiene from the cracked gasoline from their ethylene crackers but the total requirements in this country are not large.

Cyclopentadiene has been proposed as the starting point for the manufacture of synthetic drying oils but the process does not appear to have been commercially successful. It readily undergoes Diels–Alder reactions with other olefins or with acetylene; for example with acetylene it forms bicycloheptadiene; with maleic anhydride the product is endomethylene tetrahydrophthalic anhydride (carbic anhydride). This anhydride is an intermediate for resins.

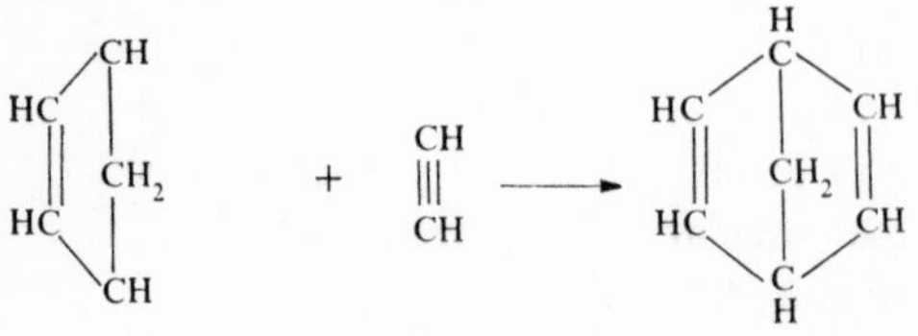

Bicycloheptadiene

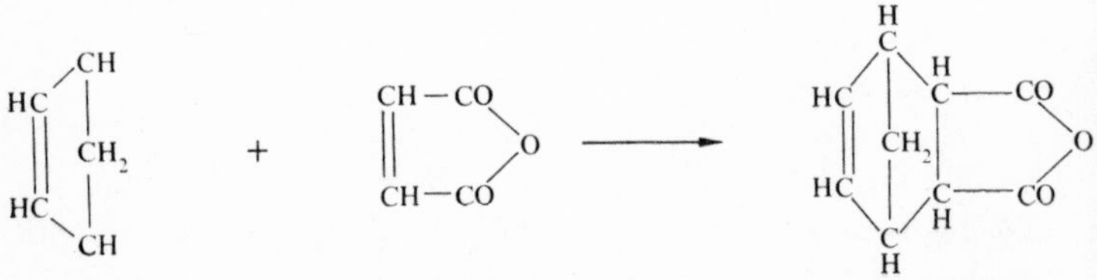

Carbic anhydride

Cyclopentadiene reacts readily with chlorine and, by a combination of addition and substitutive chlorination, followed by pyrolysis, hexachloro-cyclopentadiene may be produced. This also will undergo Diels–Alder addition to maleic anhydride to form endomethylene hexachloro-tetrahydro-phthalic anhydride (chlorendic anhydride), an intermediate for a series of flame retardant resins. Hexachloro-cyclopentadiene is also the starting point for the well known chlorinated insecticides, Aldrin and Dieldrin. Aldrin is the product of the reaction between hexachloro-cyclopentadiene and bicyclo-heptadiene and Dieldrin is produced from it by epoxidation.

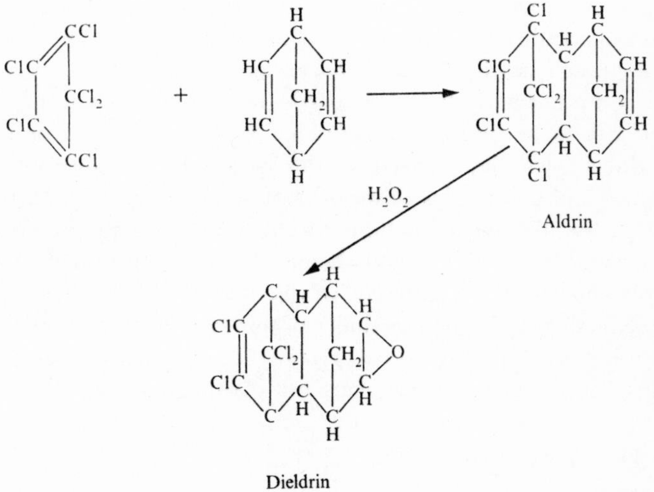

Aldrin

Dieldrin

Although they are produced on a substantial scale by Shell in Holland and in the U.S.A., these compounds are not really heavy organic chemicals. Their future, too, must be considered uncertain until the current differences of expert opinion on the long-term effects of using long lasting insecticides of this type have been resolved.

Like many other by-products from large-scale operations, cyclopentadiene is relatively cheap within the limits of its availability as a by-product. If required in excess of these quantities, it would be much more expensive. There is, however, much potential cyclopentadiene not yet recovered from cracked gasoline and no immediate shortage is foreseen.

DERIVATIVES OF HIGHER HYDROCARBONS

So far, it has been possible to classify heavy organic chemicals according to the chain length of the hydrocarbon from which they may be regarded as having been derived. Above C_5 the number of possible isomers increases so rapidly that the use of pure single compounds on an industrial scale becomes the exception rather than the rule. At this point, therefore, a change of approach has been made and materials have been classified partly by chemical type and partly by end use. Many of the products to be dealt with are either raw materials for or by-products from the detergent industry which is dealt with in another volume in this series on surface-active agents. In this field, also, the use of natural products has not been entirely superseded by synthetics and chemical, as opposed to detergent, applications of these materials will be described. The chemicals to be dealt with in the remainder of this chapter have, therefore been divided into three broad groups—detergent raw materials, higher aliphatic carboxylic acids and plasticizer alcohols.

DETERGENT RAW MATERIALS

This is a large and heterogeneous collection of chemical products which are used mainly in the manufacture of detergents, emulsifiers and surface-active agents of all kinds. It is by no means exclusive; reference has already been made to the non-ionic detergents and surface-active agents based on the alkylene oxides and there are other specialized detergents which will fall outside this section. The compounds do, however, have one thing in common; they contain a basic hydrophobic hydrocarbon structure with which a hydrophilic element, conferring the necessary surface-active properties, may readily be combined.

The manufacture of synthetic detergents received a great deal of attention in Germany in the decade before the Second World War because of the need to minimize imports of natural fats and in furtherance of the Hitler policy of self-sufficiency. Many ingenious syntheses were evolved but, in general, they centred round the hydrocarbon fractions of about C_{12}–C_{18} chain length which were produced by the Fischer–Tropsch plants (see page 65). These were perhaps the first hydrocarbon raw materials used commercially for synthetic detergent production. A good example is the "Mersolate" series, produced by the I.G. Farbenindustrie, which were made by reacting a hydrogenated straight chain Fischer–Tropsch hydrocarbon fraction with sulphur dioxide and chlorine under ultraviolet light. This yielded a monosulphonyl chloride which could be hydrolysed with aqueous caustic soda to form the sodium sulphonate. This was blended with other materials such as inorganic soluble phosphates for use in both domestic and industrial detergents.

Much experimental work on the manufacture of synthetic detergents was also going on in other countries at about this time and the sodium salts of secondary alkyl sulphates with a chain length of C_8–C_{18} were test marketed in the U.K. in 1938/9 by Technical Products Ltd., a Shell subsidiary which later became Shell Chemicals, under the trade name "Teepol". This trade name is still in use and now covers a range of synthetic detergents, including the original secondary alkyl sulphates which, on the basis of price per unit of cleansing power, have remained competitive in many applications with more sophisticated materials developed more recently.

The secondary alkyl sulphates are made by reacting sulphuric acid with straight chain α-olefins produced by cracking paraffin wax. The wax is cracked in a conventional cracking furnace in presence of steam at temperatures of 450–500°C and at substantially atmospheric pressure. A yield of about 60% of olefins with chain lengths from C_5–C_{18} is obtained and may be split into fractions as desired. Many uses for specific fractions from this range of olefins have now been developed which far exceed in total quantity the requirements for secondary alkyl sulphate manufacture. These newer uses have demanded a higher quality olefin fraction with less cyclic and branched chain compounds than were found in the original product from slack wax cracking and it has been necessary to produce a specially purified wax. This is produced by extraction of slack wax with a urea solution which forms a clathrate compound with the straight chain waxes, from which they may later be recovered, while the urea is recycled.

Shell Chemicals still carries out some wax cracking at its Stanlow plant but there is a much larger plant, together with a urea wax extraction unit, at the Shell plant near Rotterdam.

In the U.S.A. alkyl benzene sodium sulphonates became the favoured active material in synthetic detergent formulations quite early in the development and their use has since become almost world-wide. At first the alkyl side chain was provided by a hydrogenated hydrocarbon fraction in the kerosine boiling range with a chain length of C_{12}–C_{14}. Alkylation was carried out by first chlorinating the hydrocarbon to give a monochloride followed by a reaction with benzene in the presence of aluminium chloride. The product was usually called keryl benzene or detergent alkylate and was first produced in this country by Monsanto Chemicals at a newly established plant near Newport, Mon., about 1950.

The kerosine soon gave place as an alkylating agent in the U.S.A. to dodecene (propylene tetramer) and dodecyl benzene has, until recently, been the standard detergent alkylate throughout the world. Originally, the propylene tetramer was a cut from the mixed C_3 polymers prepared in oil refineries for addition to gasoline but, as demand grew, plants were built specially to make it. Propylene was generally polymerized over a phosphoric acid catalyst at about 200°C and 220 psig; a mixture of trimers, tetramers and pentamers of which the tetramer is the main constituent is obtained from which a tetramer cut is isolated by fractionation. The economics of the operation depend on being able to dispose of the associated trimers and pentamers to gasoline blending or other use.

Alkylation is carried out by reacting the olefin with benzene in the presence of sulphuric acid, aluminium chloride or hydrogen fluoride as catalysts. The reaction may be carried out batchwise but, in modern plants, continuous operation is more usual. Propylene tetramer is added to benzene containing hydrogen fluoride in solution; water must be rigidly excluded and all reagents must be pre-dried. The alkylation reaction is exothermic and cooling is necessary to maintain the temperature at about 10°C. The reaction mixture is distilled to yield recovered benzene and hydrogen fluoride for recycle, a monododecyl benzene product and some di- and tri-dodecyl benzenes which may go to fuel or be used for the preparation of special oils. Product quality is assessed on the extent to which it can be sulphonated, since any unsulphonated oil will appear in the final spray dried detergent and cause stickiness, odour and discoloration; commercial alkylates will normally be better than 98% sulphonatable. The final stage of making a synthetic detergent by sulphonation of the alkylate with oleum or sulphur trioxide followed by blending of the sodium sulphonate with various other reagents to act as builders, foam promoters etc. is normally carried out by detergent manufacturers as a combined operation.

Dodecyl benzene was first marketed in this country by Shell Chemicals about 1954, the material being produced in their refinery at Curacoa from propylene tetramer made in this country at Stanlow. A continuous process unit using hydrogen fluoride catalyst was brought into operation at Shell Haven in 1955 and now provides large quantities of alkylates for this country and for export. A joint company, Grange Chemicals, was formed by B.P., D.C.L. and California Chemical Co. (now called Chevron Chemical Co.) of the U.S.A. to produce alkylate using California "know how". A plant was built adjacent to the B.H.C. plant at Grangemouth and drew its propylene tetramer at first from the B.P. Grangemouth refinery and later from B.H.C. During this period Monsanto also changed over to propylene tetramer as alkylating agent at their South Wales plant.

As these new materials gradually replaced soap in domestic and industrial detergents, it was found that they were not being degraded by biological action in sewage treatment plants and were passing out virtually unchanged in the treated effluents. This resulted in the formation of masses of foam on rivers at effluent discharge points and served to demonstrate both how well the synthetic detergents would foam in hard water and how effective the foam stabilizers used in the original formulation could be. It also caused considerable public concern and much attention was given by manufacturers and public health authorities to finding a cure. The trouble was quickly traced to the branched chain structure of the propylene tetramer alkyl group; experimental work showed that an alkyl benzene sodium sulphonate with a straight chain alkyl group would be sufficiently degraded in the sewage treatment process to avoid trouble. Straight chain hydrocarbon fractions in the C_{12} range are not, however, easy to produce at short notice, especially in the price range of propylene tetramer. Shell Chemicals was particularly well placed since it had ready to hand a supply of straight chain α-olefins from wax cracking although not sufficient in quantity to supply the total requirements of the British market for detergent alkylate.

It was found that olefins from wax cracking could be directly substituted for propylene tetramer in the alkylation process and in 1958 Shell Chemicals began marketing an alkylate prepared from a-olefins in the C_{10}–C_{15} range. During this period a remarkable experiment—the Luton Experiment—involving the collaboration of government departments, public health authorities, detergent manufacturers and producers of detergent alkylate was carried out. An area centred on Luton, which was self-contained from a drainage point of view, was selected and an effort was made to ensure that all synthetic detergents supplied to the area itself and to the immediately surrounding areas were based on the straight chain biologically "soft" alkylate. An extensive programme of analysis was undertaken, both before and during the experiment, of the rivers and drainage effluents in the area to determine whether use of the new alkylates would lessen the concentration of unchanged synthetic detergent in the natural water supplies of the area. It was necessary to develop entirely new methods of analysis to detect the very small concentrations of alkyl aryl sulphonate present in river water and to differentiate between the propylene tetramer and cracked wax olefin based materials. The experiment showed conclusively that the use of biologically soft materials could be expected to lead to a substantial reduction in the amount of unchanged synthetic detergent in sewage plant effluents; it also showed how long it takes to eliminate stocks from a multiplicity of shops and that a surprisingly large number of people bought their detergents outside the area.

The biologically soft alkylate has now largely replaced the propylene tetramer variety in this country; other countries, especially West Germany and the U.S.A., have had a similar experience to Britain and are now changing over to "soft" alkylates or to other bio-degradable synthetic detergents. Other sources of straight chain hydrocarbons are being developed, of which one of the most promising is the separation of fractions of specific chain length by means of molecular sieves from suitable fractions distilled from paraffinic crude oils. The paraffins may be converted to substantially straight chain olefins by chlorination followed by dehydrochlorination and then used for alkylation as at present. Esso has developed a process in the U.S.A. in which C_{15}–C_{18} normal paraffins are sulphonated with sulphur trioxide under the influence of gamma radiation and the resulting sulphonic acid neutralized with caustic soda, thus producing compounds similar to the early "Mersolates" of the I.G. referred to on page 181.

In this country Monsanto has closed down its alkylation plant, thus leaving two manufacturers, Shell Chemicals and Grange Chemicals, both of which export large quantities of alkylates. U.K. consumption of detergent alkylate is probably approaching 50,000 t/a. B.P. has announced that it will build a 50,000 t/a paraffin separation plant adjacent to its Kent refinery on the Isle of Grain and this will give Grange Chemicals its own supply of straight chain hydrocarbon raw material.

Many other routes to biologically soft synthetic detergents are possible and may become important in the future. The fatty alcohol sodium sulphates of the type $C_nH_{(2n+1)}OSO_3Na$ are excellent detergents but natural alcohols are too expensive, except for specialist uses; the search for a sufficiently cheap route to synthetic alcohols has not, so far, been successful. This problem is further dealt with in the section on plasticizer alcohols. With straight chain paraffins of C_{15}–C_{18} chain length becoming available, the production of synthetic fatty acid soaps which would match the soaps produced from natural oils and fats appears a possibility but it has not yet been realized on a commercial scale. The problem of synthetic fatty acids is dealt with in the next section.

HIGHER CARBOXYLIC ACIDS

This section will deal with both synthetic acids and those derived from natural fats and oils which, with their derivatives, are sometimes referred to as oleochemicals.

The usual route to an acid is by oxidation of a hydrocarbon, an alcohol or an aldehyde. Hydrocarbon oxidation may be successfully applied to the production of short chain aliphatic acids but, the longer the carbon chain of the hydrocarbon, the more easily it is broken down and it has not been possible to make oxidation processes sufficiently selective for production of long-chain acids from the corresponding hydrocarbon. Olefins may, however, be converted to either aldehydes or alcohols and these may, in turn, be oxidized to acids; they may also be converted to acids or esters directly by the Koch reaction. The olefin is reacted with carbon monoxide and water at high temperature and pressure in the presence of sulphuric acid to form an acid containing one more carbon atom than the original olefin. If an alcohol is substituted for water, the corresponding ester is formed directly. The Koch reaction takes place at a tertiary carbon atom and, therefore, produces only branched chain acids; if the olefin does not contain a tertiary carbon atom, then one is formed by isomerization during the reaction. Thus, either isobutene or 2-butene will yield pivalic acid.

Koch acids may replace naturally occurring napthenic acids recovered during petroleum refining operations and are generally used in the form of their metal salts. The lead, manganese and cobalt salts are useful as paint driers and this is probably the largest tonnage outlet. The copper salts have insecticidal and fungicidal properties and are used in solution in kerosine for wood preservation. Some of the salts have surface-active properties and may be used as lubricating oil additives and as emulsifiers. The acids may be reacted with epichlorohydrin to give glycidyl esters and these will combine with phthalic anhydride to form non-drying alkyd resins which have considerable potential in the surface-coating industries.

The Koch reaction has not yet been exploited in this country but Shell Chemicals are importing some acids, glycidyl esters and resins from the Shell plant in Holland which uses selected fractions of wax cracked olefins as feedstock.

The natural naphthenic acids referred to above are extracted on a scale of a few thousand tons per annum by washing heavy kerosine and gas oil fractions with aqueous caustic soda followed by acidification to release or "spring" the acids. The acids are separated and vacuum distilled to give the required molecular weight product. The molecular weight of commercial acids varies from 180 to 350, according to the petroleum fraction from which they have been separated. Chemically they are complex mixtures of which some constituents, such as methyl cyclopentane and methyl cyclohexane carboxylic acids, have been identified.

Only petroleum refiners can be basic producers of naphthenic acids but it is usual for refiners to sell their naphthenic oils (crude acids) to processors who convert them to refined acids. The main naphthenic acid producers are Manchester Oil Refinery and Lobitos, both now subsidiaries of the Burmah Oil Co., Burts and Harvey, Esso, Shell Chemicals and Petro-Derivates. The last company is the biggest in this field and sells material made from crude acids imported into this country and redistilled by the Universal Oil Co. of Hull. As for the synthetic Koch acids, the most important use is for paint driers but wood preservatives, cutting oils, emulsifiers, etc., absorb a significant proportion of the total amount available.

Application of the OXO process to straight chain olefins gives a mixture of normal and 1-alkyl branched chain aldehydes with one more carbon atom than the original olefin and these may readily be oxidized to the corresponding acids. Starting from olefins with 15 or 17 carbon atoms, the normal acids obtained would, of course, be identical with natural palmitic and stearic acids obtained from fat splitting. Unfortunately the yield of normal acids from the OXO process is only 60%, or less under some conditions, of the total product and, so far, the synthetic processes have not proved competitive with natural fats as a source of straight chain acids. An important branch of the organic chemical industry, the "oleochemicals" industry, has grown up around the separation of individual natural fatty acids and their conversion to derivatives.

The natural fats and oils are, in general, glyceryl esters of fatty acids; it is unusual to find only one acid radical and most fats give a mixture of acids on hydrolysis, the most usual being palmitic, stearic and oleic acids although coconut oil yields a good proportion of lauric acid. Special mention must be made of the drying oils, such as linseed and tung oils, which yield highly unsaturated acids. Fat splitting processes have been described in Chapter 2; the separated fatty acids are usually purified by vacuum distillation at about 5 mm absolute pressure, either batchwise or in a continuous process. The stills are constructed of stainless steel and heated by circulating "Dowtherm" or other heat exchange liquid.

Separation of the solid palmitic and stearic acids from mixed fatty acids of animal and vegetable origin has been carried out for many years, one of the pioneer companies being Price's (Bromborough) Ltd., now part of the Unilever Group. The original aim was to obtain purified solid acids (stearines) for manufacture of non-sputtering candles. The by-product liquid acids (oleines) were at first thought to be useless but a market was found for them in the processing of wool. There is still a large market for stearine candles in Scandinavia and other West European countries but, in this country, it has greatly decreased and, in what remains, the stearines have been largely replaced by paraffin wax from petroleum. A wide range of uses for fatty acids and their derivatives has, however, developed in many industries and great advances in the technology of separating, purifying and chemically reacting fatty acids have been necessary to meet these needs.

The old process of pressing cakes of mixed acids to express the liquid oleic acid is still used but it is being replaced by a solvent extraction process. The "Emersol" process, developed in the U.S.A., is used by Price's (Bromborough) Ltd. and employs methanol as a selective solvent. The feed, usually vacuum distilled bone grease fatty acids, is mixed with a crystal promoter and dissolved in 93% methanol to give a 25% solution; the solution is refrigerated and the solid acids which crystallize out are removed by vacuum filtration, the filter cake being washed with further quantities of solvent to remove entrained liquid acids. Methanol is recovered by distillation from both the filter cake and filtrate and recycled, while the produced oleines and stearines are removed to storage tanks. The process may be applied to other feedstocks, for example the fatty acids from semi-drying oils, to concentrate fatty acids with particular properties.

Finally, hydrogenation may be employed to convert unsaturated acids to the corresponding saturated compounds. For example, oleic acid may be converted to stearic and ricinoleic to 12-hydroxy stearic acids. The hydrogenation process is generally referred to as fat hardening, since it converts the liquid unsaturated acids to the solid saturated compounds. It is carried out batchwise at a temperature of 160°–180°C and a pressure of 400 psig using a non-pyrophoric nickel catalyst. The hydrogenation plant operates on the "dead end" principle; a 7-ton batch of oil contained in a stainless steel reactor is mixed with catalyst, brought to reaction temperature and supplied with hydrogen under pressure. As the reaction proceeds, any impurities in the hydrogen accumulate in the space above the oil and may stop the reaction unless vented from time to time. For this reason it has been usual to use electrolytic hydrogen of 99·9% purity for fat hardening but, more recently, purified hydrogen from petroleum sources has become available cheaply enough to make its use worth while in spite of the additional venting required. The catalyst is removed from the final product by filtration.

The chemical constitution of fatty acids from different natural fats and oils is now well understood and constitutes a major study in itself; by combinations of the processes of saponification, solvent extraction and hydrogenation already described, specific acids may be separated in a fairly pure state. For heavy organic chemicals only the cheaper sources of acids need be considered; these are the common oils and fats of commerce such as bone grease, tallow, palm kernel oil, various nut oils, drying oils such as linseed and tung oils and tall oil—a by-product of the wood pulp industry.

The acids have a great diversity of uses, especially in the textile and surface-coating industries. These uses depend, in general, on the lubricating and surface-active properties of the acids and these inherent properties may be enhanced or modified by compounding or by conversion to derivatives such as esters, amides, ethers and anhydrides.

The industry is so diverse that it is not possible to make a sharp division between the detergent manufacturers and those companies processing natural oils for purely chemical purposes. Price's (Bromborough) Ltd., originally famous for candles, are important producers and offer a wide range of acids and their derivatives as chemicals. Their main products are stearines and oleines from bone grease but they also market distilled fatty acids prepared from most of the common non-drying, semi-drying and drying oils of commerce including ricinoleic and 12-hydroxy stearic acids prepared from castor oil and hydrogenated castor oil respectively. Many derivatives of these acids such as esters, amides and anhydrides are available in commercial quantities and still more are produced in development quantities and are potentially available for large-scale use if required.

Other important producers are the Universal Oil Co. Ltd. of Hull, J. Bibby & Sons Ltd. of Liverpool, Victor Woolf Ltd. of Manchester and Armour Hess Chemicals Ltd. of Littleborough, Lancs. Marchon Products Ltd. of Whitehaven, part of the Albright and Wilson Group, do not market fatty acids but do much processing of natural oils for production of their own specialities including, it is believed, some high pressure hydrogenation of fatty acids to alcohols. The first two companies are traditionally vegetable oil processors who are expanding into oleochemicals; Victor Woolf produces chemical specialities for, among others, the textile and leather trades. Armour Hess Chemicals Ltd. first started producing fatty acids under the name of Hess Products Ltd. and built a high vacuum fatty acid fractionation plant at Littleborough in 1951 to produce the "Distec" brand of fatty acids. These operations were later extended to the production of various fatty amines and other nitrogen derivatives on behalf of Armour Chemical Co. Ltd., the British offshoot of the large U.S. meat packing company, which has diversified widely into the chemical and fertilizer industries. The two companies then amalgamated and have still further expanded their range of fatty acid nitrogen derivatives.

The feed for the Littleborough plant is obtained from a conventional fat splitting operation by the autoclave process (see page 23) but this will be replaced by high-pressure steam splitting. The acid fractionation is carried out in stainless steel equipment under high vacuum and the separated acids may be sold as such or processed further to derivatives. The first stage of conversion to nitrogen derivatives is reaction of the acid with ammonia in the presence of a catalyst to form a nitrile.

$$RCOOH + NH_3 \longrightarrow RCN + 2 H_2O$$

The nitrile is then hydrogenated to the amine

$$RCN + 2 H_2 \longrightarrow RCH_2NH_2.$$

By submitting the primary amine to suitable temperature treatment, the well known de-amination reaction may be brought about to give secondary and tertiary amines

$$2 RCH_2NH_2 \longrightarrow (RCH_2)_2NH + NH_3$$

$$3 RCH_2NH_2 \longrightarrow (RCH_2)_3N + 2 NH_3$$

The amines can be converted to acetate salts or reacted with ethylene oxide to form polyoxyethylene derivatives. This range of products has a large number of applications as corrosion inhibitors, waterproofing agents, flotation agents and fuel additives and in the formulation of paints and cutting oils, to mention but a few. The tertiary amines may be converted to quaternary ammonium compounds which find their main applications as cationic detergents.

DICARBOXYLIC ACIDS

Many dicarboxylic acids of the type $HOOC(CH_2)_nCOOH$ are known but few of them have attained the status of heavy organic chemicals. The simplest of them is, of course, oxalic acid in which $n = 0$. This, although an important organic chemical, is produced on a relatively small scale in this country, but it might rank as a heavy organic chemical in the U.S.A. where annual production is around 15,000 tons. It is produced from sodium formate which is converted to sodium oxalate by heating to 350°–400°C. It may also be made by oxidation of carbohydrates or of ethylene glycol. The second member of the series, malonic acid, is mainly an intermediate for pharmaceuticals while succinic acid, in which $n = 2$, also has only small scale outlets. Hydroxy succinic, or malic, acid is becoming important in the food industries and is made by hydration of maleic acid.

$$\begin{array}{cc} \text{CHCOOH} & \text{CH(OH)COOH} \\ \| \qquad + \text{H}_2\text{O} \longrightarrow & | \\ \text{CHCOOH} & \text{CH}_2\text{COOH} \end{array}$$

Maleic acid itself is described in Chapter 9 as also is adipic acid $(n = 4)$, the most important, tonnage wise, of all the dibasic acids.

Glutaric acid, in which $n = 3$, is of small commercial importance but the monosodium salt of its amino derivative, glutamic acid, is being produced on a very large scale in the U.S.A. and Japan as a food flavouring material. It is made from by-product liquor from beet sugar manufacture or by hydrolysis of wheat or corn gluten by dilute sulphuric acid.

$$\text{Gluten} + \text{H}_2\text{O} + \text{H}_2\text{SO}_4 \longrightarrow \begin{array}{c} \text{H}_2\text{NCHCOOH} \\ | \\ \text{CH}_2\text{CH}_2\text{COOH} \end{array}$$

The acid is crystallized from the hydrolysate and converted to its monosodium salt with caustic soda.

The immediate homologues of adipic acid, viz. pimelic, suberic, azelaic and sebacic acids in which $n = 5, 6, 7$ and 8 respectively, are possible alternatives to adipic acid as intermediates for polyamide plastics and fibres; they would probably be more widely used if they were cheaper.

Some dibasic acids may be made from natural fatty acids, for example, oxidation of oleic acid with air containing ozone yields equimolar proportions of pelargonic and azelaic acids.

$$\text{C}_8\text{H}_{17}\text{CH} = \text{CHC}_7\text{H}_{14}\text{COOH} \longrightarrow \begin{array}{l} \text{C}_8\text{H}_{17}\text{COOH} \\ + \text{HOOC(CH}_2)_7\text{COOH} \end{array}$$

Sebacic acid may be obtained by destructive distillation of castor oil; the ozone oxidation process may be applied to other long-chain unsaturated acids for the production of shorter chain dibasic acids but these methods are all relatively expensive. The C_8 and C_{12} acids, suberic and dodecane dioic, may be made by oxidation of the cyclic dimer and trimer of butadiene, cyclo-octadiene and cyclo- dodecatriene, respectively and this might be a commercial route to these acids in the future.

The foregoing account of the fatty acids has necessarily been sketchy since the subject is too big to be dealt with adequately in a book of this kind. The possibility of duplicating natural fats and oils by synthetic means has always been the subject of much study because of the vast markets for them as detergent bases and as foodstuffs. Satisfactory synthetic alternatives for many detergent applications are now available and the remaining difficulty in producing synthetic straight chain fatty acids, and from them the fats, lies in the provision of a sufficiently cheap raw material. Natural synthesis is beautifully selective in producing, almost exclusively, carbon chains with an even number of carbon atoms, whereas the process of natural breakdown has been less selective and has produced a mixture of hydrocarbons. The separation of straight chain paraffins by means of molecular sieves has already been referred to and further developments along these lines, or perhaps by means of large-scale chromatographic processes, may yet provide the elusive normal paraffins with 12, 14, 16 and 18 carbon atoms cheaply enough to be the basis of synthetic fats manufacture; the possibilities for growth in this field of chemistry are enormous.

PLASTICIZER ALCOHOLS

The heading indicates the main tonnage products to be described but this section will include a general description of all higher aliphatic alcohols with large scale uses. Cetyl, stearyl and oleyl alcohols, corresponding to palmitic, stearic and oleic acids, may be obtained by hydrolysis of sperm oil which is remarkable in containing fatty acid esters of these higher alcohols; other fatty alcohols may be made by high pressure hydrogenation of the corresponding fatty acids. Price's of Bromborough produce a number of grades of oleyl, oleyl/cetyl and cetyl/stearyl alcohols from sperm oil and Marchon Products at Whitehaven carry out high pressure hydrogenations on a substantial scale, especially for lauryl alcohol.

The fatty alcohols and their derivatives, like the fatty acids, tend to find uses which depend on their lubricating and surface active properties. A specific use for the saturated cetyl/stearyl alcohols depends on their ability to spread over a water surface in the form of a monomolecular layer. This suppresses evaporation of the water and offers a large potential outlet for water conservation in static reservoirs, especially in hot arid climates.

The possible use of fatty alcohol sodium sulphates as bio-degradable synthetic detergents has been referred to on page 186 but the realization of this on a really large scale would depend on the provision of cheap synthetic alcohols; the possibilities and problems of fatty alcohol synthesis are dealt with later in this section.

An industrial application for primary alcohols in which synthetic alcohols have been successfully used, and which absorbs large tonnages, depends on the fact that their esters with dibasic acids are excellent plasticizers for PVC. The first plasticizer esters used from 1930 onwards were based on the acids and alcohols available at that time and various phosphoric acid esters, as well as diethyl and dibutyl phthalates, were tried. Dibutyl phthalate was fairly successful but the need for plasticizers of higher molecular weight became evident and a search began for higher primary alcohols which could be made sufficiently cheaply. One of the first used commercially was 2-ethyl hexanol, made from butyraldehyde as described on page 171. Di-(2-ethyl hexyl) phthalate is an excellent plasticizer and would probably be used more widely if it could be produced more cheaply.

When Shell Chemicals began production of the secondary alkyl sulphate detergents in the early part of the last war from

C_8–C_{18} cracked wax olefins, the co-produced C_6–C_8 olefins were not required and were disposed of as fuel. After the war, demand for PVC, and consequently for plasticizers, grew rapidly and when I.C.I. set up an OXO plant at Billingham for production of normal and isobutanol, the extension of this to processing the Shell Chemical C_6–C_8 olefins for production of mixed C_7–C_9 primary alcohols was obviously attractive.

Shell and I.C.I., therefore, entered into a joint arrangement for manufacture and marketing of primary alcohols produced by I.C.I. from Shell C_6–C_8 α-olefins—hence the name "Alphanol" for these materials; the arrangement also covered the production of some isononanol from di-isobutene. This joint arrangement is still in force and produces large tonnages annually of plasticizer alcohols for the British market and for export. I.C.I. has further extended its OXO operations to the production of iso-octyl alcohol from a mixed C_7 propylene/butylene co-polymer supplied by Esso and some quantities of decyl and tridecyl alcohols are made from propylene trimer and tetramer respectively. The OXO process is a versatile method of producing primary alcohols and, when a mixture of straight chain and 1-alkyl branched chain alcohols is acceptable as a product,, may be used with any suitable olefin feedstock.

Another method of obtaining primary alcohols is by hydrolysis of trialkyl aluminium compounds produced from olefins. This is based on the work of Professor Ziegler and may be accompanied by polymerization of the olefin. Thus with ethylene as feed the reaction may be written·

$$Al + 1\tfrac{1}{2}H_2 + 3\ C_2H_4 \longrightarrow Al(C_2H_5)_3$$

$$Al(C_2H_5)_3 + 3(n-1)\ C_2H_4 \longrightarrow Al(C_{2n}H_{4n+1})_3$$

$$Al(C_{2n}H_{4n+1})_3 + 3\ H_2O \longrightarrow Al(OH)_3$$
$$+ 3\ CH_3(CH_2)_{n-2}CH_2OH$$

A range of carbon chain lengths is obtained and the product may be fractionated to give narrow cuts of mixed alcohols with, of course, an even number of carbon atoms in the chains. The process is carried out commercially by the Continental Oil Co. which has plants offering a range of primary alcohols in the U.S.A. and in Western Europe. It has not yet been exploited on a commercial scale in this country.

By using a pure α-olefin to form the aluminium alkyl, followed by hydrolysis without further addition of olefin, it is possible to obtain a pure normal primary alcohol with the same number of carbon atoms as the olefin. This offers a practicable process of producing synthetically a duplication of the natural fatty alcohols and thence, by oxidation, of the natural fatty acids. The α-olefin feedstock would have to be cheap, however, for the product to be commercially competitive with natural sources under present conditions; even as a producer of mixed alcohols, it has not yet been shown that the process is competitive with other primary alcohol processes.

CONCLUSION

At present, many natural products still have a part to play in the industrial production of the higher aliphatic alcohols and acids and their derivatives and, where specific pure compounds are required, their replacement by synthetic processes is still some way off. Synthetic materials can, however, replace the natural products over a wide range of uses and there is likely to be rapid development in methods for the separation of higher hydrocarbons of specific types from petroleum and in their conversion into chemicals for the plastics, synthetic fibre and detergent industries.

READING LIST

1. *The Manufacture of Glycerol*, by G. Martin and H. J. Strausz. The Technical Press Ltd., London, 1956.
2. *Tall Oil and its Uses*. Edited by L. G. Zachary, H. N. Bajak and F. J. Eveline. Published by McGraw-Hill for the Information and Training Services Division of the F. W. Dodge Co. New York.
3. *The Chemical Constitution of Natural Fats*, by T. P. Hilditch and P. N. Williams. Chapman & Hall, London, 1964.
4. OXO Alcohols, by G. U. Ferguson. *Chemistry and Industry*, 13 March 1965,

CHAPTER 9

Chemicals Derived from Aromatic Hydrocarbons

IN DESCRIBING the industrial uses of aromatic hydrocarbons, and of chemicals derived from them, it is difficult to differentiate between aromatics as coal carbonization products, aromatics as dyestuffs intermediates, both of which are being described in other volumes in this series, and aromatics as heavy organic chemicals which properly belong here. This chapter deals, in the main, with those products which are already produced, or are likely shortly to be produced, on a large scale from petroleum feedstock. This means that a number of chemicals which are traditionally coal-based, or which are normally regarded as dyestuffs intermediates, have only been mentioned briefly although they may be produced in large tonnage; for example, nitrobenzene and aniline, T.N.T. and naphthalene derivatives are barely mentioned.

In 1948, the total production of crude benzole in this country was about 375,000 tons and the total demand for chemically pure benzene about 30,000 tons. By 1964 the crude benzole production had risen only to 410,000 tons, whereas the demand for benzene for chemical purposes was 300,000 tons in that year. By 1970 the corresponding rates are expected to be 450,000 t/a and 500,000 t/a respectively. The very slow rate of increase in crude benzole production is due to the fact that the switch to oil feedstocks in the gas-making industry and the changes in steel-making processes, which have largely decreased the requirements of coke per ton of steel, have more than compensated for the growth in demand for gas and steel. In any case, even without these changes, it is unlikely that production of coal-based aromatics would have been sufficient for the increased demands of the heavy organic chemicals industry. Only the crude benzole from coke ovens is suitable for the production of chemical grades of benzene and the need for additional sources of pure aromatics began to be felt about 1959 when, for the first time, consumption of chemical benzene exceeded the amount of aromatics from coal carbonization going to motor fuel.

The preferential rate of excise duty levied on light aromatic hydrocarbons produced in this country from coal and the complicated regulations surrounding the drawbacks of duty which could be claimed have, for many years, militated against the use of petroleum based aromatic hydrocarbons for chemical synthesis, while their value as octane rating improvers for gasoline has tended to make them expensive as chemical feedstocks. This situation is now changing; petroleum based light aromatic hydrocarbons have been imported in large quantities for some years past, the preferential excise duty on "indigenous" light hydrocarbons has been abolished from the end of 1964 and large-scale manufacture of benzene, toluene and xylenes from petroleum has been established in this country and is expanding rapidly.

The first petroleum based aromatics production in this country was by Petrochemicals Ltd. from 1949 onwards; this amounted to only a few thousand tons annually and was mostly exported because of the preferential excise duty situation. When Shell took over Petrochemicals Ltd. in 1955, it already had a captive need for benzene for detergent alkylate production and this was subsequently increased by the addition of an ethyl benzene and styrene plant to the facilities at Carrington. Although benzene recovery increased as ethylene output was raised, it supplied only a part of Shell's U.K. needs and was insignificant in the overall aromatics situation. Shell also supplied mixed xylenes from the Stanlow catalytic reformer to I.C.I. for terephthalic acid manufacture but still in fairly small quantities. During the late 1950's and early 1960's, British Celanese changed to a naphtha cracking feedstock and began to recover the light aromatic hydrocarbons from their cracked distillate and B.P. set up a xylenes plant at the Isle of Grain to produce ortho and para xylenes from mixed xylenes from the catalytic reformer there. Progress was, however, slow and this was probably due to the existence of an over-capacity situation for aromatics in the U.S.A. and Western Europe, due to ultra rapid expansion of petroleum based aromatics production, which made it possible to import benzene and mixed xylenes at low prices. The supply situation has become more stable recently and the necessary facilities are in course of erection to supply most of the country's needs. I.C.I. has almost completed a 400,000 t/a aromatics plant at Wilton and is planning an even larger one of 500,000 t/a. These are likely to supply all of the I.C.I. captive requirements and give substantial quantities for general sale. Gulf Oil Co. is building a 200,000 t/a plant at Milford Haven and Continental Oil Co. will include a 100,000 t/a aromatics plant in its planned refinery on the Humber Estuary.

Extraction processes for producing aromatics from cracker and reformer distillates have been described in Chapter 2, page 31. The liquid fraction from some ethylene crackers may be rich enough for direct recovery of pure benzene, toluene and xylenes without recourse to extraction processes; azeotropic distillation with methanol may be used for removal of small amounts of paraffins from benzene and toluene fractions. For pure benzene, Shell Chemicals now use the Newton Chambers freeze process in which a C_6 cut from the cracker distillate is refrigerated to around $-20°C$ and the crystallized benzene is centrifuged out. In reforming processes benzene, which is in greatest demand, is the most difficult hydrocarbon to form and there is usually an excess of toluene and, sometimes, of xylenes. In such a case, the balance may be corrected by conversion of the excess toluene and xylene to benzene by catalytic hydro-dealkylation and a number of commercial processes for this conversion have been developed in the U.S.A. such as the "Hydeal" and "Detol" processes of

Universal Oil Products and Houdry Process Corporation respectively. In these processes toluene or xylene vapour is mixed with hydrogen and passed over a catalyst at about 600°C. Methyl groups are removed as methane and benzene is condensed and purified by distillation.

The industrial applications of the light aromatic hydrocarbons are legion. Benzene, toluene and the mixed xylenes are excellent solvents and are widely used as such in the surface-coatings industries; they also have many uses in the production of dye-stuffs, pharmaceuticals and fine chemicals. The really large tonnage outlets, however, are as intermediates for the manufacture of synthetic fibres, synthetic rubbers, detergents, plastics and plasticizers; it is the rapidly increasing requirements in these fields that have stimulated the large-scale manufacture of the light aromatic hydrocarbons from petroleum.

STYRENE

Of some 300,000 t/a of pure benzene currently being used for chemical synthesis in this country, styrene manufacture takes approximately one-third. This is probably still the largest single outlet although it is rapidly being overtaken by the requirements for nylon. Present consumption of styrene, mainly for polystyrene and styrene/butadiene rubber is about 130,000 t/a and is still increasing. Styrene is made by catalytic dehydrogenation of ethyl benzene which, in turn, is produced by alkylation of benzene with ethylene.

In a typical alkylation process, ethylene and a 60% excess of pre-dried benzene are fed into a glass-lined reactor where they are brought into intimate contact with the catalyst; a small amount of ethyl chloride is added to act as a source of hydrogen chloride and to provide some additional ethylene during the reaction. The catalyst consists of a complex of aluminium chloride with hydrocarbons; it is a reddish brown oil with the approximate composition shown in Table 8 and is insoluble in the benzene/ethyl benzene reaction mixture.

TABLE 8. COMPOSITION OF CATALYST
COMPLEX FOR ETHYL BENZENE PROCESS

	Wt.%
Combined $AlCl_3$	26
Free $AlCl_3$	1
Benzene/ethyl benzene	48
High molecular wt. hydrocarbons	25

Ethylene is almost completely absorbed and there is no recycle, any unreacted gases being passed to flare or, after washing, to fuel. The reaction is exothermic and the temperature is maintained at about 90°C by circulating cooling water. Some higher alkyl benzenes are always formed and their formation is suppressed by returning the higher alkyl benzene fraction, separated in the distillation section, to the reactor; some versions of the process treat this fraction in a separate de-alkylation step. The reactor product is cooled and passed to a settler where the catalyst complex separates out and is returned to the alkylation vessel. The hydrocarbon layer is washed with water and caustic soda solution and passed to the distillation system. Catalyst quality is maintained by taking two small bleed streams from the reactor effluent; one is washed with water to decompose the catalyst complex into an upper hydrocarbon layer, which is passed to the washers with the product from the settler, and a lower layer consisting of aluminium chloride solution and some tarry residues. The second bleed stream is diverted to a small vessel, fitted with a stirrer, where dry granular aluminium chloride is added and the mixture is then returned to the alkylation vessel. A flowsheet for the alkylation process is shown in Fig. 16.

The crude product from the alkylation system, containing benzene, ethyl benzene and higher alkyl benzenes, is separated in a conventional distillation train to give recovered benzene for return to the drying column, higher alkyl benzenes for recycle to

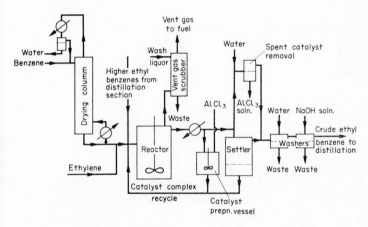

FIG. 16 Alkylation Process for Ethyl Benzene.

the reactor and ethyl benzene of better than 99% purity to go forward to the dehydrogenation step.

There are several versions of the ethyl benzene dehydrogenation process which are operated commercially; they differ chiefly in the way in which the heat for the endothermic reaction is added and in the composition of the catalyst used. In the "isothermal" process the dehydrogenation is carried out in an externally heated reactor and heat is supplied as the reaction proceeds. In the "adiabatic" process, on the other hand, ethyl benzene vapour is preheated almost to reaction temperature, mixed with sufficient steam superheated above the optimum reaction temperature to supply the amount of reaction heat required, and discharged into the reaction chamber where the temperature falls as dehydrogenation proceeds. Various catalysts have been tried and generally they consist of one or more of the oxides of zinc, chromium, iron or magnesium on a base of activated charcoal, alumina or bauxite. The adiabatic process is now generally preferred and will be described.

Purified ethyl benzene is vaporized with steam and preheated by exchange with reaction products to about 500°C. Steam is superheated to around 710°C, first by heat exchange with reaction products, and then in a furnace, mixed with the preheated ethyl benzene in the proportion of about 2·5 lb of steam per lb of ethyl benzene and the mixture is fed continuously to the reactor. When the catalyst is new, a reactor inlet temperature of about 600°C is aimed at but, as the catalyst ages, this is gradually raised to about 660°C to maintain conversion at about 35% per pass. The temperature falls through the reactor as dehydrogenation proceeds and the products leave at about 560°C; they are cooled in heat exchangers, first by incoming ethyl benzene and then by steam. The products are further cooled in a spray cooler, which also washes out tarry materials, and liquefied in a final condenser. The liquid hydrocarbon product, containing ethyl benzene and styrene with small quantities of toluene, benzene and tars is separated from water and passed forward to the distillation stage. The vent gases, consisting mainly of hydrogen with some oxides of carbon and hydrocarbons, may be passed to fuel or purified to give hydrogen streams for other processes. A flowsheet of the dehydrogenation process is shown at Fig. 17.

The crude styrene is first passed through a vessel containing solid sulphur, sufficient being dissolved to act as a polymerization inhibitor, and then goes to the first vacuum column. Benzene and toluene are taken overhead and separately distilled for recovery of the pure hydrocarbons; the column bottoms pass on to the second vacuum column where ethyl benzene is taken overhead and recycled to the dehydrogenation system. The bottom product, consisting of styrene with some tar and sulphur, is purified in the final column to give pure sytrene overhead and a tarry residue which is discarded. A polymerization inhibitor, usually *p*-tertiary butyl catechol, is added to the top of the final column; the distillate from this column is better than 99·7%

pure styrene and passes to receivers where more inhibitor is added to give a concentration of 10 ppm before it goes to final storage. The overall yield on benzene and ethylene is 86–87%.

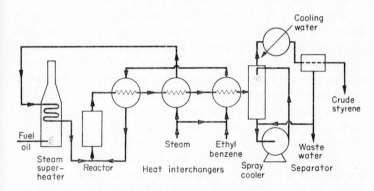

Fig. 17 Dehydrogenation of Ethyl Benzene.

There are only two manufacturers of styrene in this country at present—Forth Chemicals with plants at Grangemouth and Baglan Bay, and Shell Chemicals with a plant at Carrington. Total capacity is sufficient for the current U.K. requirements although appreciable quantities of styrene are still imported, especially from Canada by the Polymer Corporation. There have been rumours from time to time that other manufacturers intend to enter the market but, so far, these have not materialized.

In addition to its major outlets for manufacture of polystyrene and SBR, styrene has a number of smaller, but important, uses; it is employed as a cross linking agent in unsaturated polyester resin compositions and in some surface-coating resins; substantial amounts are also used for production of the high styrene/butadiene resins and latices described in Chapter 7, page 165.

CYCLOHEXANE

Cyclohexane may be separated from a C_6 cut from naphthenic based crude oils by modern close fractionation methods; the amount of cyclohexane present in the cut may first be increased by a hydroforming operation to convert methyl cyclopentane to cyclohexane. Petroleum derived cyclohexane is produced on a large scale in the U.S.A., but high purity is difficult and costly to achieve and the preferred route, both there and in Europe, is hydrogenation of benzene; this reaction takes place in high yield at temperatures below 200°C with the aid of a conventional hydrogenation catalyst such as nickel. This is, in effect, a reversal of the process by which aromatics are produced in catalytic reforming operations; the fact that the benzene ring may be hydrogenated or dehydrogenated according to conditions and with good yields in either direction forms the basis of several industrial processes; for example the oxidation of benzene to phenol has not yet been achieved commercially but its hydrogenation to cyclohexane, oxidation of this to cyclohexanol followed by dehydrogenation of the cyclohexanol to phenol is a feasible commercial process.

In this country requirements for cyclohexane have, in the past, been met by hydrogenation of coal-based benzene, particularly by I.C.I. and Howards of Ilford. In recent years, however, a sudden upsurge in demand caused by expansion of nylon production has exceeded both hydrogenation capacity and benzene availability. In consequence large quantities of cyclohexane have been imported, mainly from the U.S.A. This situation is now being remedied; I.C.I. is building the world's largest benzene hydrogenation plant as part of its new 400,000 t/a aromatics plant at Wilton. The actual capacity has not been published but it is estimated that the I.C.I. demand for cyclohexane will rise to about 150,000 t/a in a few years. The Gulf Oil plant at Milford Haven will also include a 60,000 t/a cyclohexane unit and other manufacturers, including the National Coal Board, are planning new facilities.

Cyclohexane may be oxidized to cyclohexanol and cyclohexanone; these two compounds are valuable solvents which, together with methyl cyclohexanol, have been manufactured and marketed in this country for many years by Howards of Ilford.

It is to their use as intermediates for nylon, however, that the great increase in demand for these materials is due; by further oxidation both cyclohexanol and cyclohexanone are converted to adipic acid.

$$HOOC\ (CH_2)_4\ COOH\ +\ H_2O$$
Adipic acid.

Nylon is produced by dehydration of the salt formed when adipic acid and hexamethylene diamine react together in equimolar proportions. Hexamethylene diamine is made by reacting adipic acid with ammonia to form adiponitrile which is then hydrogenated to the diamine.

$$HOOC(CH_2)_4COOH + 2\ NH_3 \longrightarrow NC(CH_2)_4CN + 4\ H_2O$$

$$+ 2H_2$$

$$H_2NCH_2(CH_2)_4CH_2NH_2$$

$$n\ H_2N(CH_2)_6NH_2 + n\ HOOC(CH_2)_4COOH \longrightarrow$$
$$(-HN(CH_2)_6NHCO(CH_2)_4CO-)_n + 2\ H_2O$$
Nylon.

Only limited information is available on the process details of adipic acid production. The process of the Scientific Design Co.

is a two-stage oxidation of cyclohexane; in the first stage cyclo-hexane, with cobalt naphthenate in solution to act as oxidation catalyst, has air blown through it at a pressure of about 350 psig and a temperature of 125°–135°C until 8–10% of the hydro-carbon has been converted. The unconverted cyclohexane is then stripped off and the cyclohexanol/cyclohexanone mixture is sub-mitted to a further oxidation with air at a pressure of 100 psig and temperature of 80°–85°C. When conversion is complete, adipic acid, which is a solid melting at 152°C and only slightly soluble in water, is separated and purified by conventional crystallization processes. I.C.I. also uses a two-stage process; the first stage is similar to the first stage of the Scientific Design process described above while the second stage oxidation of the mixed cyclohexanol/cyclohexanone is carried out with 50% nitric acid at about 80°C in the presence of a copper/vanadium catalyst. dupont in the U.S.A., the world's largest producer of nylon, is believed to use a similar process. Another possible route to cyclohexanol would be by hydrogenation of phenol if this were cheap enough.

For the other half of the nylon molecule, hexamethylene diamine, adiponitrile is required. This is generally made from adipic acid and ammonia as described above but other routes are possible. One method which offers good possibilities for commercial application, starts from butadiene. When butadiene is chlorinated, 1.4 addition of chlorine predominates to give 1.4-dichlorobutene which may be converted to 1.4-dicyano-butene by reaction with sodium cyanide.

$$CH_2 = CHCH = CH_2 + Cl_2 \longrightarrow CH_2ClCH = CHCH_2Cl$$

$$CH_2Cl\ CH = CHCH_2Cl + 2\ NaCN \longrightarrow$$
$$NCCH_2CH = CHCH_2CN + 2\ NaCl$$

Hydrogenation of the 1.4-dicyano-butene gives first adiponitrile and then hexamethylene diamine. Direct production of adiponi-trile from butadiene and hydrogen cyanide is believed to have been achieved in good yield but not yet on a commercial scale. Another most interesting possibility is electrochemical production from acrylonitrile according to the process developed by Monsanto in the U.S.A. The electrolysis is carried out in aqueous solution using a mercury cathode and a platinum anode; a salt, such as tetraethyl ammonium *p*-toluene sulphonate, is added to increase the solubility of the acrylonitrile in water and to raise the conductivity of the solution. Solution is continuously withdrawn from the system, the adiponitrile is extracted, and unchanged acrylonitrile and solubilizing salt are recycled. If adiponitrile could be made cheaply enough, it could also provide the adipic acid required by hydrolysis; it is clear, however, from the vast expansion of cyclohexane capacity which is planned, that the manufacturers in this country do not expect serious competition from other processes for many years.

Conventional nylon is designated 6:6 from the number of carbon atoms in the two halves of the molecule. Nylon type molecules may obviously be produced from other diamines and dibasic acids and nylon 6:10, in which the adipic acid is replaced by sebacic acid has found some applications; other possibilities have been mentioned in the section on dibasic acids (Chapter 7, page 193). A more likely contender for a substantial share in the nylon market appears to be nylon 6 produced from caprolactam, the internal anhydride of amino-caproic acid. The raw material for caprolactam manufacture is again cyclohexanone, produced from cyclohexane or phenol as noted above.

A 5% excess of cyclohexanone is mixed with an aqueous solution of hydroxylamine sulphate and ammonia is passed in until the solution is neutral. The crude oxime separates as an oily liquid containing about 5% of water; it is reacted with 98% sulphuric acid at temperatures below 140°C, when it undergoes a Beckmann rearrangement to form the caprolactam, which is withdrawn continuously as a vapour and purified by distillation. Ammonium sulphate is recovered from the aqueous layer from the first stage reaction and the value which can be given to this by-product has a marked effect on the cost of the caprolactam.

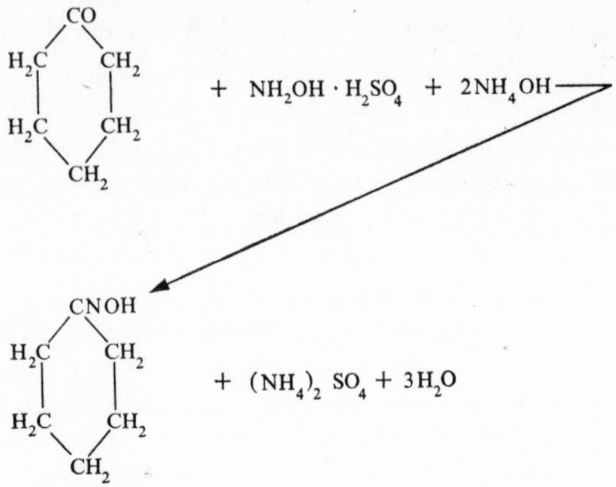

$$+ \ NH_2OH \cdot H_2SO_4 \ + \ 2NH_4OH \longrightarrow$$

$$+ \ (NH_4)_2 \ SO_4 + 3H_2O$$

Cyclohexanone
Oxime

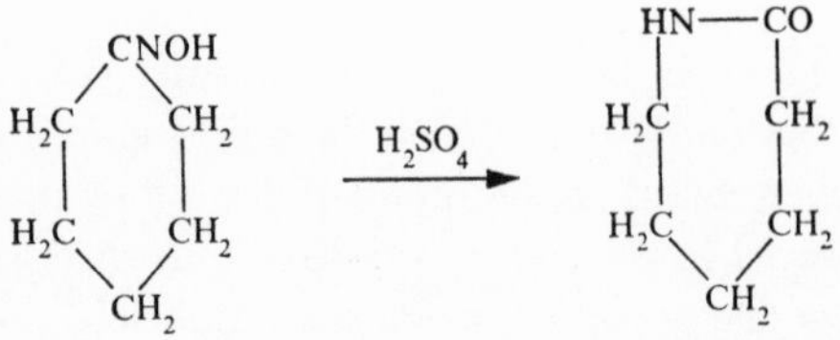

$$\xrightarrow{H_2SO_4}$$

Capralactam

A number of alternative processes for preparation of the oxime have been tried of which the Snia Viscosa Process is probably the best known. This starts with the oxidation of toluene to benzoic acid followed by reduction to hexahydrobenzoic acid; this is then treated, in a molar ratio of $1:3$, with nitrosyl sulphuric acid and ammonia. The oxime is produced in good yield with ammonium sulphate as a by-product. Another route is benzene $\rightarrow$ nitrobenzene $\rightarrow$ aniline $\rightarrow$ cyclohexylamine $\rightarrow$ cyclohexanone oxime; the final stage is accomplished by oxidation with 30% aqueous hydrogen peroxide. Caprolactam is not made in this country but it is likely that both Fisons and Courtaulds will build plants in the near future. Substantial quantities are at present being imported for U.K. manufacture of nylon 6.

PHENOL

The phenol naturally occurring in coal tar has been supplemented for many years by synthetic phenol produced from coal based benzene. Two processes were commonly used which involved the initial preparation of chlorobenzene or benzene sulphonic acid which were then decomposed by caustic soda under high temperature conditions to form phenol

Many attempts have been made to produce phenol by direct air oxidation of benzene but, so far, yields have not been high enough to make the process commercially viable. With continued development of organic oxidation processes, this may still be the process of the future. About 1950 the D.C.L. in this country and the Hercules Powder Co. in the U.S.A. independently evolved processes for the air oxidation of cumene (isopropyl benzene) to cumene hydroperoxide which may be hydrolysed to phenol and acetone. The companies subsequently entered into an arrangement for the exchange of patents and for joint licensing. The process proved to be more economic than the established chlorobenzene and benzene sulphonic acid processes and plants have been built under license in many parts of the world.

The process starts with the alkylation of benzene with propylene to form cumene. This is a simple alkylation and the process is similar to that for ethyl benzene described on page 201; a phosphoric acid catalyst may be preferred to aluminium chloride. Cumene is oxidized in a stream of air in the liquid phase at a temperature of 110°–130°C; a small amount of a metal salt such as cobalt naphthenate is used as catalyst and the reaction mixture is kept slightly alkaline at a pH of 8·5–10. Conversion is about 30% per pass. A stream of the reaction mixture is continuously withdrawn and the unconverted cumene recovered by vacuum distillation and recycled. The crude cumene hydro-peroxide, now at about 80% concentration, is hydrolysed by dilute aqueous sulphuric acid at 45°–60°C and both products, phenol and acetone, are purified by distillation. Both α-methyl styrene and acetophenone are produced in small amount as by-products.

The process produces about 0·6 tons of acetone per ton of phenol and its economics depend to a considerable extent on the sales value which can be assigned to this co-product; this can be a disadvantage in a well-supplied acetone market. Other synthetic phenol processes which do not have this disadvantage are the Dow process, which proceeds via air oxidation of toluene to benzoic acid followed by decarboxylation of the acid in the presence of air, and the modified Raschig process developed by the Hooker Chemical Co. in the U.S.A. The Hooker process is claimed to be highly efficient and to avoid the formation of by-products.

The first stage is an oxychlorination reaction between benzene, hydrogen chloride and air over a copper/iron catalyst at about 300°C to form monochlorobenzene. Conversion is only about 10% per pass; the monochlorobenzene is separated by distillation while unreacted benzene is recycled. In the second stage monochlorobenzene is hydrolysed over a siliceous catalyst at about 500°C to form phenol and hydrogen chloride. The phenol is redistilled and the hydrogen chloride returned to the first stage of the process.

$$C_6H_6 + HCl + \tfrac{1}{2} O_2 \longrightarrow C_6H_5Cl + H_2O$$

$$C_6H_5Cl + H_2O \longrightarrow C_6H_5OH + HCl$$

Until comparatively recently, synthetic phenol in this country was produced mainly by I.C.I. and Monsanto using the chlorobenzene and benzene sulphonic acid routes respectively. In 1960 B.H.C. brought the first cumene oxidation plant on stream with a capacity of 13,000 t/a and this has since been enlarged to 27,000 t/a. I.C.I. is at present in the process of enlarging its capacity to an estimated 50,000 t/a and, at the same time, changing over to the cumene oxidation process. B.H.C. is the major manufacturer of cumene and will probably supply the I.C.I. requirements as well as producing for its own needs and supplying large quantities for export.

The major use for phenol is in the manufacture of phenolic plastics and these absorb the lion's share of total output; other important applications are in the production of insecticides, herbicides, disinfectants, fine chemicals and dyestuffs. The total production capacity of around 75,000 t/a indicated above is expected to be sufficient for the country's needs for a few years but continued growth in demand is foreseen for many years to come

MALEIC ANHYDRIDE

Maleic anhydride has attained considerable importance as an organic chemical and is made by a number of companies. The route is the same in each case—oxidation of benzene with air—but there are variations in the way in which the process is carried out and in the catalysts used.

$$
\text{C}_6\text{H}_6 + 4\tfrac{1}{2}\,\text{O}_2 \longrightarrow
\begin{array}{c}
\text{CH}\!-\!\text{CO} \\
\| \qquad \rangle\text{O} \\
\text{CH}\!-\!\text{CO}
\end{array}
+ 2\,\text{H}_2\text{O} + 2\text{CO}_2
$$

Some details of the Scientific Design Co.'s process have been published. Benzene and air are preheated and passed to a multitubular reactor containing the catalyst and jacketed for cooling. After reaction the mixture is cooled in stages, first in a waste heat boiler, then in a feed gas preheater and finally in a water cooled condenser. The gases are scrubbed with water to remove maleic acid which is then dehydrated to the anhydride.

Maleic anhydride is a very important constituent of some polyester resins, described later in this chapter, since the double bond provides a reactive point in the polymer chain from which cross linking can take place; the acid itself has a number of applications as a dibasic acid and may be converted to the *trans* isomer, fumaric acid, by catalytic isomerization. Fumaric acid is widely used in the food industries as an acidulant where it competes with malic acid which may be made by hydration of maleic acid.

There are several producers of maleic anhydride and fumaric acid of which Monsanto Chemical Co. is the largest with an estimated capacity of 8000 t/a of maleic anhydride, based on the Scientific Design process, and 2500 t/a of fumaric acid. Alchemy Ltd., a Burt, Boulton and Haywood subsidiary, has a maleic anhydride plant for which capacities from 2000 to 5000 t/a have been quoted. Bowmans Chemicals of Widnes has also recently commenced production of maleic anhydride and fumaric acid.

OTHER USES OF BENZENE

Many uses of benzene for production of dyestuffs, fine chemicals and pharmaceuticals have been omitted from this chapter since the products are not generally regarded as heavy organic chemicals. Some of these applications, such as dyestuffs manufacture, are still expanding slowly but there is always the likelihood that new processes will become commercially important— for example the cyclohexylamine route to caprolactam is a possibility—and the availability of cheap, and virtually unlimited, supplies of benzene from petroleum can be expected to stimulate further developments in the future.

TOLUENE

Toluene, like benzene, has traditionally been regarded as a by-product of coal carbonization and the main outlets for it have been as a solvent and as an intermediate in manufacture of dyestuffs, explosives, fine chemicals and pharmaceuticals. With the exception of explosives manufacture in war time, none of the applications calls for large tonnages and chemical applications for toluene have not developed on the same scale as for benzene. On the other hand, war time demands for high octane gasoline and the post war increase in production of petroleum-based benzene have made large quantities of petroleum-derived toluene potentially available, especially in the U.S.A.; this has led to efforts to substitute toluene in some of the large-scale outlets for benzene. The most obvious place for substitution is vinyl toluene as a plastics monomer instead of styrene. At least two large vinyl toluene plants were erected in the U.S.A. at the time of the Korean crisis but the polymers have not proved commercially acceptable and the plants have since been abandoned.

Toluene may be oxidized with air in the presence of manganese or cobalt naphthenates to form benzoic acid and this is the first step in the Dow process for phenol already described. Air oxidation of toluene has proved to be cheaper than the standard method of decarboxylation of phthalic anhydride as a route to benzoic acid and it is now becoming the preferred process. W. J. Bush and Co., a member of the Albright and Wilson group, has recently installed a 6000 t/a benzoic acid plant at Widnes using this process. In recent years benzoic acid has become an important anti-oxidant and food preservative and the market for it is growing. It is also the starting point for the Henkel process for terephthalic acid manufacture referred to later in the chapter.

Benzyl dichloride, or benzal chloride, produced by controlled chlorination of toluene, may be hydrolysed to benzaldehyde, an important perfumery intermediate. The reaction is carried out by passing chlorine into boiling toluene to the point of maximum formation of benzal chloride. The reaction mass of crude benzal chloride is then hydrolysed with water containing a trace of alkali and the resulting benzaldehyde purified by distillation.

$$C_6H_5CH_3 + 2\ Cl_2 \longrightarrow C_6H_5CHCl_2 + 2\ HCl$$

$$C_6H_5CHCl_2 + H_2O \longrightarrow C_6H_5CHO + 2\ HCl$$

As well as in perfumery, benzaldehyde has uses in food flavouring and as an intermediate for dyestuffs and pharmaceuticals. It is claimed that the product from the chlorination process still contains enough residual chlorine compounds to make it unsuitable for the highest grade of perfumery and an alternative toluene oxidation process has been developed. The yield is less than 50% and the process is unlikely to achieve large-scale importance.

By stopping the chlorination reaction short at an earlier stage, good yields of benzyl chloride may be obtained and this may, in turn, be hydrolysed to benzyl alcohol.

$$C_6H_5CH_3 + Cl_2 \longrightarrow C_6H_5CH_2Cl + HCl$$

$$C_6H_5CH_2Cl + H_2O \longrightarrow C_6H_5CH_2OH + HCl$$

The benzoic acid ester of benzyl alcohol has become of considerable importance for use in delousing sprays and ointments under war conditions in tropical countries.

CRESOLS

The hydroxy toluenes, or cresols, are produced from coal tar by distillation and it has not yet been necessary to establish manufacture of synthetic cresols in this country; if required they could be made from toluene sulphonic acid or *p*-cymene by adaptation of processes used for the production of phenol. They are used, with formaldehyde, for the manufacture of resins but can substitute for phenol only to a limited extent in this application. Tricresyl phosphate is an important plasticizer for PVC and is produced by Boake Roberts (Albright and Wilson) on a scale greater than 10,000 t/a.

NITRO AND AMINO COMPOUNDS OF TOLUENE

Toluene may readily be nitrated to form mono-, di-, or trinitro derivatives; the tri-nitro compound is, of course, well known because of its use as an explosive; it will not be further described as it is covered in the volume in this series on high explosives and propellants. The nitro-toluenes are easily reduced to the corresponding amino compounds and tolylene diamine has become very important as an intermediate for polyurethane manufacture. 2.4-Tolylene diamine, either alone or mixed with up to 35% of the 2.6 isomer, is reacted with phosgene in solution in a high boiling inert solvent at about 50°C; the reaction is carried out in stages in which phosgene is added on to first one and then the second amino group, followed by removal of hydrogen chloride by blowing with inert gas at 110°C,

$$CH_3C_6H_3(NH_2)_2 + COCl_2 \longrightarrow CH_3C_6H_3{\overset{\displaystyle /NH_2Cl}{\underset{\displaystyle \backslash NHCOCl}{}}} + HCl$$

$$CH_3C_6H_3{\overset{\displaystyle /NH_2Cl}{\underset{\displaystyle \backslash NHCOCl}{}}} + COCl_2 \longrightarrow CH_3C_6H_3{\overset{\displaystyle /NHCOCl}{\underset{\displaystyle \backslash NHCOCl}{}}} + HCl$$

$$CH_3C_6H_3(NHCOCl)_2 \xrightarrow{\text{heat}} CH_3C_6H_3(NCO)_2 + 2\ HCl$$

The di-isocyanate will react with a polyhydroxy compound, such as a polyoxypropylene derivative (see page 158), to form polyurethanes which have been briefly described in Chapter 6.

Tolylene di-isocyanate manufacturers are dupont in Northern Ireland and I.C.I. at Hillhouse, near Fleetwood, Lancs. I.C.I. also manufacture MDI (diphenyl methane 4.4'-di-isocyanate) which is used mainly for rigid polyurethane foams; other polyisocyanates may be developed in the future which may affect the demand for the toluene derivative. Some di-isocyanates are imported but the demand is mainly met by the two manufacturers mentioned. Consumption is unknown with certainty but total demand for all iso-cyanates may be estimated at 30,000 t/a and the growth prospects are good.

XYLENES

The three possible xylene isomers are all produced during coal carbonization but in relatively small quantities. Whereas one ton of coal will yield about 0·072 ton of benzene, it will only give 0·012 ton of mixed xylenes. In contrast, it is easier to produce xylenes from petroleum by catalytic reforming than it is to make benzene. As the demand for xylenes for chemical synthesis has grown, more and more of these hydrocarbons have been produced from petroleum. All three isomers, together with ethyl benzene, are produced during catalytic reforming and the composition of a typical C_8 aromatics cut from a reformate and the boiling points of individual isomers are shown in Table 9.

TABLE 9. COMPOSITION OF CATALYTIC REFORMATE

	Isomer content Wt.%	Boiling point °C	Melting point °C
Ethyl benzene	12	136·2	−95
p-xylene	18	138·5	13·2
m-xylene	50	139·3	−47·4
o-xylene	20	144	−25

A mixed xylene cut of this composition is quite suitable for use as a solvent and large quantities are used in this way. For certain chemical applications, however, pure isomers are required; the separation of the pure isomers from each other and from ethyl benzene presents interesting problems. Inspection of the physical properties given in Table 9 shows that *o*-xylene can be separated as a residue product by efficient fractionation while fractional crystallization could provide a means of separating the para isomer. The ethyl benzene content of the mixed xylenes cut may vary widely; it may even be up to 20%, and this can have a considerable effect on *p*-xylene crystallization, while the relative proportions of the other xylene isomers tend to approach equilibrium values of about 50% for meta and 25% for each of the ortho and para compounds. It is possible to separate ethyl benzene by distillation and a super fractionation process has been operated in the U.S.A. by the Cosden Petroleum Co. which is claimed to produce an ethyl benzene fraction sufficiently pure for conversion to polymerization grade styrene. A number of separation schemes based on fractional distillation, fractional crystallization and isomerization can therefore be devised according to the requirements of pure isomers.

It is mainly the ortho and para isomers which are required; there is little demand for the meta compound which, unfortunately, is the major constituent of the equilibrium mixture. For preparation of pure *p*-xylene, it is desirable to start with a mixed xylene cut containing a maximum of 10–12% of ethyl benzene;

I

p-xylene is crystallized by cooling to about −35°C and the crystals separated in a centrifuge. These crystals are remelted and again crystallized in a second stage refrigeration step; the mother liquor from this second stage contains about 50% *p*-xylene and is returned to the first stage. The mother liquor from the first stage crystallization may be submitted to an isomerization process over a silica/alumina catalyst at about 450°C to reform the equilibrium mixture of isomers which is then blended with the fresh feed. Ethyl benzene is unchanged by the isomerization process and the rate at which it builds up in the feed limits the amount of recycle to isomerization which can be tolerated. Clearly a higher yield of the para isomer would be obtained if the ethyl benzene were first removed, when a much higher rate of recycle to isomerization would be possible; any ortho xylene required for sale could be recovered as part of the ethyl benzene distillation process. So far, however, the high fuel and capital costs of the ethyl benzene separation have not made it worth while to adopt the process in this country; the relatively high value of the xylene/ethyl benzene mother liquors for solvent purposes and gasoline blending have contributed to this situation.

p-Xylene is the starting point for production of terephthalic acid which will form high molecular weight polyesters with dihydric alcohols. Polyethylene glycol terephthalate is well known as the I.C.I. synthetic fibre "Terylene", also produced now in many other countries under various trade names.

Various processes for the oxidation of *p*-xylene to terephthalic acid have been tried commercially such as one-stage oxidation with nitric acid, when both methyl groups are oxidized simultaneously to carboxyl, or two-stage oxidation in which *p*-toluic acid is first formed from *p*-xylene, esterified to its methyl ester and then further oxidized, either with air or nitric acid, to monomethyl terephthalate. The process which is currently preferred was developed by the Standard Oil Co. of Indiana and the Scientific Design Co. and employs a one-stage oxidation of *p*-xylene at about 195°C and 200 psig; the catalyst may be

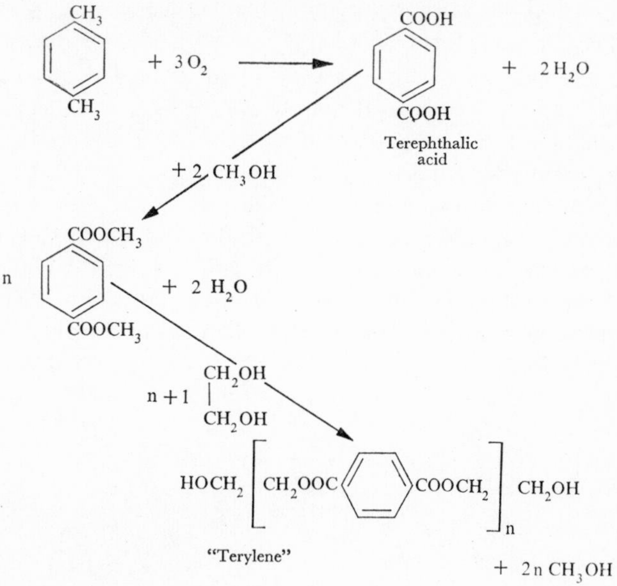

CH_3-benzene-CH_3 $+ 3 O_2 \longrightarrow$ $COOH$-benzene-$COOH$ $+ 2 H_2O$

Terephthalic acid

$+ 2 CH_3OH$

n $COOCH_3$-benzene-$COOCH_3$ $+ 2 H_2O$

$n+1$ $\begin{array}{c} CH_2OH \\ | \\ CH_2OH \end{array}$

$$HOCH_2 \left[CH_2OOC \!-\! \bigcirc \!-\! COOCH_2 \right]_n CH_2OH$$

"Terylene"

$+ 2n\, CH_3OH$

manganese acetate promoted with ammonium bromide. Whichever process is used the terephthalic acid is esterified to the dimethyl ester and purified by distillation; the pure ester is then reacted directly with ethylene glycol. Oxidation of di-isopropyl benzene instead of *p*-xylene has been proposed but the process has not reached commercial application. Another interesting process which has not been used commercially in this country is the Henkel process developed in Germany. In this process potassium benzoate is passed over a catalyst with carbon dioxide at high temperature; a disproportionation takes place to form benzene and potassium terephthalate.

I.C.I. is, at present, the only producer of dimethyl terephthalate in this country. At first the mixed xylenes were obtained from Shell's Stanlow refinery and nitric acid was used for the oxidation. More recently the one-stage air oxidation has been adopted and

I.C.I. has built its own plant for production of aromatic hydro-carbons. Capacity for terephthalic acid is believed to be about 40,000 t/a.

B.P. also has a xylenes separation plant at its Isle of Grain refinery; the *o*-xylene is used mainly for the Grange Chemical Co. phthalic anhydride plant at Hull and the *p*-xylene is produced for sale, mainly for export.

o-Xylene may be oxidized in a similar way to the para isomer to form orthophthalic acid or its anhydride. Manufacture of the anhydride has, in the past, been based entirely on the oxidation of coal tar naphthalene and every student is familiar with the story of the broken thermometer which first led to the discovery of this reaction.

$$\text{naphthalene} + 4\tfrac{1}{2}\,O_2 \longrightarrow \text{phthalic anhydride}$$

$$+ \; 2CO_2 \; + \; 2H_2O$$

In recent years, a decline in coal carbonization and a rapid increase in consumption of phthalic anhydride has led to a shortage of naphthalene while *o*-xylene has become plentiful and cheap. At first the yield of phthalic anhydride from *o*-xylene oxidation was not satisfactory. It is now claimed, however, that the difficulties have been solved and the process has been widely applied, especially in the U.S.A.

$$\text{o-xylene} + 3\,O_2 \longrightarrow \text{phthalic anhydride} + 3\,H_2O$$

Grange Chemical Co. is the only producer in the U.K. using the *o*-xylene process in a plant specially designed for the purpose but it is believed that both I.C.I. and Monsanto have adapted their plants to use some *o*-xylene; there are several other producers depending on naphthalene feedstock. Total consumption of phthalic anhydride in this country in 1963 was estimated at about 60,000 t/a and it is still rising.

The use of phthalic acid esters of primary alcohols as plasticizers for PVC has been referred to in Chapter 8; this outlet absorbs the greater part of the available anhydride and is likely to grow still further as consumption of PVC increases. Production of alkyd resins for the paint industry is also a large outlet which is not increasing very rapidly as other acids are becoming competitive. While terephthalic acid is used for the fibre forming saturated polyesters, phthalic anhydride or *o*-phthalic acid is used in admixture with an unsaturated acid, such as maleic acid, to form polyesters with unsaturated groups in the chain which may be cross linked by reaction with other compounds such as styrene. Unsaturated polyesters of this type form the resin component in many polyester resin/glass fibre moulding operations and their use is growing rapidly.

Increasing consumption of ortho- and para-xylenes for chemical purposes has thrown up a large excess of *m*-xylene for which the only outlets are solvent use, isomerization or return to motor gasoline. Strenuous efforts have been made in the U.S.A. to develop commercial outlets for isophthalic acid, the product of *m*-xylene oxidation, as an intermediate for resins and plasticizers. These have had only a limited success and isophthalic acid is not made in this country although imported material is available, if required.

POLYCYCLIC COMPOUND

The major use for polycyclic compounds such as phenanthrene and anthracene is in dyestuffs manufacture, which also absorbs much naphthalene. The hydrocarbons can be recovered from coal tar and this source has, so far, proved adequate to meet all requirements. They can be formed by severe thermal treatment of petroleum and significant quantities were present in the fuel oil fraction from the original "Catarole" cracking plant of Petrochemicals Ltd. None of the polycyclics can, at present, be regarded as a heavy organic chemical and none of them, with the possible exception of naphthalene in the U.S.A. and, to a very small extent in this country, has been produced in commercial quantities from petroleum.

MISCELLANEOUS AROMATIC BASED CHEMICALS

In addition to the very large-scale uses for light aromatic hydrocarbons already described in this chapter, there are many aromatic based compounds used as insecticides, herbicides and detergents and as intermediates for resins and plastics on a scale which would justify their inclusion as heavy organic chemicals but which are being more fully described in other volumes of this series. Only a very brief description, therefore, is given here.

Of the insecticides, the simplest is benzene hexachloride, made by direct addition of chlorine to benzene and sold under various trade names of which the I.C.I. "Gammexane" is probably the most familiar in this country. Only the γ isomer is effective and the art of manufacture lies in maximizing the yield of this isomer. Of other chlorinated insecticides the best known is D.D.T. (dichlorodiphenyl trichloroethane) produced from the reaction between monochlorobenzene and chloral.

$$CCl_3CHO + 2\ C_6H_5Cl \xrightarrow{\ H_2SO_4\ } CCl_3CH(C_6H_4Cl)_2 + H_2O$$

Chloral is produced by direct chlorination of ethyl alcohol or acetaldehyde. As an indication of the scale of operations, the production of both benzene hexachloride and D.D.T. in the U.S.A. exceeds 50,000 t/a and many chlorine and phosphorus based insecticidal derivatives are made in large quantities.

A characteristic of the chlorinated insecticides is their stability, which allows them to remain effective over long periods of time, but which has also led to fears that they may build up to undesirable levels in the countryside. The long-term effects of such a build up are not known but there is currently some restriction on the use of certain compounds while the effects are being further investigated.

The best known and most commonly used selective weed killer is 2.4-Dichloro-phenoxy acetic acid (2.4-D). This is made from 2.4-dichloro-phenol and monochloroacetic acid and is a major outlet for these compounds.

$$Cl_2C_6H_3OH + CH_2ClCOOH + NaOH \longrightarrow$$
$$Cl_2C_6H_3O\ CH_2COOH + NaCl + H_2O$$

The corresponding derivatives based on propionic and butyric acids have also become important and a constant search is going on for more efficient and more selective herbicides.

The use of alkyl phenols as a base for non-ionic detergents by reaction with ethylene oxide, has already been mentioned and this application absorbs some thousands of tons of alkyl phenols annually, mainly octyl and nonyl derivatives. When the longer side chain alkyl phenols are substituted for cresols, or for phenol itself, in the reactions with formaldehyde, the resulting resins are soluble in drying oils and are used in the paint industries. Some alkyl phenols have also achieved importance as anti-oxidants. A good example is 2.6-ditertiary butyl 4-methyl phenol, made from isobutene and *p*-cresol, and sold by I.C.I. as "Topanol" A and by Shell Chemicals as "Stavox". It is an excellent anti-oxidant for oils and fats and is widely used in petroleum products. It has also been used in many food products without apparent ill effect but its long-term biological safety is not yet (1965) fully established.

Among the aromatic chemicals described above there is little that is new; what is new in most cases is the very large increases in production which have been made possible by the availability of unrestricted supplies of cheap light aromatic hydrocarbons produced from petroleum. This may be expected to stimulate further growth in the aromatic chemicals field in the future.

READING LIST

1. The Hooker Phenol Process, by Walter Prahl. *The Chemical Engineer*, Sept. 1964, pp. CE 199–CE 201.

2. Recent Developments in Aromatics Oxidation, by R. Landau. *Chemistry & Industry*, No. 2, pp. 70–75, 1962.
3. New Methods of Terephthalic Acid Manufacture, by David Brown. *Oil & Gas Journal*, **63**, No. 6, 1965, pp. 103–7.
4. *Unsaturated Polyesters*, by H. V. Boenig. Elsevier, Amsterdam, 1964.
5. *Polymer Technology*, by D. C. Miles and J. H. Briston. Temple Press, London, 1965.

See also the reading list for Chapter 5.

CHAPTER 10

Miscellaneous Heavy Organic Chemicals

THERE are a few chemicals which are produced on a large scale but which do not fit easily into the system of classification adopted in this monograph and which do not merit a chapter to themselves; they have, therefore, been brought together in this final chapter.

CELLULOSE

Cellulose has been described in a volume published by the American Association for the Advancement of Science as *The Chemical that Grows*. It is a remarkable material and, is literally, part of the very fabric of our lives. Perhaps the most remarkable thing about it in this day and age is that no-one has yet suggested that synthetic manufacture would be cheaper and more efficient than the natural process. Nevertheless, its properties can be modified chemically in a variety of ways and these processes consume large quantities of organic chemicals. It was the basis for the first plastic material more than a century ago; it has been the mainstay of wars all over the world for about a hundred years and has provided the basis for proving that the pen is mightier than the sword for some thousands of years. Today it is still the most widely used fibre forming material, both in its natural state and as xanthate and acetate rayon, and cellulose compounds are constantly finding more uses in the plastics industry.

The raw material for chemical use is usually either cotton linters, the short fibres separated in the processing of natural cotton, or wood pulp prepared from soft woods. The wood pulp industry is ever expanding to provide paper for the world's growing population and the wider spread of literacy and itself provides other chemical raw materials such as rosin, tall oil, lignin, furfural and ethanol as by-products of the cellulose separation process.

Several process are available for the preparation of cellulose from wood and the one chosen will depend on the kind of wood being treated and the end use of the product. The best known is probably the sulphite process applied generally to the soft woods from coniferous forests. In this process the wood is first reduced to chips and is then digested with a sulphite liquor, containing 5–10% of sulphur dioxide with ammonia or caustic soda, for up to 12 hr at about 100 psig and 150°C. The resulting pulp is washed, separated from knots and undigested chips and rolled into sheets which are packed into bundles for sale. If required, it may be bleached with hypochlorous acid. The spent sulphite liquor, or black lye as it is called in the industry, may be worked up for recovery of various by-products which will vary with the wood which has been treated.

As might be expected, a large part of this country's cellulose requirements are imported from countries with large areas of coniferous forest such as Canada or Scandinavia. A considerable tonnage of home-produced wood is, however, processed by the major British paper manufacturers and a large new pulp mill has recently been established near Fort William to use wood from the Forestry Commission's woodlands in Scotland. As the large areas of forest planted by the Forestry Commission over the past forty years become fully productive, the production of cellulose in this country can be expected to increase.

CARBON DISULPHIDE

It is appropriate that a description of carbon disulphide manufacture should follow the section on cellulose since it is the production of regenerated cellulose films and fibres that accounts for much more than half of the total consumption of this chemical.

Carbon disulphide is formed in small quantities during the carbonization of coal and appears in the fore-runnings from crude benzole recovered from coal gas. The traditional method of manufacture is by direct combination of charcoal and sulphur at about 1000°C. The reaction is carried out in direct-fired, refractory-lined cast iron vessels or in an electric resistance furnace. In either case the vessel is charged with charcoal, brought to the required temperature and sulphur is fed in from the bottom. As it vaporizes and rises through the hot charcoal, it reacts to form carbon disulphide which passes out at the top of the reactor; fresh charcoal is added from the top as required. A special grade of coke may be used as the source of carbon instead of wood charcoal. The crude carbon disulphide is separated from unchanged sulphur and hydrogen sulphide by conventional scrubbing and distillation processes.

The direct process described above is gradually being replaced by a more modern process based on the reaction of sulphur with natural gas; this process produces large quantities of by-product hydrogen sulphide from which the sulphur has to be recovered for recycle.

$$CH_4 + 4\,S \longrightarrow CS_2 + 2\,H_2S$$

$$2\,H_2S + 3\,O_2 \longrightarrow 2\,SO_2 + 2\,H_2O$$

$$2\,H_2S + SO_2 \longrightarrow 3\,S + 2\,H_2O$$

Sulphur vapour and methane are preheated separately to about 600°C and mixed together with the sulphur in slight excess. The mixture is then passed through a superheater before going to the converter packed with a catalyst such as silica gel. The reaction is endothermic and, by proper control of the superheater temperature, a conversion of 90% molar per pass may be obtained. Carbon disulphide is recovered from the reactor gases by conventional cooling and scrubbing equipment and is purified by distillation; the hydrogen sulphide is decomposed in a Claus kiln for recovery of sulphur which is recycled.

The largest user of carbon disulphide, Courtaulds, is also the largest producer and has a plant at Trafford Park, near Manchester, with an estimated capacity of 70,000–80,000 t/a.

Originally this plant used the direct reaction process but this was replaced a few years ago by the methane/sulphur process. The plant draws its methane by pipeline from the Petrochemicals Ltd. works of Shell Chemicals a few miles away at Carrington. I.C.I. also has a plant at Hillhouse, near Fleetwood, Lancs., which is apparently worked intermittently according to the state of supply and demand.

Apart from the main use in rayon manufacture, carbon disulphide is the raw material for carbon tetrachloride manufacture (see page 92); it also has smaller scale applications in the production of rubber processing chemicals, flotation agents and insecticides.

FURFURAL

Furfural, or furfuraldehyde,

$$\begin{array}{c} CH = CH \\ | \qquad \diagdown O \\ CH = C\ CHO \end{array}$$

is recovered from agricultural residues, such as oat hulls, corn cobs and sugar cane bagasse by hydrolysis of the pentosans which they contain, followed by dehydration of the resulting pentoses to furfural. Waste liquor from wood pulp processes also contains pentoses and could be a source of furfural.

Ground oat hulls are digested with dilute sulphuric acid of about 10% concentration under moderate steam pressure for some hours. When the pressure is released, the furfural, together with some by-products such as methanol and acetic acid, flashes off and is passed to a distillation system for recovery of furfural. The pure material darkens readily on exposure to air and requires an oxidation inhibitor to stabilize it.

The major, if not the only, manufacturer in the world is the Quaker Oats Co. in the U.S.A., and its British subsidiary imports the relatively small quantity of furfural needed in this country.

Furfural has been used in several applications as an extractive solvent in the refining of 1.3-butadiene and in the separation of aromatic hydrocarbons from petroleum. Furfuryl alcohol, produced by the Quaker Oats Co. at Greenford, Middx., by selective hydrogenation of the aldehyde, has substantial applications in combination with urea/formaldehyde resins as a sand core binder in foundries. Furoic acid is offered by Lloyds Research Ltd. and has potential uses in the production of pharmaceuticals, dyestuffs, plastics and perfumery.

In general, it may be said that furfural is an interesting and reactive chemical, potentially available in vast quantities from natural waste products, which has not yet found any very large-scale industrial uses but for which success always appears to be just around the corner.

SORBITOL

Sorbitol is produced by hydrogenation of glucose at about 2500 psig using Raney nickel as catalyst; the reaction is rapid, so that a contact time of a few minutes only is required, and conversion is complete.

$$
\begin{array}{l}
CH_2OH \\
CHOH \\
CHOH \\
CHOH \quad + H_2 \longrightarrow \\
CHOH \\
CHO
\end{array}
\qquad
\begin{array}{l}
CH_2OH \\
CHOH \\
CHOH \\
CHOH \\
CHOH \\
CH_2OH
\end{array}
$$

After filtering off the catalyst, which is reprocessed and used again, it is usual to pass the sorbitol solution through ion exchange resins to remove inorganic cations and anions before it goes to the distillation plant for concentration. The product may be sold as a concentrated aqueous solution or the pure alcohol, melting point $97 \cdot 7°C$, may be crystallized out.

Sorbitol is made on a scale of about 6000 t/a by Howards of Ilford (Laporte Group) which also manufactures a number of derivatives. As a polyhydric alcohol it competes with other compounds of this class such as glycerol and penta-erythritol in the resin, plasticizer and printing ink fields. Its fatty acid and polyoxyethylene esters have some outlets in the food and specialized detergents fields.

Sorbitol and its derivatives may be regarded as typical of a large number of compounds which can be prepared from sugars; because of the general acceptability of sugars as constituents of food materials, some of these compounds could have large potential uses in the food processing and packaging industries. Because of the great complexity of sugar chemistry, the possibilities are almost endless but, so far, sugars have been comparatively little used as chemical raw materials. Sugar cane will yield a larger tonnage of food per acre than any other crop but the amount which can be incorporated in human diets is limited; it is, therefore, an ideal natural raw material for chemical processing.

HYDROGEN CYANIDE

Hydrogen cyanide is regarded with awe by the uninitiated because of its reputation as a poison. Its tendency to polymerize with explosive violence, unless very pure or containing a stabilizer, is less well known but may be equally hazardous and was a limiting factor to its commercial development for many years. It is now, however, an important industrial chemical and may even be transported in tank cars in the liquid state.

The traditional route to hydrogen cyanide is decomposition of sodium cyanide produced by the reaction between sodamide and carbon.

$$NaNH_2 + C \xrightarrow{-H_2} NaCN$$

$$2\,NaCN + H_2SO_4 \longrightarrow 2\,HCN + Na_2SO_4$$

This method is both cumbersome and expensive and many other routes involving interaction of hydrocarbons with nitrogen or ammonia have been tried but only one of these—the reaction between methane and ammonia—has been developed on a commercial scale.

$$CH_4 + NH_3 \longrightarrow HCN + 3 H_2$$

This reaction is highly endothermic and requires a temperature of around 1200°C for reasonable reaction rates. The first successful large-scale process was developed by Andrussov in the early 1930's; the reaction heat was supplied by burning part of the methane with air, thus giving a reaction which may be represented by the equation

$$2 CH_4 + 2 NH_3 + 3 O_2 \longrightarrow 2 HCN + 6 H_2O$$

This process may be regarded as the first example of a commercial "ammoxidation" process such as is described on page 154 for the production of acrylonitrile; it may have considerable potential for future development.

Approximately 1 volume of methane, 0·9 volume of air and an excess of ammonia are mixed at a pressure of about 20 psig and passed into the reactor containing a platinum or platinum/ iridium catalyst. Oxidation of part of the methane maintains the reaction temperature at about 1100°C and supplies the heat required for formation of hydrogen cyanide. The reactor effluent is quenched in a waste heat boiler and passed to the work-up system. Where a ready outlet for ammonium sulphate exists, the excess of ammonia is removed by scrubbing with dilute sulphuric acid and the sulphate is recovered from the scrubber liquor. It is generally found more economic to recover the excess ammonia for recycle by a regenerative scrubbing process using aqueous mono-ammonium phosphate or polyhydroxy boric acid as the scrubbing liquid. Ammonia may be distilled out of the saturated absorbent and the regenerated lean absorbent is recycled to the scrubber. In either case, the vapours from the ammonia scrubber are washed with water acidulated with sulphuric acid to dissolve the hydrogen cyanide which is then stripped off and refined by distillation in the presence of small quantities of sulphur dioxide as a stabilizer. A flow sheet of the process is shown in Fig. 18.

A variation of the process has been developed on a commercial scale by Degussa in Germany in which the reaction is carried out in an externally heated catalyst chamber. This greatly reduces

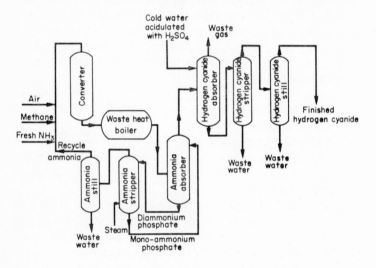

FIG. 18 Andrussov Process for Hydrocyanic Acid.

the volume of gases to be handled and, in consequence, the capital cost of the plant required is much lower. Hydrogen cyanide is likely to become increasingly available in the future as the by-product of other ammoxidation reactions; for example, the 40,000 t/a acrylonitrile plant of Border Chemicals Ltd. at Grangemouth is estimated to produce 6000 t/a of by-product hydrogen cyanide.

The only manufacturer in this country is I.C.I. which originally used the sodamide process and changed to an Andrussov-type process in recent years. The scale of operations is not known but is believed to be substantial since preliminary preparation of hydrogen cyanide is now the most economic route to metallic cyanides. Commercial manufacture of hydrogen cyanide is, however, carried out on a larger scale in Germany and, especially, in the U.S.A. where production in 1963 was about 150,000 tons. Development of the ammoxidation process for acrylonitrile and the apparent intention of I.C.I. to concentrate on the cyclo-hexane route to nylon appears to limit the prospects for growth of hydrogen cyanide output. There will, however, be a continuing demand for metallic cyanides for electroplating and ore extraction.

CYANAMIDE AND MELAMINE

When nitrogen is brought into contact with finely powdered calcium carbide at about 1000°C, it reacts to form calcium cyanamide and carbon.

$$CaC_2 + N_2 \longrightarrow CaCN_2 + C$$

This reaction formed the basis for the first commercial process for the fixation of atmospheric nitrogen and very large quantities of the crude calcium cyanamide were used as fertilizers in the early years of this century, especially in Germany and the U.S.A. where the American Cyanamide Co. pioneered development. This market disappeared with the advent of the Haber process for pressure synthesis of ammonia after the 1914–18 war.

More recently, however, calcium cyanamide has made a "come-back", since it may be regarded as the calcium salt of cyanamide which may be obtained from it by acid hydrolysis. The reaction is carried out by passing carbon dioxide into an aqueous suspension of finely powdered calcium cyanamide.

$$CaCN_2 + H_2O + CO_2 \longrightarrow N \equiv CNH_2 + CaCO_3$$

The precipitated carbonate and insoluble matter are filtered off and the resulting aqueous solution of cyanamide may be concentrated, with the aid of stabilizers, to give crystals of cyanamide melting at 45°C.

Cyanamide is best known in the form of its dimer—dicyan-diamide or, more correctly, cyano-guanine—which is a stable, non-hygroscopic crystalline solid of melting point 209°C. A measure of its importance is given by the estimate of non-Communist world production in 1962 as 100,000 tons.

$$2 \, N \equiv CNH_2 \longrightarrow H_2NC = NC \equiv N$$
$$| \atop NH_2$$

Dicyandiamide is used almost entirely for conversion to melamine via the intermediate compound, guanyl melamine.

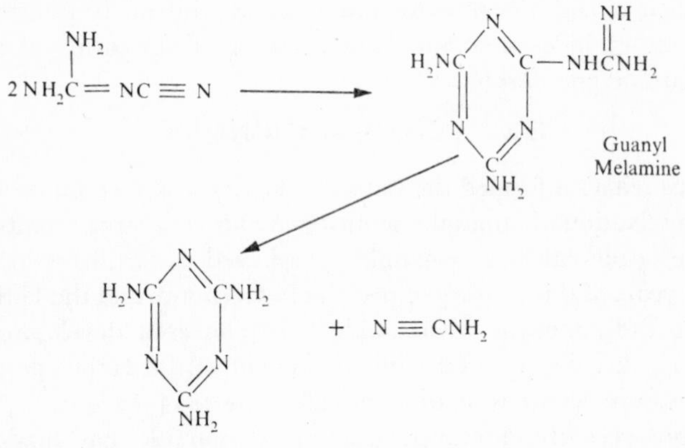

Guanyl
Melamine

Melamine

The reaction takes place when dicyandiamide is heated, but yields are poor and much ammonia is evolved. By carrying out the reaction under ammonia pressure, the de-ammoniation may be suppressed and high yields of melamine obtained.

Melamine is a white crystalline solid of melting point 350°C and is the precursor of a valuable series of melamine/formaldehyde resins which are strongly water and heat resistant. They are, perhaps, best known to the general public in the form of the laminate "Formica", a product of the De la Rue company. There are, of course, many other fabricators of melamine plastics and the resins have numerous applications in the plastics and adhesives industries.

There are two manufacturers of melamine in this country— British Oxygen Chemicals Ltd., which depends ultimately on calcium carbide manufactured by the B.O.C. Norwegian associates, and Cyanamide of Great Britain Ltd. at Gosport, which uses dicyandiamide imported from the Canadian branch of the American Cyanamid Company. Total capacity is around 10,000 t/a, with British Oxygen the larger producer.

Melamine has immense possibilities as a plastic but is still relatively expensive. Successful operation of several other processes has been claimed; the most promising would appear to be the one starting from urea. On paper, the reaction may be written as the dehydration and condensation of three molecules of urea:

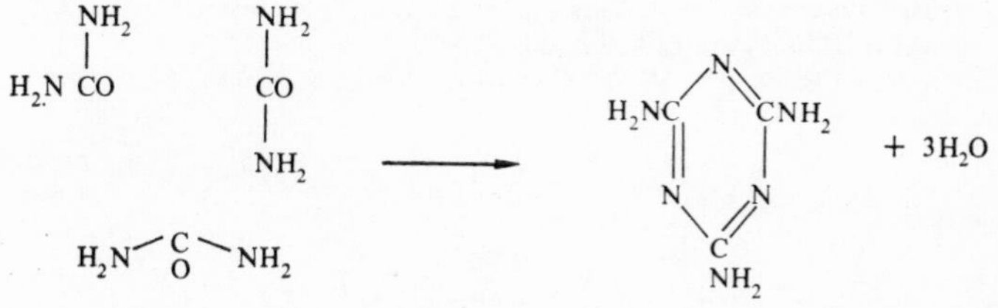

In practice, the reaction is not so simple and ammonia and carbon dioxide are always produced and isocyanic acid is certainly an intermediate product. The complete series of reactions might, therefore, be written:

$$6\ CO(NH_2)_2 \longrightarrow 6\ HCNO + 6\ NH_3$$

$$6\ HCNO \longrightarrow C_3H_6N_6 + 3\ CO_2$$

$$3\ CO_2 + 6\ NH_3 \longrightarrow 3\ CO(NH_2)_2 + 3\ H_2O$$

The process has not yet been applied commercially in this country, but a number of plants are either operating or under construction in the U.S.A. and continental Europe. The process may be summarized as the treatment of urea at elevated temperature and pressure in the presence of ammonia and a suitable catalyst, although at least one version of the process claims to operate at atmospheric pressure. Comparatively little has been published about the process, but the yield on urea is believed to be rather low and the process to be subject to trouble with corrosion. These facts may account for its apparently slow rate of commercial development.

Dicyandiamide will react with nitriles to form guanamines which, like melamine, are triazine derivatives. These too will form resins with formaldehyde which are even more water resistant than the melamine resins. High cost of manufacture, however, limits their commercial use.

READING LIST

1. *Pulping Processes*, by Sven A. Rydholm. Interscience Publishers, London, 1965.
2. *Cellulosic Plastics*, by V. E. Yarsley, W. Flavell, P. S. Adamson and N. G. Perkins. Iliffe Books Ltd., London, 1964.
3. Hydrogen Cyanide, by P. W. Sherwood. *Petroleum Engineer*, **31**, C22–C31, 1959.

Conclusion

IN THE preceding pages many fields of organic chemistry have
been touched on, in the main somewhat superficially, since this
is a book about industry and large-scale manufacture and not a
textbook. During the period of a year over which it was written
there were so many changes in the heavy organic chemicals
industry that quite substantial revisions were necessary before the
book went to press.

In a climate of such rapid change, it is impossible to do justice
to a commercial situation, especially in an industry which is not
noted for the amount of reliable statistical information published
about it. The information given is believed to be accurate at the
time of going to press in the last quarter of 1965; much effort
has been expended in checking it and the author apologizes for
any inaccuracies which appear in the descriptions of the operations of individual firms.

During the monograph references have been made to the
probable lines of future development of some chemicals. This
seems likely to continue at a rapid rate for many years to come;
new compounds will become industrially important and new
processes will be devised, while there will be a continuing struggle
to improve the existing processes in order that they can remain
competitive. A very important trend, which can already be seen,
is likely to be towards the elimination of complete steps in
multistage syntheses; the steadily rising capital charges associated
with large modern organic chemical plants provide an even
greater incentive than saving in operating cost to the
elimination of process stages and will pay for some deterioration
in yield.

Since many important industrial organic chemicals contain

oxygen, the use of oxidation processes for their production from hydrocarbons is certain to grow; examples, such as the production of acetic acid from naphtha and of acetaldehyde from ethylene, have been given and others will almost certainly follow. The use of oxidation combined with other reactions as in oxychlorination and ammoxidation offers great possibilities for further expansion. Another technique which may be more widely applied can be described as "beating the reaction rates". This involves heating the reactants extremely rapidly to a high temperature at which useful yields of the desired product are formed, followed by ultra-rapid cooling to avoid decomposition. Production of acetylene by oxidative cracking of methane is an example of this. The carrying out of high-temperature reactions in gas turbines to provide both power and product, or in plasmas with temperatures of 10,000°C or more have been suggested but have not, so far as is known, been applied on a commercial scale as yet.

Many of the processes described in this book operate continuously; this is especially true of those using petroleum feedstocks where oil refinery thinking, based on quantities which are astronomical by chemical industry standards, has influenced process and plant design. Economic pressures now provide a great incentive to achieve the cost reductions which are usually possible through large-scale continuous operation; many existing batch processes, therefore, are likely to be changed to continuous operation as soon as the demand for their products has risen sufficiently to make the change practicable.

Continuous processing also brings its problems, since a shutdown means a complete cessation of production. It is customary, therefore, to operate these plants to a planned maintenance schedule. This allows the stocks required for sale during the shut-down period to be accumulated according to plan and, at the same time, permits efficient deployment of the maintenance labour force. Continuous processes also demand accurate control methods; in a batch process there is time to correct temporary errors in control of process variables whereas, for continuous working, the conditions should be held always at the optimum. Responsive control instruments are, therefore, a necessity and modern continuous plants are equipped with an impressive array of instruments which are steadily growing in accuracy, sophistication and cost. The use of both analogue and digital computors for process control has begun but is, as yet, in its infancy; it is likely to become commonplace during the next five years. In particular, digital computors may be used both for controlling the process variables at the ideal values and for determining what the optimum values are under a given set of conditions. This latter calculation is often complex and can only be carried out, in time for it to be of use, by electronic methods. The technique is known as "process optimization"; it is likely to be widely used, especially in the complexes of inter-connected plants which occur in many modern chemical factories.

As economic pressures are influencing the lines of technological development, they are also likely to have a dominating influence on chemical engineering for organic chemical plants and on the whole structure of the organic chemical industry. Plants seem constantly to get larger, in order to achieve maximum economy, and equipment must also increase in size to keep in step and to provide integrated units which will operate continuously without standby equipment. This tendency may be particularly noted in the capacity of ethylene plants currently being built; a better known example is the increase in optimum size of turbo-generators in the electricity supply industry. This industry is large enough to support a number of optimum-sized units; what happens in the organic chemical industry when the market is only large enough to support one plant of optimum size has yet to be worked out. As always, it is change in the economic factors which will determine the future shape of the industry and these are even less predictable than technological changes. It seems certain, however, that they will favour continued growth and greater concentration of the industry into large units, probably inter-connected by pipelines, and with some form of overall co-ordination of operations.

Index

(Page numbers in italic type refer to more important references)